Designing the Internet of Things

Adrian McEwen,
Hakim Cassimally

WILEY

This edition first published 2014
© 2014 John Wiley and Sons, Ltd.

Registered office
John Wiley & Sons Ltd, The Atrium, Southern Gate, Chichester, West Sussex,
PO19 8SQ, United Kingdom

For details of our global editorial offices, for customer services and for
information about how to apply for permission to reuse the copyright material
in this book please see our website at www.wiley.com.

A catalogue record for this book is available from the British Library.

ISBN 978-1-118-43062-0 (paperback); ISBN 978-1-118-43063-7 (ebook);
978-1-118-43065-1 (ebook)

Set in 9.5/11.5pt Minion Pro by Indianapolis Composition Services

Printed in the United Kingdom by TJ International

About the Authors

Adrian McEwen is a creative technologist and entrepreneur based in Liverpool. He has been connecting devices to the Internet since 1995—first cash registers, then mobile phones, and now bubble machines and lamps. He founded MCQN Ltd., an Internet of Things product agency and (along with Hakim and others) is co-founder of DoES Liverpool, a hybrid co-working/makerspace that incubates Internet of Things startups in NW England. He is also CTO of Good Night Lamp, a family of Internet-connected lamps. He was one of the first employees at STNC Ltd, which built the first web browser for mobile phones and was acquired by Microsoft in 1999. Adrian concentrates on how the Internet of Things intersects with people's lives and how heterogeneous networks of devices should work together, and lectures and speaks on these issues internationally. You can find him on the Internet at www.mcqn.net or follow him on Twitter as @amcewen.

For Jean, Les, and Christine, and in memory of Karen.

—Adrian

Despite an education in Italian and English literature, once **Hakim Cassimally** discovered software development, he hasn't looked back. He is a staunch proponent of Perl and was one of the organisers of YAPC::EU 2010 in Pisa. These days, however, he is likely to be writing Python for 3D printers or for civic hacking projects with mySociety.org. He co-founded (with Adrian and others) DoES Liverpool. His website is at greenokapi.net.

For my parents. This time I didn't start with the page numbers.

—Hakim

PUBLISHER'S ACKNOWLEDGEMENTS

Some of the people who helped bring this book to market include the following:

Editorial and Production
VP Consumer and Technology Publishing Director: Michelle Leete
Associate Director–Book Content Management: Martin Tribe
Associate Publisher: Chris Webb
Executive Commissioning Editor: Craig Smith
Project Editor: John Sleeva
Copy Editor: Chuck Hutchinson
Technical Editors: Daniel Soltis, Aaron Crane,
Alexandra Deschamps-Sonsino
Editorial Manager: Jodi Jensen
Senior Project Editor: Sara Shlaer
Editorial Assistant: Annie Sullivan

Marketing
Associate Marketing Director: Louise Breinholt
Marketing Manager: Lorna Mein
Senior Marketing Executive: Kate Parrett
Marketing Assistant: Polly Thomas

Composition Services
Compositor: Jennifer Mayberry
Proofreader: Susan Moritz
Indexer: Potomac Indexing, LLC

Acknowledgements

First off, we'd like to thank Craig Smith at Wiley for persuading us that capturing some of what we know into a book would be a good thing. Thanks also to the rest of the Wiley team and everyone who helped edit the book: John Sleeva, Daniel Soltis, Alexandra Deschamps-Sonsino, Chuck Hutchinson, and Aaron Crane. Despite our grumbling at the additional work of rewriting sections, the book is much better as a result.

We'd also like to thank everyone at DoES Liverpool for putting up with our sometimes distracted have-book-to-write periods in the run up to deadlines, and in particular our fellow organizers, John McKerrell, Andy Goodwin, Paul Freeman, Patrick Fenner, Steve Sparrow, and Ross Jones, who had to take up the slack in running the space.

—Adrian and Hakim

The acknowledgements section was one I never normally paid a lot of attention to, as it was the author thanking a load of people I didn't know. Having written a book, and realised how much help and support are given to the authors, I have a newfound appreciation for this section.

I'd like to thank Hakim for agreeing to join me in the adventure of actually doing the writing. Andy Huntington, Lawrence Archard, and Christopher Pett were all generous with their time and sharing their expertise in areas where I'm only in the early stages of exploring.

For endless encouragement and keeping me sane in the difficult bits, I need to thank my family and friends, especially Francis Irving, Andrew Dixon, Rob Stock, Neil Sowler, Kieran MacCourt, Jen Forakis, Colette MacCourt, Dan Lynch, and Neil Morrin.

And, finally, thanks to Bubblino for helping get me into this mess in the first place.

—Adrian

I tend to at least skim the acknowledgements and knew (in theory) that writing a book was a huge, collaborative effort. Experiencing it firsthand was awe-inspiring. We will almost certainly have forgotten to thank somebody: if that's you, we would love to make it up to you over a beverage of your choice.

Firstly, thanks to Adrian for suggesting we work together on the book; it's been an interesting project. Dave Cross, Kieren Diment, and Jodi Schneider gave invaluable early advice about publishing. Georgina Voss pointed me in the right direction on the ethics chapter, and Coen van Wyk kindly proof-read the first draft. Tomas Doran gave useful suggestions on asynchronous web programming for the online components chapter, and Aaron Crane stepped in as technical editor. Kelvin Lawson advised us on the current state of real-time operating systems, while Kiel Gilleade and Jen Allanson provided insights into physiological computing. Guy Dickinson gave his usual enthusiasm and support, and Jim Hughes has kept me regularly up-to-date with interesting ideas. Thanks, also, to Shaun Myhill at Electric Imp, Aaron at .:oomlout:., Antony McLoughlin, Ross Jones, and Francis Fish for donating or lending microcontrollers and books without which writing this book would have been impossible. My colleagues at mySociety have been exceptionally tolerant of my last-minute time off to finish the final drafts.

Having the opportunity to attend or speak at events such as OpenIoT, the IoT Howduino, TSB IoT round table, BBC's PlayIoT unconference, MadLab's IoT workshop, Internet World, LivLug, and SMC Liverpool helped shape the ideas of the book. Thanks to Alex Deschamps-Sonsino, Ed Borden, Usman Haque, Adam Greenfield, Hannah Goraya, Nick O'Leary, Ben Ward, Thomas Amberg, Charalampos Doukas, Stefan Ferber, Chris Adams, Gavin Sparks, Peter Bihr, Andrew Back, Laura James, Russell Davies, Rob van Kranenburg, Erik van der Zee, Martin Spindler, Matt Biddulph, Fiddian Warman, Rachel Jones, Alistair MacDonald, Natasha Carolan, Mark Holmes, Pat Link, Cefn Hoile, Thom Shannon, Alistair Houghton, Chris Holgate, Alastair Somerville, Matthew Hughes, Jessi Baker, Aine and Aidan McGuire, Grey Povey, Hwa Young Jung, Andy Piper, Sue Black, Travis Hodges, Bob Ham, Neil Morrin, Dan Lynch, Francis Irving, Conrad Mason, Pete Thomas. In addition, I have had great discussions online and offline with Javier Montaner, Paul Kinlan, Luke Petre, Paul Ede, and have received helpful comments and suggestions from Rob Nightingale, Zarino Zappia, Aldo Calpini, David Jones, Kirsty Sparrow, and Arto Nabito.

I worked with Greg McCarroll back in 2005. Though I didn't know it at the time, his connected train-aware alarm clock was the first Internet of Things object I ever came across. Greg was a gentleman as well as an innovator, and will be dearly missed.

Thanks, also, to Claire, Lolita, Rumplestiltskin, Sheri My, Wolfie, and Helvetica. Definitely.

—Hakim

Contents

Introduction

A COMPUTER PROCESSOR such as Intel's i486 used to cost around the same as a small car. Nowadays a chip with similar power is the price of a chocolate bar.

When processing power is so cheap, you can afford to put processors in places that you couldn't before—not just a business workstation or a home PC but also a telephone, an electricity meter, a bedside lamp, or a teddy bear. We can make objects intelligent. We can make them think and speak. Pundits have dubbed this "physical computing", "ubiquitous computing" or "ubicomp", or "the Internet of Things". Whatever you choose to call it, we are really talking about making magical things, enchanted objects.

In this book we look at the kinds of computer chips that can be embedded in objects ("microcontrollers" such as the Arduino) and take you through each step of the process from prototyping a Thing to manufacturing and selling it. We explore the platforms you can use to develop the hardware and software, discuss the design concepts that will make your products eye-catching and appealing, and show you ways to scale up from a single prototype to mass production.

WHAT THIS BOOK IS NOT

For starters, this book is not a specific guide to any given microcontroller. Although we look at the Arduino, Raspberry Pi, and other options, this detailed technical information will necessarily date more quickly than the rest of the material in the book. So we are more interested in showing the criteria for evaluating and choosing a platform.

Nor is this book a guide to particular cool projects to make. Rather, we survey some groundbreaking Things but mostly look at the general design principles that will, we hope, encourage you to make something fresh, beautiful, useful, and magical.

Finally, this isn't an academic treatise on the business infrastructure of tomorrow's Internet of Things—technologies such as 6LoWPAN and emerging M2M standards. We are far more interested in how to design, manufacture, and sell consumer-facing Things that will delight *people*.

WHO SHOULD READ THIS BOOK?

We certainly hope that this book, as a technical publication, will help software engineers, web developers, product designers, and electronics engineers start designing Internet of Things products. Indeed, we cover microcontrollers, electronics, embedded programming, and web APIs, among other technical topics of interest.

The book is also targeted at entrepreneurs, "makers" (designers, artists, craftspeople, and hobbyists), academics and educators, and anyone interested in getting an overview of this exciting upcoming technology. Even if you have little or no technical background in IT, much of the material is accessible to a general reader, and our coverage extends beyond the purely digital to topics in design, ethics, and business.

HOW TO USE THE BOOK

As we mentioned previously, this is not a "how-to" book, so you don't need any particular tools to read along. The more technical chapters do give some suggestions for microcontroller hardware or web development frameworks that you may choose to investigate further in parallel.

We have designed the book to flow from principles through prototyping to manufacture and business considerations, so you *can* certainly read it from cover to cover. However, you may prefer to take alternative paths through the book. Depending on your background and concerns, some chapters may be of greater interest, whereas others you may prefer to skip for now.

Part I, "Prototyping", introduces the Internet of Things and moves onto experimenting and creating your prototype project.

We recommend that all readers start with Chapter 1, "The Internet of Things: An Overview", which describes what the Internet of Things is and why it's happening now, and Chapter 2, "Design Principles for Connected Devices", where we set out a manifesto for consumer-facing Things for humans.

Chapter 3, "Internet Principles", is designed to be an accessible introduction which will be helpful to keep your ideas clear while you are building your Thing and thinking about how it communicates with the world. If you have a background in the Internet and web family of protocols, you can certainly skip this one.

The next chapters will be of most interest if you are planning to build a Thing yourself. To get a better understanding of the field, it is certainly worth reading Chapter 4, "Thinking About Prototyping", for general considerations about technology choices. For the engineer, maker, or technical person responsible for making a device, Chapter 5, "Prototyping Embedded Devices", applies the general principles to specific devices (at time of publication); Chapter 6, "Prototyping the Physical Design", discusses how to build the physical design of your prototype; and Chapter 7, "Prototyping Online Components", describes building the online components as web APIs.

Although many readers will have at least some general knowledge of programming, writing code for the small computers which often power connected devices has its own challenges. Chapter 8, "Techniques for Writing Embedded Code", presents some lessons learned in the trenches and will be useful to makers involved in projects with more complex computational requirements.

Part II, "From Prototype to Reality", moves beyond the world of making and prototyping and looks at what happens when your project meets the real world.

If you are an entrepreneur hoping to make money from your Internet of Things project, Chapter 9, "Business Models", examines business models which go far beyond simply selling devices. Of course, if you *are* planning to sell devices, then moving to manufacture presents a whole new set of problems, such as creating PCBs, sourcing materials, and getting certification, as we discuss in Chapter 10, "Moving to Manufacture".

Finally, technology always changes the world, and not always for the better. We began the book with design principles for making enchanted objects, and Chapter 11, "Ethics", discusses how ethical and moral principles are also essential if we want to keep the enchantment from going bad.

You can find more information about the book and the authors at `book.roomofthings.com` or by following `@aBookOfThings` on Twitter.

PRODUCTION NOTES

They say travel broadens the mind. It also helps you write. Parts of the book were written on a couple of flights, but much more on countless train journeys—mostly between Liverpool and London, but also elsewhere in the UK and in northern Italy. Former transport systems worked, too: the High Line in New York was an excellent venue for writing during an extended visit there early in the book's life.

The rest was written in and around Liverpool. In DoES Liverpool, in my flat by the cathedrals, holed up in Bold St. Coffee, or on the third floor of the majestic Central Library. When the weather permitted, even some down at the Pier Head, overlooking the river Mersey.

The main text was written in Vim in Markdown, on a Sony Vaio laptop running Ubuntu, and then edited in Microsoft Word on Windows on the same laptop.

—Adrian

Before even touching a keyboard, Adrian and I had several long, wide-ranging conversations about the Internet of Things in general and the content we wanted for the book. As I was quite new to the topic, this helped me form an understanding by getting to ask silly questions and challenge assumptions. The discussions helped us to reach a common "voice" for the book. We drafted a chapter together (which eventually became Chapter 4, "Thinking About Prototyping") and then split the remaining chapters evenly in accordance with our interests and knowledge. We have consistently reviewed each other's chapters before submitting them, which has helped maintain that shared voice through the whole process.

My drafts were written in Vim, converted from Markdown using Pandoc, and edited in LibreOffice, originally on an aging ThinkPad and then, when that finally gave up the ghost, on a MacBook Pro. Dropbox was invaluable for sharing the latest version of every document immediately. We wrote blog posts in Markdown, too, and published them with Jekyll.

—Hakim

PROTOTYPING

1

THE INTERNET OF THINGS: AN OVERVIEW

THE FIRST QUESTION that we should attempt to answer is, of course, what *is* the Internet of Things? Although the concepts we call on throughout this book are relatively straightforward, people have many different visions of what the phrase means, and many of the implications are hard to grasp. So we will take this question slowly in this chapter and look at it from a number of different angles.

What does the phrase "Internet of Things" mean? And how does it relate to the earlier buzzword "ubiquitous computing"? For those who are interested in the history of technological progress, where does the Internet of Things sit in the broad sweep of things, and why are we talking about it *now*? For those who understand best through metaphors, we look at the idea of *enchanted objects*, an image which has described technology for millennia but which is especially potent when describing the Internet of Things. For the more practical readers who understand by seeing examples of real things, we sketch out some of the exciting projects that give a good flavour of this exciting field. Let's start with this last approach, with a short piece of "design fiction".

THE FLAVOUR OF THE INTERNET OF THINGS

The alarm rings. As you open your eyes blearily, you see that it's five minutes later than your usual wake-up time. The clock has checked the train times online, and your train must be delayed, so it lets you sleep in a little longer. (See `http://makezine.com/magazine/make-11/my-train-schedule-alarm-clock/`.)

In your kitchen, a blinking light reminds you it's time to take your tablets. If you forget, the medicine bottle cap goes online and emails your doctor to let her know. (See `www.vitality.net/glowcaps.html`.)

On your way out of the house, you catch a glow in the corner of your eye. Your umbrella handle is lit up, which means that it has checked the BBC weather reports and predicts rain. You sigh and pick it up. (See `www.materious.com/#/projects/forecast/`.)

As you pass the bus stop on the way to the station, you notice the large LCD display flash that the number 23 is due. It arrives when you turn the next corner. When the bus company first installed those displays, they ran on the expected timetable information only, but now that every bus has GPS tracking its location, they simply connect to the bus company's online service and always give the updated information. Various transport organizations have implemented this. London's TfL has some useful information on their signs at `www.tfl.gov.uk/corporate/projectsandschemes/11560.aspx`.

When you get to the station, your phone checks you in automatically to a location-based service (such as Foursquare). On your mantelpiece at home, an ornament with a dial notices the change and starts to turn so that the text on it points to the word "Travelling". Your family will also see later that you've arrived at "Work" safely. (See `http://wheredial.com`.)

On your lunch break, a pedometer in your training shoes and a heart monitor in your wrist band help track your run around the block. The wrist band's large display also makes it easy to glance down and see how fast you are running and how many calories you've burned. All the data is automatically uploaded to your sports tracking site, which also integrates with your online supermarket shopping account to make it easy to compare with how many calories you've eaten. (See `http://nikeplus.nike.com/plus/`.)

As you can see from the preceding links, each of these products is feasible with today's technology. Each has been prototyped, and many of them exist as craft or mass-market products.

THE "INTERNET" OF "THINGS"

We've looked at a number of examples of the Internet of Things, so what is the common thread that binds them together? And why the name? All the cases we saw used the *Internet* to send, receive, or communicate information. And in each case, the gadget that was connected to the Internet wasn't a computer, tablet, or mobile phone but an object, a *Thing*. These Things are designed for a purpose: the umbrella has a retractable canopy and a handle to hold it. A bus display has to be readable to public transport users, including the elderly and partially sighted and be able to survive poor weather conditions and the risk of vandalism. The sports bracelet is easy to wear while running, has a display that is large enough and bright enough to read even when you are moving, and will survive heat, cold, sweat, and rain.

Many of the use cases could be fulfilled, and often are, by general-purpose computers. Although we don't carry a desktop PC around with us, many people do carry a laptop or tablet. More to the point, in almost every country now, most people do carry a mobile phone, and in many cases this is a smartphone that easily has enough power for any task one could throw at a computer. Let's see how well one could replicate these tasks with a smartphone.

Viewing your bus provider's timetable with a smartphone web browser seems to fulfil the same function at first glance. But just consider that last phrase, "at first glance". On arriving at the bus stop, one can simply glance at the computerised timetable and see when the next bus is due. With a smartphone, if you have one and can afford the data use (which may be prohibitive if you are a foreign tourist), you have to take the phone out of your pocket or bag, unlock it, navigate to the right website (this may be the slowest and most complicated part of the process, whether you have to type the URL or use a QR code), and read the data from a small screen. In this time, you are not able to fully concentrate on the arriving buses and might even miss yours.

You can track your runs with an app on your smartphone, and many people do: the phone has GPS, many other useful sensors, processing power, an Internet connection, and a great screen. But it turns out that such a phone isn't easy to carry on a run without worrying about dropping it or getting it wet. Plenty of carrying options are available, from a waist bag to an arm strap. The latter, in theory, enables you to read the device while you are running, but in practice reading details on the screen can be hard while you are jiggling up and down! To get around this difficulty, apps such as RunKeeper provide regular audio summaries which can be useful (`www.runkeeper.com`). Ultimately, a phone is a perfectly capable device for tracking your run, and most runners will find it a sufficient, comfortable, and fun way of logging their running data. However, others may well prefer a device worn as a watch or wristband, designed to be read on the move, worn in the rain, and connected to peripherals such as heart monitors.

Of course, no mobile phone (or even tablet or laptop) is large enough or waterproof enough to use as an umbrella. However, you could pair a smartphone with a normal "dumb" umbrella, by checking an app to see whether it is likely to rain later, before you leave the house. Unlike a calm, subtle light in the umbrella stand, glimpsed from the corner of your eye as an ambient piece of information to process subconsciously when you pass it on the way out of your home, an app requires you to perform several actions. If you are able to establish and maintain the habit of doing this check, it will be just as effective. Rather than having greater capabilities, the smart umbrella simply moves the same intelligence into your environment so that you don't have to change your routine.

So the idea of the Internet of Things suggests that rather than having a small number of very powerful computing devices in your life (laptop, tablet, phone, music player), you might have a large number of devices which are perhaps less powerful (umbrella, bracelet, mirror, fridge, shoes). An earlier buzzword for roughly the same concept was "ubiquitous computing", also known by the ugly portmanteau "ubicomp", and this also reflects the huge number of possible objects that might contain computing technology. Now that the Internet is a central pipe for data, it's hard to imagine, for example, a PC that doesn't have an always-on broadband connection. Younger readers may never have seen such a thing. As technologist and columnist Russell Davies joked at the 2012 Open Internet of Things Assembly in London:

> *I can't understand why teddy bears did not have wifi before. A bear without wifi is barely alive, a semi-bear.*
> —http://storify.com/PepeBorras/opent-iot-assembly

The definition of ubicomp, however, would also include the Glade air fresheners which release scent when they detect movement in the room as part of its domain. That is to say, such a device is an intelligently pro-grammed computer processor, driven by sensors in the real world, and driving output in the real world, all embedded into an everyday object. These factors make this ubicomp, and it is only differentiated from the "Internet of Things" by the fact that these days most of the really interesting things done with computing also involve an Internet connection.

But what does it mean to "connect an object to the Internet"? Clearly, sticking an Ethernet socket into a chair or a 3G modem into a sewing machine doesn't suddenly imbue the object with mysterious properties. Rather, there has to be some flow of information which connects the defining characteristics of the Thing with the world of data and processing represented by the Internet.

The Thing is present, physically in the real world, in your home, your work, your car, or worn around your body. This means that it can receive inputs from your world and transform those into data which is sent onto the Internet for collection and processing. So your chair might collect information about how often you sit on it and for how long, while the sewing machine reports how much thread it has left and how many stitches it has sewn. In subsequent chapters, we talk a lot about "sensors".

The presence of the Thing also means that it can produce outputs into your world with what we call "actuators". Some of these outputs could be triggered by data that has been collected and processed on the Internet. So your chair might vibrate to tell you that you have received email.

We could summarize these components in the following appealingly simple (though, of course, also simplistic) equation:

Physical Object

+

Controller, Sensor, and Actuators

+

Internet

=

Internet of Things

An equation for the Internet of Things.

Note that in all the cases we've looked at, the form of the object follows the function of the Thing: your chair is designed to sit on, the sewing machine to sew at, and so on. The fact of also being connected to the Internet and having general-purpose computing capabilities doesn't necessarily have an impact on the form of the object at all. (One might argue that current-generation smartphones and tablets are in forms optimized for use as general-purpose computers, not as portable telephony devices. Certainly, on seeing the number of phones with scratched screens, one could ask whether they are designed to be easy to hold securely and resistant to drops and the impacts of everyday use.)

THE TECHNOLOGY OF THE INTERNET OF THINGS

In starting to define the Internet of Things, we compared it to the earlier concept of ubiquitous computing. We could compare that, in turn, with Bill Gates's famous vision in 1977 of "a computer on every desk and in every home" (`http://danbricklin.com/log/billg_entwof.htm`) and again with the earlier notion of a computer as an astonishingly expensive and specialised machine, accessible only to universities, some forward-thinking global corporations, and the military. It is worth taking a little time to look at the Internet of Things through a lens of the history of technology to more clearly understand how and where it fits.

Technology's great drivers have initially been fundamental needs, such as food and water, warmth, safety, and health. Hunting and foraging, fire, building and fortifications, and medicine grow out of these needs. Then, because resources for these things are not always distributed where and when one might like, technological advances progress with enabling and controlling the movement of people, their possessions, livestock, and other resources. Trade develops as a movement of goods from a place where they are plentiful and cheap to one where they are rare and valuable. Storage is a form of movement in time—for example, from harvest time, when food is plentiful and cheap, to the following winter, when it is highly valued.

Information becomes key, too—hence, the development of language to communicate technology to others. Travellers might pass on messages as well as goods and services, and an oral tradition allows this information to pass through time as well as space. The invention of writing makes this communication ever more important and allows, to some extent, human lives to be preserved in words by and about writers, from the ancient philosophers and poets to the present day. From writing, via the telegraph, radio, and television, to digital information, more and more technology has been about enabling the movement of information or doing interesting things with that information.

But the other human needs we looked at haven't ceased to exist, nor will they. We still need to eat and drink. We still need light and warmth. We still need love and friendship. We still need chairs, clothes, and shoes; means of transport and communication; and ways to entertain ourselves. The shape and details of all of these things will change but not the needs they address.

As technology has progressed, new categories of objects have been created: in the electronic age, they have included telephones, radios, televisions, computers, and smartphones. As with most new technology, these devices tended to start out very expensive and gradually come down in price. Demand drives down prices, and research leads to optimization and miniaturisation. Ultimately, it becomes not just possible but also feasible to include functionality that would previously have required its own dedicated device *inside* another one. So although a television screen would originally have physically dominated a living room, not only are today's flat-screen panels more compact, but the technology is so ubiquitous that a high-resolution screen capable of displaying television content can be embedded into a door frame or a kitchen unit, and of course, even smaller screens can find their way into music players and mobile phones.

Similarly with computers, it has become so cheap to produce a general-purpose microchip in devices that your washing machine may contain a computer running Linux, the cash register at the supermarket may run on Windows, and your video player may run a version of Apple's OS X. But as we've already hinted at, mere computing power isn't a sufficient precondition for the Internet of Things. Rather, we are looking at computing power linked on the one hand to electronic sensors and actuators which interact with the real world and on the other to the Internet. It turns out that the rapid sharing and processing of *information* with services or other consumers is a huge differentiator.

As an example, let's consider the computers that exist in modern cars: they have myriad sensors to determine how well the car is running—from oil gauge and tyre pressure to the internals of your engine. As well as diagnostics, computerized brakes may assist the driver when the processor spots conditions such as the wheels locking or spinning out of control. All this is local information, and although the processing and analysis of this data may be highly sophisticated, it will be limited to whatever your car manufacturer has programmed. But perhaps your car also tracks your location using GPS: this is external (although not necessarily Internet-related) data. High-end cars may communicate the location back to a tracking service for insurance and anti-theft purposes. At this point, the car carries computing equipment that is able to not just passively consume data but also to have a dialogue with an external service. When your car's computer is connected to the Internet (regularly or permanently), it enables services such as responding to traffic conditions in real time by rerouting around them. Your GPS might already supply such data, but now it can be created in real time by "social route planning" based on the data aggregated from what other connected drivers nearby are doing. When the previously internal data gets connected to the Internet, the ways it can be processed, analysed, aggregated, and remixed with other data open up all the possibilities that we've seen in existing connected areas and indeed new ones that we can't yet imagine.

So there is a real change to an object or appliance when you embed comput-ing power into it and another real change when you connect that power to the Internet. It is worth looking at why this latter change is happening *now*.

When the Internet moved out of academia and the military, with the first commercial Internet service providers (ISPs) opening for business in the late 1980s, the early adopters of the consumer Internet may have first gone online with a computer running an Intel 486 chip, costing around £1500, or around the price of a small car. Today a microchip with equivalent power might set you back around £0.50, or the price of a chocolate bar. The rapid rise of processing power, and the consequent cost decrease, is not a new insight: it is widely known as Moore's law (the rule of thumb, suggested by the co-founder of Intel, that says the number of transistors you can fit on a silicon chip will double every 18 months).

However, the kind of price difference we've mentioned isn't merely a question of degree: it is a *qualitative* as well as a quantitative change. This is a "long tail" phenomenon through which we have now hit the right price/performance sweet spot that means the cost of the computing horsepower required to talk to the Internet has fallen to a level where adding a network or computing capability is akin to choosing what type of material or finish to use—for example, whether to use a slightly more expensive wood veneer. Either option would add a little to the cost of the product but could also add disproportionately to its value to the customer. When Internet-capable computing cost thousands of pounds, this wasn't an option, but now that it costs tens of pence, it is.

So the price of computing power has come down to affordable levels, but this is only part of the story. Manufacturers of electronic products have started to incorporate general-purpose computer CPUs into their products, from washing machines to cars, as they have seen that it has become, in many cases, cheaper to do this than to create custom chips. The wealth of pro-gramming and debugging resources available for these platforms has made them attractive to hobbyists and the prototyping market, leading to the proliferation of the microcontrollers, which we look at in Chapter 4, "Thinking About Prototyping", and Chapter 5, "Prototyping for Specific Devices".

Internet connectivity is also cheaper and more convenient than it used to be. Whereas in the past, we were tied to expensive and slow dial-up connec-tions, nowadays in the UK, 76% of adults have broadband subscriptions, providing always-on connectivity to the Net. Wired Ethernet provides a fairly plug-and-play networking experience, but most home routers today also offer WiFi, which removes the need for running cables everywhere.

While having an Internet-accessible computer in a fixed location was useful to those who needed to use it for work or studies, it would often be monopolized disproportionately by male and younger members of the family for general browsing or gaming. Now that the whole family can go online in the comfort of the living room sofa or their own room, they tend to do so in greater numbers and with ever greater confidence.

> *We hope the reader will excuse the preceding generalisation. As shown in the following figure, computer use in the UK between genders for the 16–24 age group is near identical since 2002. For the 55–74 group, there is a clear gap which persists, despite increasing take-up for both genders, until a tipping point around 2010 (http://w3.unece.org/pxweb/database/STAT/30-GE/09-Science_ICT/). Our hypothesis is that the shift is due, at least in part, to processing power and connectivity becoming cheap, widely available, and convenient. Not entirely coincidentally, these are the same factors we suggest help give rise to the Internet of Things.*

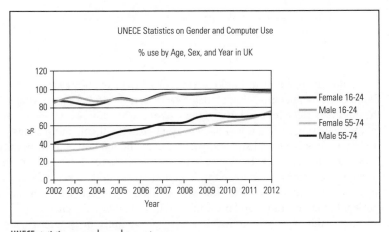

UNECE statistics on gender and computer use.

For situations in which a fixed network connection isn't readily available, mobile phone connectivity is widespread. Because the demand for connectivity is so great now, even embryonic solutions such as the whitespace network are available to use the airspace from the old analogue TV networks to fill gaps.

Another factor at play is the maturity of online platforms. Whereas early web apps were designed to be used only from a web browser, the much heralded "Web 2.0", as well as bringing us "rich web apps", popularized a style of programming using an Application Programming Interface (API), which allows other programs, rather than just users, to interact with and use the services on offer. This provides a ready ecosystem for other websites to "mash up" a number of services into something new, enables mobile phone "Apps", and now makes it easy for connected devices to consume.

As the online services mature, so too do the tools used to build and scale them. Web services frameworks such as Python and Django or Ruby on Rails allow easy prototyping of the online component. Similarly, cloud services such as Amazon Web Services mean that such solutions can scale easily with use as they become more popular. In Chapter 7, "Prototyping Online Components", we look at web programming for the Internet of Things.

ENCHANTED OBJECTS

The best known of Arthur C. Clarke's "three laws of prediction" states

> *Any sufficiently advanced technology is indistinguishable from magic.*
> —http://en.wikipedia.org/wiki/Clarke's_three_laws

We've already seen how technology has evolved to meet our needs and desires. The parallel invention of magic serves largely similar goals. After all, the objects in folktales and fairy tales are often wish-fulfilment fantasies to fill the deepest desires: if only I had enough to eat; if only my mother was well again; if only I could talk to my friend even though I'm far away; if only I could get home; if only I didn't have to work every hour of the day to earn enough money for my family to eat. Literary and anthropological scholars have long studied fairy tales for the lessons that can be learnt about the basic rules of human narrative and meaning and have analysed the characters, storylines, and objects found within them. For example, the formalist scholar Vladimir Propp categorized the folktales of his native Russia and categorised their plot elements into 31 functions, including "violation of interdiction", "villainy", "receipt of a magical agent", "difficult task", and so on.

More recently, and from the point of view of a Silicon Valley entrepreneur and technologist, David Rose has talked about Enchanted Objects at TEDx Berkeley (http://tedxtalks.ted.com/video/TEDxBerkeley-David-Rose-Enchant) and has categorised various objects drawn from fairy tales and fantasy literature in ways that apply as much to technological objects. For *Protection*, just as magical swords and helmets protected the protagonists of fairy tales from their enemies, so has much of the development of science and technology throughout history been driven by the need for military superiority, for the purpose of security or conquest. *Health* has been a driver for many quests to find an ingredient for a health potion and for research into various branches of medicine, pharmacology and surgery, physiotherapy, and diet. Humans have always desired *Omniscience*, from Snow White's wicked stepmother asking "Mirror mirror on the wall, who's the fairest of them all?" to the friends settling an argument of fact by looking up articles from Wikipedia on their smartphones. *Human Connection,* even when one's loved ones are far away, is an urgent, aching need: the Finnish hero Lemminkäinen's family know that he has been hurt when the enchanted comb that he left on the mantelpiece starts to bleed. Similarly, the postal service, telephones, and social networking help keep us in touch with our family and friends. The ancient storytellers yearning for *Effortless Mobility* invented seven-league boots, flying carpets, and even teleportation. Through technology, we have invented cars and railways, bicycles, and aeroplanes. The need for *Creative Expression* is fulfilled in stories by the enchanted paintbrushes or magic flutes and harps, while we have always used technology to devise such creative outlets, from charcoal to paint to computer graphics, or from drums to violins and electronic synthesisers.

So, technology has always been associated with magic, and so this will be true almost by default for the Internet of Things. But there is more to it than that: a key element of many enchanted objects is that above and beyond their practical enchantment they are given a name and a personality—implying an intelligence greater than strictly necessary to carry out the task for which they are designed. Examples of this abound, each with its own personality and morality, from the Finnish mill of plenty, named the Sampo, and the Arthurian Excalibur, to the malevolent intelligences of Tolkien's One Ring and Moorcock's Stormbringer. Just as these enchanted mills, swords, and rings are capable of more than just their functional specification, so our connected devices, or Things, have processing and communicating capabilities well beyond the needs of the average lamp, umbrella, or bubble machine.

WHO IS MAKING THE INTERNET OF THINGS?

Although we look at various theoretical aspects in this book, we are largely interested in the practice of actually *designing* and *making* Internet-connected Things. As Internet of Things thought leader and entrepreneur Alexandra Deschamps-Sonsino noted at the Victoria and Albert Museum's Power of Making Symposium, both these words mean many things to

different people. The following graphic depicts her initial attempt to map out
the meaning of making things:

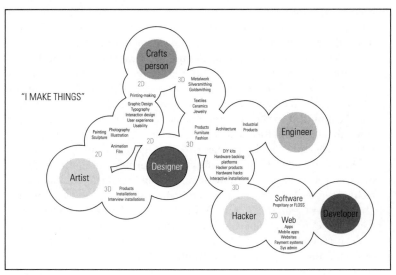

"I Make Things".

There are many crossover points between all the disciplines listed. Artists may
collaborate with designers on installations or with traditional craftspeople on
printmaking. Designers and engineers work closely to make industrial products,
and hobbyist "hackers" (in the sense of tinkerers and amateur engineers), by
their nature, are a diverse group encompassing various technical and artistic
interests and skills. The map isn't complete, and one could raise issue with
omissions: no role of "architect" is listed, only the discipline of architecture,
straddling the roles of engineer, designer, and craftsperson.

A more striking omission, given Deschamps-Sonsino's pedigree as an
Internet of Things innovator, is the role of "builder of the Internet of Things".
And, of course, this is not accidental. Rather, the Internet of Things straddles
all these disciplines: a hacker might tinker at the prototype for a Thing; a
software developer might write the online component; a designer might turn
the ugly prototype into a thing of beauty, possibly invoking the skills of a
craftsperson, and an engineer might be required to solve difficult technical
challenges, especially in scaling up to production. Finally, as we will see in
Chapter 2, "Design Principles for Connected Devices", the Internet of Things
is, or should be, the "Internet of Beautiful Things", and every object, as well
as being a crafted, designed, and engineered object, is, or could be, the work
of an artist also.

Of course, it is a rare Renaissance individual who covers all these disciplines with the fluency and ease that are conducive to creating a truly successful product. If you fit only one or a handful of these roles, you can still learn enough of the others to get things going. Getting additional expertise to make a project work, from prototype to production, is no bad thing and is something that we touch on in Chapter 9, "Business Models", and Chapter 10, "Moving to Manufacture". The most important lesson, however, is that whatever your interest as a creative person, you are abundantly qualified to get involved in the exciting field of the Internet of Things!

SUMMARY

We began by looking at some examples of the Internet of Things in action. Throughout the book, we discuss many similar projects, from the perspective of creating the first prototypes in Part I, to the extra effort required to manufacture and distribute them commercially in Part II. The Internet of Things can be characterised as joining the physical object, the computer embedded into it, and communication and code on the Internet itself. We focus on these three elements in both the prototyping and the manufacturing sections.

We compared Internet-connected devices to enchanted objects, and we will come back to this theme throughout the book, starting with the next chapter on design principles. These principles will, we hope, give rise to elegant, usable, interesting devices which delight their users. Creating a delightful and magical object may seem a daunting task, and as we saw in the previous section, the expertise required to make an Internet "Thing" is vast. However, this means that the playing field for making such a connected device is astonishingly level. Whatever your own skills and interests, you are as well placed as anyone to start experimenting and building. There really is no better time to enter the exciting world of the Internet of Things.

2

DESIGN PRINCIPLES FOR CONNECTED DEVICES

THIS BOOK IS called *Designing the Internet of Things,* so does that mean we think design is an important part of building a connected device?

For some applications, you may think that design isn't important at first glance. Who cares what the box holding a production-line sensor looks like in a factory? Surely form is defined by function?

Although the physical design of your connected device may be less important than that of something you're going to set on your mantelpiece, the extra functionality regarding how it will interact with the rest of the factory and its control systems is something you should consider and think through rather than just leave to chance.

If you haven't spent much time with designers, you might be forgiven for thinking that design is merely concerned with the shape and look of an object—something ornamental, to give it a pleasing appearance. However, design is a much wider field than that.

Industrial design (sometimes also called *product design*) does include the form and decoration of the item, but it also covers functional aspects such as working out how the product will be constructed or ensuring the controls are easily understood.

The user interface to the object—be that on a screen or the more traditional buttons and switches—is also something of interest to the discipline of experience design. That takes the perspective of the end user of the design as its focus and seeks to create the best solution for the user. Obviously "best" is subjective and could aim to make using the device as enjoyable as possible, or perhaps as efficient as possible, depending on the priorities of the designer or her team.

The rise of digital services, particularly those which take advantage of the Internet and the network effects it enables, has led to design specialists who take a wider view of the design of the whole system. Service design has the broadest view of the service in its entirety, whereas interaction design also looks at how different parts of the system interrelate, and especially how the user features in that interaction.

There are no hard boundaries between these differing facets of design, but we think designers of all types would agree that design is about more than just the surface look of the device.

In this chapter we look at some of the overarching principles that can be applied when designing an Internet of Things system, and then visit some of the techniques you can use to help explore the problem space and end up with a stronger product. Not all the techniques apply in all cases, but they provide some useful rules of thumb in approaching your work.

CALM AND AMBIENT TECHNOLOGY

The Internet of Things has its roots in the work done by Mark Weiser at Xerox PARC in the 1990s. His work didn't assume that there would be network connectivity but was concerned with what happens when computing power becomes cheap enough that it can be embedded into all manner of everyday objects. He coined the term *ubiquitous computing*, or *ubicomp* for short, to describe it, and through his research and writing sought to explore what that would mean for the people living in such a world.

With its focus on computing power being embedded everywhere, ubicomp is often also referred to as *ambient computing*. However, the term "ambient" also has connotations of being merely in the background, not something to which we actively pay attention and in some cases as something which we seek to remove (e.g., ambient noise in a sound recording).

We prefer, as did Mark Weiser, the term *calm technology*—systems which don't vie for attention yet are ready to provide utility or useful information when we decide to give them some attention.

Such proliferation of computing devices into the world comes with all manner of new challenges. Issues include configuration, how to provide power to all these items, how they talk to each other, and how they communicate with us.

The power and networking challenges are purely technical and are driving developments such as 6LoWPAN (`www.ietf.org/dyn/wg/charter/ 6lowpan-charter.html`). This is a standards drive from a working group of academics, computing professionals, and others to take the next-generation Internet protocol (IPv6) to the simplest and lowest-power networked sensors. (It is revisited when we look at future developments in the next chapter.) It aims to provide the scale of addresses and lower power usage needed by so many sensors.

Configuration and user interaction, however, obviously involve people and so are difficult problems to solve with just technical solutions. This is where good design can aid in adoption and usability. You can see this with the introduction of the Apple iPod in 2001. It wasn't the first portable MP3 player, but the combination of the scroll-wheel user interface and the companion iTunes software made it much easier to use and turned them into mass market gadgets.

Designing a connected device in isolation is likely to lead you to design decisions which aren't ideal when that object or service is placed into the seething mess that is the real world. To bastardize Eliel Saarinen's maxim on design, we suggest you think of how the connected device will interact as one of a wealth of connected devices.

In addition to thinking of a device in the physical context one step larger— Saarinen's "Always design a thing by considering it in its next larger context—a chair in a room, a room in a house, a house in an environment, an environment in a city plan"—we should do the same for the services.

For connected devices which are just sensing their world, or generally acting as *inputs*, as long as their activity doesn't require them to query the people around them, there shouldn't be any issues. They will happily collect information and deposit it into some repository online for processing or analysis.

When the devices start interacting with people, things get more complicated. Already we're seeing the number of notifications, pop-ups, and indicator noises on our computers and mobile phones proliferate. When we scale up this number to include hundreds of new services and applications and then spread that across the rest of the objects in our world, it will become an attention-seeking cacophony.

Mark Weiser and John Seely Brown proposed an antidote to such a problem by suggesting we design ubiquitous computing systems to seek to blend into their surroundings; in so doing, we could keep them in our peripheral perception until the right time to take centre stage:

> *Calm technology engages both the center and the periphery of our attention, and in fact moves back and forth between the two.*
> —Designing Calm Technology, Mark Weiser and John Seely Brown,
> Xerox PARC, December 21, 1995

A great example of this approach is *Live Wire*, one of the first Internet of Things devices. Created by artist Natalie Jeremijenko when she was in residence at Xerox PARC under the guidance of Mark Weiser, Live Wire (also sometimes called Dangling String) is a simple device: an electric motor connected to an eight-foot long piece of plastic string. The power for the motor is provided by the data transmissions on the Ethernet network to which it is connected, so it twitches whenever a packet of information is sent across the network.

Under normal, light network load, the string twitches occasionally. If the network is overloaded, the string whirls madly, accompanied by a distinctive noise from the motor's activity. Conversely, if no network activity is occurring, an unusual stillness comes over the string. Both extremes of activity therefore alert the nearby human (who is used to the normal behaviour) that something is amiss and lets him investigate further.

> *Not all technology need be calm. A calm videogame would get little use; the point is to be excited. But too much design focuses on the object itself and its surface features without regard for context. We must learn to design for the periphery so that we can most fully command technology without being dominated by it.*
> —Designing Calm Technology, Mark Weiser and John Seely Brown,
> Xerox PARC December 21, 1995

The mention of the distinctive sound from the motor when the Live Wire is under heavy load brings up another interesting point. Moving the means of conveying information away from screens and into the real world often adds a new dimension to the notification. On a computer, updating the screen is purely visual, so any additional senses must be engaged explicitly. Like Live Wire, Bubblino—Adrian's Internet of Things bubble machine which searches Twitter and blows bubbles when it finds new tweets matching a search phrase (see the case study in Chapter 4)—is a good example in which the side effect of the motor is to generate an audible notification that something is happening. With their Olly (`www.ollyfactory.com`) device, agency Mint Digital combines the motor with a deliberate olfactory indicator to provide a smelly notification of one of a number of social media events.

These noisy "side effects" are something that we should also be wary of losing with a move to "better" technology. Years ago all airport and railway arrival and departure boards were built using split-flap displays. They consisted of a number of flaps on a roll—sometimes with full place names printed onto the flap, and in other times as individually controllable characters—which could be rotated until they showed the correct item.

In most locations these split-flap displays have been phased out in preference for dot-matrix LED displays. The newer displays are much easier to update with new destinations. They also have capabilities such as horizontally scrolling messages which were impossible to add with the split-flap technology. Sadly, in doing so they have lost one important characteristic: the flurry of clacking as the display updates. As a result, passengers waiting in a station terminal must stare endlessly up at the display waiting for their train to be announced, rather than attending to other tasks and checking the departures board only when a change occurs.

That is not to say that screens are never the right choice, merely that in this age of mobile phones and tablets they are often chosen without realising a choice is being made. If you start from a position of trying *not* to use a screen, then if you return to it you will have worked out that a screen is the best solution.

There has been some interesting experimentation in the use of screens around what has been called *glanceable displays*. These are secondary screens, meant to sit away from your immediate surroundings in the same sort of places in which you might place a picture frame.

They aren't all screens. For example, Russell Davies, agitator for the recently possible, built Bikemap (`http://russelldavies.typepad.com/planning/2011/04/homesense-bikemap.html`), a handful of LEDs inserted into specific places on a printed-out map. The map shows the area around his home, and each LED marks the location of a bike stand for the London city bike rental scheme. If there are more than five bikes available at a stand, the corresponding LED lights up. It is mounted into a picture frame and hangs near to Russell's front door, so a glance over to it as he leaves lets him know which direction to head in order to find a bike.

One of Russell's roles is as a partner in the Really Interesting Group, a multidisciplinary agency based in London. Others in the agency, and some of their wider network of friends, have also been exploring the area.

They have a set of AirTunes WiFi speakers in the studio, which anyone can take control of and play music through. When you were working there, you'd often wonder exactly what a particular track was but had no way of finding out short of interrupting the entire office to ask who was in charge of the music at that moment and what was playing right now.

To solve that problem, they stuck a spare monitor out of everyone's way on top of a bookcase and, through a combination of watching the network traffic and hooking into the last.fm service that they all used to record what tracks they play, built a system to display the current track and who had played it.

The screen updated only whenever the song changed, and wasn't positioned in anyone's eye-line, so it didn't distract you from your work. However, if the music distracted you, the screen was there to satisfy your curiousity.

The Bikemap also provided some inspiration for RIG studio-mate Chris Heathcote. Chris is an interaction designer and realised that every morning he would check a few different apps on his phone to find out things like the weather forecast, his appointments for the day, and how the trains on the London Underground were running.He didn't have any power sockets near to his front door, and so settled on a bedside information display instead. Given that it would be always on and next to where he sleeps, a standard monitor or other LCD display, with its persistent glow, wouldn't be suitable. The e-ink display on a Kindle, however, was ideal. He took advantage of the WiFi connectivity and computing power in the Kindle to make it a self-contained device and configured it to just display a web page, which refreshed every few minutes.

The resultant device, which Chris called the Kindleframe (`http://anti-mega.com/antimega/2013/05/05/kindleframe`), would then always display up-to-date information from the mash-up of websites that he pulled together to collect all the information that he needs at the start of the day.

MAGIC AS METAPHOR

One of the main issues with introducing any new technology or service that is radically different from the norm is getting people to understand and accept it. Early adopters are generally happier looking a bit strange or doing things somewhat awkwardly to reap the benefits of the new gadgets; however, for the technology/service to catch on, you need to persuade the majority to take it up.

In addition to the technology becoming capable of a particular action, we often need *society*, for wont of a better term, to be ready to accept it. There are many examples when the main difference between a failed technology and a wildly successful one is that the successful one arrived a few years later, when people were more receptive to what was offered.

Technology blogger Venkatesh Rao came up with a good term to help explain how new technology becomes adopted. He posits that we don't see the present, the world that we live in now, as something that is changing. If we step back for a second, we do *know* that it has changed, although the big advances sneak up on us over time, hidden in plain sight. Rao called this concept the *manufactured normalcy field* (`www.ribbonfarm.com/2012/05/09/welcome-to-the-future-nauseous/`).

For a technology to be adopted, it has to make its way inside the manufactured normalcy field. As a result, the successful user-experience designer is the one who presents users with an experience which doesn't stretch the boundaries of their particular normalcy field too far, even if the underlying technology being employed is a huge leap ahead of the norm. For example, the mobile phone was first introduced as a phone that wasn't tethered to a particular location. Now broadly the same technology is used to provide a portable Internet terminal, which can play movies, carry your entire music collection, and (every now and then) make phone calls.

The way that portable Internet terminals made it into our manufactured normalcy field was through the phone metaphor. Introducing technology to people in terms of something they already understand is a tried and tested effect: computers started off as glorified typewriters; graphical user interfaces as desktops....

So, what of the Internet of Things? As we saw in the last chapter, Arthur C. Clarke has claimed that "any sufficiently advanced technology is indistinguishable from magic," and given that the Internet of Things commonly bestows semi-hidden capabilities onto everyday objects, maybe the enchanted objects of magic and fairy tale are a good metaphor to help people grasp the possibilities.

Some Internet of Things projects draw their inspiration directly from magic. For example, John McKerrell's WhereDial takes its lead from the clock in *Harry Potter* which tracked the location of the members of the Weasley family. The Weasley clock could use magic to divine the whereabouts of each family member and was therefore also aware of when they were in mortal peril. The WhereDial, by comparison, has to rely on mere technology for its capabilities; however, with the GPS chipsets in smartphones and location check-in services like FourSquare, it isn't much of a leap to also own an ornament which updates to show when you are at work, or travelling, or at a restaurant.

CASE STUDY: The WhereDial

Developer John McKerrell is passionate about maps and location. He got a job with mapping startup Multimap when he showed them a version of the slippy maps you could drag around in your web browser (something Google had only just wowed the world with at the time) using the Multimap map tiles, and by 2009 already had a couple of years of regularly logging his location on MapMe.At, a service he built to let people store and share their location.

So, when he attended a physical computing hackday in his home town of Liverpool (coincidentally organised by Adrian), a location-related project was almost a foregone conclusion.

The Harry Potter franchise was near its peak, and in it one of the families, the Weasleys, has a clock which shows where each family member is. A friend suggested that John could use that as a way to visualise some of the location data that he was already gathering.

John sourced a traditional carriage clock and rigged up a stepper motor to drive the clock mechanism, controlled by an Arduino which could talk to his MapMe.At service. The numbers on the clock face were replaced with a collection of common locations: home, work, shops, pub, restaurant, etc. Or, if the person wasn't in a specific place, it would show that they were travelling. That gave him a nice piece to sit on his sideboard and show whomever was at home the current location of both John and his wife (one hand on the clock for each).

Over the following years, John has refined the concept and turned it into an Internet of Things product. The software has been updated to hook into more location services, such as FourSquare, as their popularity has increased, and the physical form of the device itself has also evolved.

Using an existing clock for the housing and face had its issues: there's the challenge of sourcing suitable clocks in sufficient quantities, but also the problem of one of the hands only changing to a new location when the other has done a full rotation (good for showing hours and minutes, less useful for the location of two different people).

The WhereDial.

Now the WhereDial (http://wheredial.com) only shows the location of one person, and it is the location display that moves rather than a hand pointing to a location. This revised design is completely bespoke, and John can produce as many as he needs in house using the laser cutter in his workshop.

Other projects have a less obvious influence.

Enchanted mirrors seem a popular choice in design research, although they haven't quite reached the capabilities of the evil queen's "Mirror, mirror on the wall" in the Snow White tale. They tend to show information which is useful as you start or end your day, in line with the expected times when you'd use a bathroom mirror. You get the time and can check appointments and traffic and weather information while having your morning shower. Presumably, it is merely a matter of time before one shows the number of "Likes" you have on Facebook, thus turning it into the modern equivalent of the evil queen's query to know "who is the fairest of them all?"

Given David Rose's thinking around enchanted objects, it's not surprising that Ambient Devices, the company that he used to run, has a couple of examples. The ambient orb is a "single-pixel display" that can show the status of a metric of its user's choosing—the price of a stock, the weather forecast, the pollen count. Like the crystal ball whose shape the orb mimics, it shows you information from afar.

Ambient Devices then took the idea one step further and built an enchanted umbrella. It can read the weather forecast, and the handle glows gently if rain is expected, alerting you to the fact that you may need to pick it up as you head out of the house.

The magic of these devices isn't the epic magic of *The Lord of the Rings*; it's a more mundane, everyday sort of magic that makes tasks a bit easier and lives a little more fun. But that's the point: using our understanding of magic and fairy tales to help make sense of these strange new gadgets.

Of course, tales like *The Sorcerer's Apprentice* show us the danger of trying to use magic to reach beyond our capabilities. When the apprentice tries to ease his chores by using magic, that he doesn't fully understand, to enchant the broom, things get out of hand. It takes the timely return of the sorcerer to restore order. So far, our Roomba automated vacuum cleaners seem relatively well behaved, but we should be wary of creating Internet of Things devices whose seamless "magical" abilities give them behaviours or control interfaces which are hard for their owners to comprehend.

As well as trusting that your devices will do your bidding, it is also important to trust them to safeguard any data that they gather.

PRIVACY

The Internet of Things devices that we own aren't the only ones that should concern us when it comes to matters of trust. With more sensors and devices watching us and reporting data to the Internet, the privacy of third parties who cross our sensors' paths (either by accident or design) is an important consideration. Designers of an Internet of Things service will need to balance these concerns carefully.

KEEPING SECRETS

For certain realms, such as health care, privacy concerns are an obvious issue, so we cover this topic in more detail in Chapter 11, "Ethics". However, even seemingly innocuous applications can leak personal information, so you should be alert to the danger and take measures to avoid it.

This advice is perfectly illustrated with an example from an early instrumented car park in a Westfield shopping mall in Australia. Each parking bay is overlooked by a small sensor from Park Assist, which uses a cheap camera to tell whether the space is occupied. The sensors are all networked and presumably can provide analytics to the owner of the car park as to its usage. A light on the sensor can help guide drivers to a free space. All useful and harmless stuff.

The problem came with a more advanced feature of the system. The shopping mall provided a smartphone app for visitors to download so that they could find out more information about the facilities. One of the features of the app was a Find My Car option. Choosing that, you were prompted to enter the first few characters of your licence plate, and the app would then return four small photos of potential matches—from optical character recognition software processing the sensor data on the mall's server.

The returned images were only thumbnails—good enough to recognise which was your car, but not much else, and the licence plates were blurry and hard to see. However, security professional Troy Hunt found that the implementation method left a lot to be desired (www.troyhunt.com/ 2011/09/find-my-car-find-your-car-find.html).

With a fairly simple, off-the-shelf bit of software, Troy was able to watch what information the app was requesting from the server and found that it was a simple unencrypted web request. The initial request URL had a number of parameters, including the search string, but also including information such as the number of results to return.

That request returned a chunk of data (in the easily interpreted, industry standard JSON format), which included the URLs for the four images to download, but also included a raft of additional pieces of information. Presumably, it was easier for the developer of the web service to just return all the available data than to restrict it to just what was needed in this case. The extra data included, for example, the IP addresses of each of the sensor units, but more importantly, it also included the full licence plate for each vehicle and the length of time it had been parked in the space.

By altering the search parameters, Troy found that he could request many more than the four matches, and it was also possible to omit the licence plate search string. That meant he could download a full list of licence plates from all 2550 parking spaces in a single web request, whenever he liked.

Obviously, all that data is already publicly available, but there's a pretty large difference in ease of gathering it between staking out the entrance to the car park and watching cars come and go and setting up a script on a computer to check at regular intervals.

Once alerted to the problem, Westfield and Park Assist were quick to disable the feature and then work with Troy to build a better solution. However, that situation came about only because Troy was generous enough to bring it to their attention.

Don't share more than you need to provide the service.

As founder of WikiLeaks, Julian Assange, has said, "The best way to keep a secret is to never have it" (www.pbs.org/wgbh/pages/frontline/ wikileaks/interviews/julian-assange.html). If you can avoid gathering and/or storing the data in the first place, you need not worry about disclosing it accidentally.

In this day and age, it is standard practice to never store passwords as cleartext. You could also consider applying the standard mechanisms for password encryption, such as the one-way hash, to other pieces of data. This technique was suggested by Peter Wayner in his book *Translucent Databases* (CreateSpace Independent Publishing Platform, 2009). Rather than storing identifying data in the database, if you don't need to return it to its original form (that is, you just need it to be unique and associated with the same group of data), use a one-way hashed version of the information instead. Doing so still lets the originators of the data find their data (as they can provide it to be hashed again) and allows statistics gathering and reports, and the like, without storing the data in a recoverable form.

Hashes

One-way hashing is a cryptographic technique used to condense an arbitrarily sized chunk of data into a fixed-sized piece, called the hash. It's called one-way hashing because there isn't an easy way, given the resultant hash, to work out what the original data was. Hashing algorithms are so designed such that even a small difference in the input data leads to a huge difference in the output hash.

This makes them very useful for times when you want to verify that two pieces of data are identical without having to store them for comparison. That's useful when the data you want to compare is either very large or something you don't want to store in its original form.

The most common use of cryptographic hashes is in password verification. Rather than store the user's password, the service provider stores a hash of the password. When the user wants to authenticate himself in the future, the hash can be recalculated; if it matches the stored one, the service can be reasonably sure that the user has provided the correct password.

It is good practice to salt the password before applying the hash. This adds some random, non-secret extra text to the password before the hash is computed. The salt is then stored with the hash, so the service can concatenate the two again when it needs to verify a newly presented password. The salt prevents any attacker who ends up with a copy of the hash from easily comparing it to a dictionary of precompiled hashes to work out the password.

WHOSE DATA IS IT ANYWAY?

With the number of sensors being deployed, it isn't always clear whose data is being gathered. Consider the case of a camera deployed in an advertising hoarding which can check to see whether people are looking at the different adverts. Does the data belong to the company that installed the camera or to the members of the public who are looking at the adverts? Adam Greenfield, a leading practitioner of urban computing, makes a convincing argument that in a public space this data is being generated by the public, so they should at least have equal rights to be aware of, and also have access to, that data. (See point 67 at https://speedbird.wordpress.com/2012/12/03the-city-is-here-for-you-to-use-100-easy-pieces/.)

On private property, you can more easily claim that the members of the public don't have such a right, but perhaps the property owner might assert rights to the data rather than whoever installed the camera. And there are many places such as shopping malls which, to all intents and purposes, look and feel like public spaces, despite being privately owned. How do things stand in those areas?

When convening to debate such issues in the summer of 2012, the participants at the Open Internet of Things Assembly (`http://openiotassembly.com/`) coined the term *data subjects*—those people to whom the data pertains, regardless of whether they owned the sensors used to gather the data or the property where the sensors were sited. There's no clear understanding of what rights, if any, such "data subjects" will enjoy, but it is an area that deserves more debate and attention.

WEB THINKING FOR CONNECTED DEVICES

When you are thinking of the networked aspect of Internet of Things objects, it might help to draw on experiences and design guidelines from existing network deployments. The obvious choice would be to look at design guides to the World Wide Web and the Internet itself; after all, the term *Internet of Things* will look quaint in the future when we accept that it is completely natural for the Internet to be full of Things as well as computers and phones. You should aim to get into the mindset of the web and create devices which are *of* the web rather than those which just exist *on* the web.

In an early version of the specification for TCP (RFC761, `http://tools.ietf.org/html/rfc761 - section-2.10`), Jon Postel wrote: "Be conservative in what you do, be liberal in what you accept from others". Since then, that *robustness principle* has become so well known that it is commonly referred to as *Postel's Law*. It is good to bear this in mind when designing or building anything which must interact with other services— particularly when you aren't the one building the other components with which your system interacts.

SMALL PIECES, LOOSELY JOINED

Even if you are building all the components of your service, it makes sense not to couple them too tightly together. The Internet flourished not because it is neatly controlled from a central location, but because it isn't; it is a collection of services and machines following the maxim of *small pieces, loosely joined*.

What this means for the architects of a service is that each piece should be designed to do one thing well and not rely too much on tight integration with the separate components it uses. Strive also to make the components more generalised and able to serve other systems which require a similar function. That will help you, and others, to reuse and repurpose the components to build new capabilities unimagined when the initial system was commissioned.

Where possible, use existing standards and protocols rather than inventing your own. Any loss of elegance or efficiency of code size or electronics will be outweighed by the availability of standard libraries and skills for people to interact with, and build on, your system. For example, when the designers at Twitter implemented the search feature, they chose to include a more machine-readable option in the form of a feed of results in the standard Atom syndication format (`http://tools.ietf.org/html/rfc4287`). I'm fairly certain that they didn't expect it to be consumed by an Arduino, which would then use it to activate a bubble machine to blow bubbles for each new tweet.

Similarly, because Bubblino was made to understand and consume Atom feeds to look for new tweets, it can now be repurposed to monitor anything with such an interface. So new entries in a blog are trivial to monitor, and most web languages have libraries to generate suitable Atom feeds for any other notifications that you would like to visualise as bubbles.

This meant it was trivial for one customer to get their Bubblino to trigger whenever one of their developers submitted some code which failed their automated tests. They just wrote a small web service that took the test results and presented them as an Atom XML feed. Once their Bubblino was configured to use that new service, it would then blow bubbles whenever the tests failed.

FIRST-CLASS CITIZENS ON THE INTERNET

An extension of the concept of loose coupling is to strive to make your devices first-class citizens on the Internet. What do we mean by that? Where possible, you should use the same protocols and conventions that the rest of the Internet uses.

In the early days of any new development, it is tempting to compromise and choose protocols which are easier to implement. Indeed, many middleware providers encourage that practice, claiming that such low-powered end-points are not capable enough (in processing power or RAM or in the networks they use). There is an element of truth to this—though not as much as you will be led to believe—but a good rule of thumb for the past 20 years or more has been to expect the IP protocol to penetrate everywhere. We see no reason for it not to continue into the Internet of Things.

In the few cases where the existing protocols don't work, such as in extremely low-powered sensors, a better solution is to work with your peers to amend existing standards or create new open standards which address the issue within the conventional standards groups.

The evolution of the mobile web serves as a good cautionary example. When mobile phones were first being connected to the Internet, it was deemed too difficult for them to talk to web servers directly, and a whole suite of new protocols, Wireless Application Protocol (WAP), were developed. Handsets accessed either bespoke WAP sites or standard websites via a WAP/web gateway server. As they needed site developers to learn a whole new set of skills, the new protocols gained little traction; without the sites to visit, user adoption of the mobile web was slow.

As the handsets evolved to talk the standard protocols of the web, even though the display wasn't perfect, it was good enough for users to begin using it. With the increase in usage directly to the websites developers could then see the demand for mobile-friendly features. Given that those features could be developed with the tools with which they were already familiar, over time the mobile web has just become a facet of the web in general.

GRACEFUL DEGRADATION

Because the Internet is so welcoming and tolerant of all sorts of devices and services, the endpoints have a massively disparate and diverse range of capabilities. As a result, building services which can be used by all of them is a nearly impossible task. However, a number of design patterns have evolved to mitigate the problem.

The first is to acknowledge that the wealth of different devices is likely to be a problem and design your system to expect it. If you need to come up with a format for some data being transferred between devices, include a way to differentiate between successive versions of the formats—ideally in such a way that older devices can still mostly read newer formats. This is known as *backwards compatibility*, and although over time it will add some cruft to the format, as certain features will only persist to serve outdated devices, it will greatly extend the life and utility of your users' devices. The HTML format does this by stating that any client should ignore any tags (the text inside the <>) that it doesn't understand, so newer versions can add new tags without breaking older parsers. The HTTP protocol uses a slightly different technique in which each end specifies the version of the protocol that it supports, and the other end takes care not to use any of the newer features for that particular session.

The other common technique is to use something called *graceful degradation*. This technique involves aiming to provide a fully featured experience if the client is capable of it but then falling back—potentially in a number of levels—to a less feature-rich experience on less capable clients. This capability can even span technologies and does so in its most common usage. When trying to implement rich web applications such as Twitter and Gmail, the coder wants to use an assortment of advanced JavaScript features in modern browsers. Well-written apps check that the features are available before using them, but if those features aren't available, the apps might limit themselves to a version using simpler (and more common) JavaScript code—still validating form contents before submitting them, for example, but no longer calling over to the server to provide autocomplete. And if JavaScript isn't available at all, they fall back to basic HTML forms. This experience is not as nice as the full one but better than no experience at all!

Aside from using the same techniques when designing our connected devices, we might also be able to apply that approach to the devices themselves to give a degree of fault tolerance. The proliferation of devices and the likelihood that some of them will break in some way means that it is important that their technology continues to add what value it can, as parts cease to function. When your early-adopter Internet Fridge can no longer talk to your WiFi because it's only IPv4 and the world has moved to IPv6, you would still be able to use its touchscreen to write messages and view the photos stored in the USB stick stuck in it. And if the touchscreen breaks, you should still be able to keep the food inside it cold.

AFFORDANCES

In his book *The Design of Everyday Things*, Donald Norman defines *affordances* as follows:

> *Affordances provide strong clues to the operations of things. Plates are for pushing. Knobs are for turning. Slots are for inserting things into. Balls are for throwing or bouncing. When affordances are taken advantage of, the user knows what to do just by looking: no picture, label, or instruction is required. Complex things may require explanation, but simple things should not. When simple things need pictures, labels, or instructions, the design has failed.*
> —The Design of Everyday Things, *MIT Press, 1998*

We recommend this excellent book for anyone with an interest in design, although the section on the affordances of doors may ruin your interactions with buildings because you will encounter examples of poorly thought-out design almost daily.

As adoption of the Internet of Things gathers pace, more and more of our cities, homes, and environment will become suffused with technology. With these additional behaviours and capabilities will come additional complexity—something that successful designers of connected devices and services will need to counter.

By their very nature, many of the new capabilities bestowed upon objects will be hidden from sight or not immediately apparent from first glance, which makes intuitive design difficult. What are the affordances of digitally enhanced objects?

How do we convey to the user of an object that it can communicate with the cloud? Or that this device is capable of short-range communication such as RFID? What does it mean that a toy knows what the temperature is or when it is shaken? How do you know whether your local bus shelter is watching you or, possibly more importantly, why?

An important start is to keep the existing affordances of the object being enhanced. Users who don't realise that a device has any extra capabilities should still be able to use it as if it hasn't. Although this principle sounds like common sense, it is often discarded due to costs or difficulties in design.

For example, a "dumb" light dimmer switch is usually implemented as a rotary knob which gives the user fine-grained control over the brightness. When it is hooked up to a home-automation system, the difficulties of synchronising the state of both the knob and the light level, now that the brightness can be controlled remotely or automatically, often leads to the knob being replaced with a couple of buttons. As a result, the user loses the ability to make both rapid large changes and smaller, fine-grained adjustments. A better approach would be to adopt the system used on many stereo systems where the volume knob is a motorized potentiometer; the user can still adjust it in the conventional manner, and any changes made by the remote are instantly reflected in the position of the volume knob.

Things get trickier with interactions that are invisible—either because they use wireless communication or because they are invoked through learned gestures. However, we can still design the physical form of the object to encourage the right behaviour. Nothing inherent in RFID requires it to be laid out flat in a card, but this leads users towards the correct interaction of tapping their Oyster transport payment card onto the similarly flat reader surface when travelling on the London Underground.

Similar rules apply when designing physical interfaces. Don't overload familiar connectors with unfamiliar behaviours. For example, you shouldn't use 3.5mm audio jacks to provide power, although alternative "data-level" uses are probably okay. And if you're designing a new connector completely, think about ways to prevent users from connecting it the wrong way round. littleBits (`http://littlebits.cc/about`) faced this problem when they were designing their modular, plug-together electronic circuit building blocks. They were looking for a way to make it easy and relatively foolproof to connect things together because the product is aimed at beginners. Their solution is a nice approach in this respect, using magnets to both discourage incorrect connection whilst also encouraging the correct connection.

SUMMARY

This chapter will have given you a deeper understanding of the emerging field of the Internet of Things and some ways to direct your thinking when you are designing something to fit into the landscape.

The examples have shown how you need to think not just about the technical details of how the device will work, but also of how it will fit into the wider context of the user's life. Unlike an app on her phone, your Internet of Things product will take up physical space in the world and won't be silenced just by the user's focusing on a different app, so you need to consider that for her.

You also need to take care not to divulge any information that users wouldn't expect you to. It is a new field full of expanding possibilities which gives us opportunities for delighting and enriching people's lives, but we need to do so in a way that doesn't scare or alienate the less technical in the population.

Careful use of touchpoints such as magic and fairytales can help with this, as will systems which fail gracefully and still perform their non-computer-enhanced functions in the way to which everyone is accustomed.

Even this early in the book you will already have encountered different aspects of the network bleeding through—for example, in the description of Natalie Jeremijenko's Live Wire or the mention of HTTP protocol versions in the section on graceful degradation.

That's hardly surprising in a book about the *Internet* of Things, but we don't assume that you have a full understanding of how the network works or exactly what it can do. The next chapter looks at the common protocols on the Internet (and even what a protocol is) and how they interrelate, to give you a better understanding of how the Internet works.

3

INTERNET PRINCIPLES

IF YOU ARE reading this book, we assume that you probably use the Internet regularly—for browsing the web, reading and sending email, listening to music. But familiarity with the Internet is very much on a gradient. Using the Internet daily is a first step in understanding it; developing software or Things that speak to the Internet is another; and developing or debugging the software that runs the Internet itself is yet another.

This gradient of familiarity also applies to the authors of this book. Perhaps, like Adrian, you have implemented a full TCP/IP stack, several times. Perhaps, like Hakim, you're not entirely sure what that jargon means.

Whether you are a developer, engineer, artist, or entrepreneur, having a high-level view of the different components and technologies that make up what we call the Internet will help you understand the possibilities and the current limitations of what you can do with the Internet of Things.

This chapter is a short, high-level survey, designed to be readable rather than complete. Let's start by looking at an example of how communication over long distances could work in the real world and then compare it to how information is transmitted across the virtual world of the Internet.

INTERNET COMMUNICATIONS: AN OVERVIEW

Suppose that you wanted to send a message to the authors of this book, but you didn't have the postal address, and you didn't have any way to look up our phone number (because in this example you don't have the Internet).

You remember that we're from the UK, and London is the biggest city in the UK. So you send a postcard to your cousin Bob, who lives there.

Your cousin sees that the postcard is for some crazy hardware and technology people. So he puts the postcard in an envelope and drops it off at the London Hackspace because the guys there probably know what to do with it.

At the Hackspace, Jonty picks up the envelope and sees that it's for some people in Liverpool. Like all good Londoners, Jonty never goes anywhere to the north of Watford, but he remembers that Manchester is in the north too. So he calls up the Manchester Digital Laboratory (MadLab), opens the envelope to read the contents, and says, "Hey, I've got this message for Adrian and Hakim in Liverpool. Can you pass it on?"

The guys at MadLab ask whether anyone knows who we are, and it turns out that Hwa Young does. So the next time she comes to Liverpool, she delivers the postcard to us.

IP

The preceding scenario describes how the Internet Protocol (IP) works. Data is sent from one machine to another in a packet, with a destination address and a source address in a standardised format (a "protocol"). Just like the original sender of the message in the example, the sending machine doesn't always know the best route to the destination in advance. Most of the time, the packets of data have to go through a number of intermediary machines, called *routers*, to reach their destination. The underlying networks aren't always the same: just as we used the phone, the postal service, and delivery by hand, so data packets can be sent over wired or wireless networks, through the phone system, or over satellite links.

In our example, a postcard was placed in an envelope before getting passed onwards. This happens with Internet packets, too. So, an *IP packet* is a block of data along with the same kind of information you would write on a physical envelope: the name and address of the server, and so on. But if an IP packet ever gets transmitted across your local wired network via an Ethernet cable—the cable that connects your home broadband router or your office local area network (LAN) to a desktop PC—then the whole packet will get bundled up into another type of envelope, an *Ethernet Frame,* which adds additional information about how to complete the last few steps of its journey to your computer.

Of course, it's possible that your cousin Bob didn't know about the London Hackspace, and then maybe the message would have got stuck with him. You would have had no way to know whether it got there. This is how IP works. There is no guarantee, and you can send only what will fit in a single packet.

TCP

What if you wanted to send longer messages than fit on a postcard? Or wanted to make sure your messages got through?

What if everyone agreed that postcards written in green ink meant that we cared about whether they arrived. And that we would always number them, so if we wanted to send longer messages, we could. The person at the other end would be able to put the messages in order, even if they got delivered in the wrong order (maybe you were writing your letter over a number of days, and the day you passed the fifth one on to cousin Bob, he happened to visit Liverpool and passed on that postcard without relaying through London Hackspace or MadLab). We would send back postcard notifications that just told you which postcards we had received, so you could resend any that went missing.

That is basically how the Transmission Control Protocol (TCP) works. The simplest transport protocol on the Internet, TCP is built on top of the basic IP protocol and adds sequence numbers, acknowledgements, and retransmissions. This means that a message sent with TCP can be arbitrarily long and give the sender some assurance that it actually arrived at the destination intact.

Because the combination of TCP and IP is so useful, many services are built on it in turn, such as email and the HTTP protocol that transmits information across the World Wide Web.

THE IP PROTOCOL SUITE (TCP/IP)

The combination of TCP and IP is so ubiquitous that we often refer simply to "TCP/IP" to describe a whole suite or stack of protocols layered on top of each other, each layer building on the capabilities of the one below.

- The low-level protocols at the *link layer* manage the transfer of bits of information across a network link. This could be by an Ethernet cable, by WiFi, or across a telephone network, or even by short-range radio standards such as IEEE 802.15.4 designed to carry data over the Personal Area Network (PAN), that is to say between devices carried by an individual.
- The *Internet layer* then sits on top of these various links and abstracts away the gory details in favour of a simple destination address.
- Then TCP, which lives in the *transport layer*, sits on top of IP and extends it with more sophisticated control of the messages passed.
- Finally, the *application layer* contains the protocols that deal with fetching web pages, sending emails, and Internet telephony. Of these, HTTP is the most ubiquitous for the web, and indeed for communication between Internet of Things devices. We look at standards such as MQTT briefly in Chapter 7.

UDP

As you can see, TCP is not the only protocol in the transport layer. Unlike TCP, but as with IP itself, in UDP each message may or may not arrive. No handshake or retransmission occurs, nor is there any delay to wait for messages in sequence. These limitations make TCP preferable for many of the tasks that Internet of Things devices will be used for.

The lack of overhead, however, makes UDP useful for applications such as streaming data, which can cope with minor errors but doesn't like delays. Voice over IP (VoIP)—computer-based telephony, such as Skype—is an example of this: missing one packet might cause a tiny glitch in the sound quality, but waiting for several packets to arrive in the right order could make the speech too jittery to be easy to understand. UDP is also the transport for some very important protocols which provide common, low-level functionality, such as DNS and DHCP, which relate to the discovery and resolution of devices on the network. We look at this topic in detail in the next section.

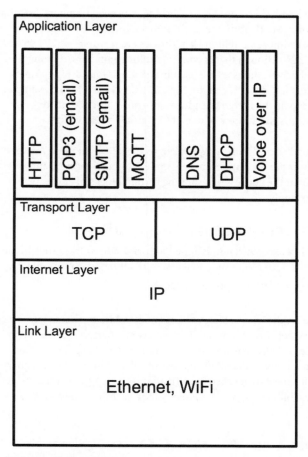

The Internet Protocol suite.

IP ADDRESSES

We mentioned earlier that the Internet Protocol knows the addresses of the destination and source devices. But what does an "address" consist of? Here is a typical human (or in this case, hobbit) address:

> Bilbo Baggins
> "Bag End", Bagshot Row
> Hobbiton
> The Shire
> Middle Earth

In the world of low-level computer networking, however, numbers are much easier to deal with. So, IP addresses are numbers. In Internet Protocol version 4 (IPv4), almost 4.3 billion IP addresses are possible—4,294,967,296 to be precise, or 2^{32}. Though that is convenient for computers, it's tough for humans to read, so IP addresses are usually written as four 8-bit numbers separated by dots (from `0.0.0.0` to `255.255.255.255`)—for example, `192.168.0.1` (which is often the address of your home router) or `8.8.8.8` (which is the address of one of Google's DNS servers).

This "dotted quad" is still exactly equivalent to the 32-bit number. As well as being simply easier for humans to remember, it is also easier to infer information about the address by grouping certain blocks of addresses together. For example,

`8.8.8.x` — One of several IP ranges assigned to Google.

`192.168.x.x` — A range assigned for private networks. Your home or office network router may well assign IP addresses in this range.

`10.x.x.x` — Another private range.

Every machine on the Internet has at least one IP address. That means every computer, every network-connected printer, every smartphone, and every Internet of Things device has one. If you already have a Raspberry Pi, an Arduino board, or any of the other microcontrollers described in Chapters 3 and 4, they will expect to get their own IP address, too. When you consider this fact, those 4 billion addresses suddenly look as if they might not be enough.

The private ranges such as `192.168.x.x` offer one mitigation to this problem. Your home or office network might have only one publicly visible IP address. However, you could have all the IP addresses in the range `192.168.0.0` to `192.168.255.255` (2^16 = 65,536 addresses) assigned to distinct devices.

A better solution to this problem is the next generation of Internet Protocol, IPv6, which we look at later in this chapter.

DNS

Although computers can easily handle 32-bit numbers, even formatted as dotted quads they are easy for most humans to forget. The Domain Name System (DNS) helps our feeble brains navigate the Internet. Domain names, such as the following, are familiar to us from the web, or perhaps from email or other services:

```
google.com
bbc.co.uk
wiley.com
arduino.cc
```

Each domain name has a top-level domain (TLD), like `.com` or `.uk`, which further subdivides into `.co.uk` and `.gov.uk`, and so on. This top-level domain knows where to find more information about the domains within it; for example, `.com` knows where to find `google.com` and `wiley.com`.

The domains then have information about where to direct calls to individual machines or services. For example, the DNS records for `.google.com` know where to point you for the following:

```
www.google.com
mail.google.com
calendar.google.com
```

The preceding examples are all instantly recognizable as website names, which is to say you could enter them into your web browser as, for example, `http://www.google.com`.

But DNS can also point to other services on the Internet—for example:

`pop3.google.com` — For receiving email from Gmail

`smtp.google.com` — For sending email to Gmail

`ns1.google.com` — The address of one of Google's many DNS servers

Configuring DNS is a matter of changing just a few settings. Your registrar (the company that sells you your domain name) often has a control panel to change these settings. You might also run your own authoritative DNS server. The settings might contain entries like this one for `roomofthings.com`:

```
book A 80.68.93.60 3h
```

This entry means that the address `book.roomofthings.com` (which hosts the blog for this book) is served by that IP address and will be for the next three hours.

STATIC IP ADDRESS ASSIGNMENT

How do you get assigned an IP address? If you have bought a server-hosting package from an Internet service provider (ISP), you might typically be given a single IP address. But the company itself has been given a block of addresses to assign. Historically, these were ranges of different sizes, typically separated into "classes" of 8 bits, 16 bits, or 24 bits:

> Class A — From `0.x.x.x`
>
> Class B — From `128.0.x.x`
>
> Class C — From `192.0.0.x`

The class C ranges had a mere 8 bits (256 addresses) assigned to them, while the class A ranges had many more addresses and would therefore be given only to the very largest of Internet organisations. The rigid separation of address ranges into classes was not very efficient; every entity would want to keep enough spare addresses for future expansion, but this means that many addresses would remain unused. With the explosion of the number of devices connecting to the Internet (a theme throughout this chapter), the scheme has been superceded since 1993 by Classless Inter-Domain Routing (CIDR), which allows you to specify exactly how many bits of the address are fixed. (See RFCs 1518 and 1519, at `http://tools.ietf.org/rfc/`.) So, the class A addresses we mentioned above would be equivalent to `0.0.0.0/8`, while a class C might be `208.215.179.0/24`.

For example, you saw previously that Google had the range

> `8.8.8.x` (which is equivalent to `8.8.8.0/24` in CIDR notation)

Google has chosen to give one of its public DNS servers the address

> `8.8.8.8`

from this range, largely because this address is easy to remember.

In many cases, however, the system administrator simply assigns server numbers in order. The admininstrator makes a note of the addresses and updates DNS records and so on to point to these addresses. We call this kind of address *static* because once assigned it won't change again without human intervention.

Now consider your home network: every time you plug a desktop PC to your router, connect your laptop or phone to the wireless, or switch on your network-enabled printer, this device has to get an IP address (often in the range `192.168.0.0/16`). You *could* assign an address sequentially yourself, but the typical person at home isn't a system administrator and may not keep thorough records. If your brother, who used to use the address `192.168.0.5` but hasn't been home for ages, comes back to find that your new laser printer now has that address, he won't be able to connect to the Internet.

DYNAMIC IP ADDRESS ASSIGNMENT

Thankfully, we don't typically have to choose an IP address for every device we connect to a network. Instead, when you connect a laptop, a printer, or even a Twitter-following bubble machine, it can request an IP address from the network itself using the Dynamic Host Configuration Protocol (DHCP). When the device tries to connect, instead of checking its internal configuration for its address, it sends a message to the router asking for an address. The router assigns it an address. This is not a static IP address which belongs to the device indefinitely; rather, it is a temporary "lease" which is selected *dynamically* according to which addresses are currently available. If the router is rebooted, the lease expires, or the device is switched off, some other device may end up with that IP address.

This means that you can't simply point a DNS entry to a device using DHCP. In general, you can rely on the IP address probably being the same for a given work session, but you shouldn't hard-code the IP address anywhere that you might try to use it another time, when it might have changed.

Even the simplest computing devices such as the Arduino board, which we look at in Chapter 5, can use DHCP. Although the Arduino's Ethernet library allows you to configure a static IP address, you can also request one via DHCP. Using a static address may be fine for development (if you are the only person connected to it with that address), but for working in groups or preparing a device to be distributed to other people on arbitrary networks, you almost certainly want a dynamic IP address.

IPv6

When IP was standardised, few could have predicted how quickly the 4.3 billion addresses that IPv4 allowed for would be allocated. The expected growth of the Internet of Things can only speed up this trend. If your mobile phone, watch, MP3 player, augmented reality sunglasses, and telehealth or sports-monitoring devices are all connected to the Internet, then you personally are carrying half a dozen IP addresses already. Perhaps you have a dedicated wallet server for micropayments? A personal web server that contains your contact details and blog? One or more webcams recording your day? Perhaps rather than a single health monitoring device, you have several distributed across your person, with sensors for temperature, heart rate, insulin levels, and any number of other stimuli.

At home you would start with all your electronic devices being connected. But beyond that, you might also have sensors at every door and window for security. More sensitive sound sensors to detect the presence of mice or beetles. Other sensors to check temperature, moisture, and airflow levels for efficiency. It is hard to predict what order of number of Internet connected devices a household might have in the near future. Tens? Hundreds? Thousands?

Enter IPv6, which uses 128-bit addresses, usually displayed to users as eight groups of four hexadecimal digits—for example, `2001:0db8:85a3:0042 :0000:8a2e:0370:7334`. The address space (2^{128}) is so huge that you could assign the same number of addresses as the whole of IPv4 to *every* person on the planet and barely make a dent in it.

The new standard was discussed during the 1980s and finally released in 1996. In 2013, it is still less popular than IPv4. You can find many ways to work around the lack of public IP addresses using subnets, but there is a chicken-and-egg problem with getting people to use IPv6 without ISP support and vice versa. It was originally expected that mobile phones connected to the Internet (another huge growth area) would push this technology over the tipping point. In fact, mobile networks are increasingly using IPv6 internally to route traffic. Although this infrastructure is still invisible to the end user, it does mean that there is already a lot of use below the surface which is stacked up, waiting for a tipping point.

IPv6 and Powering Devices

We can see that an explosion in the number of Internet of Things devices will almost certainly need IPv6 in the future. But we also have to consider the power consumption of all these devices. We know that we can regularly charge and maintain a small handful of devices. At any one moment, we might have a laptop, a tablet, a phone, a camera, and a music player plugged in to charge. The constant juggling of power sockets, chargers, and cables is feasible but fiddly. The requirements for large numbers of devices, however, are very different. The devices should be low power and very reliable, while still being capable of connecting to the Internet. Perhaps to accomplish this, these devices will team together in a mesh network. This is the vision of 6LoWPAN, an IETF working group proposing solutions for "IPv6 over Low power Wireless Personal Area Networks", using technologies such as IEEE 802.15.4. While a detailed discussion of 6LoWPAN and associated technologies is beyond the scope of this book, we do come back to many related issues, such as maximising battery life in Chapter 8 on embedded programming.

Conclusion on IPv6

Although IPv6 is, or will be, big news, we do not go into further detail in this book. In 2013, you can find more libraries, more hardware, and more people that can support IPv4, and this is what will be most helpful when you are moving from prototype to production on an Internet of Things device. Even though we are getting close to the tipping point, existing IPv4 services will be able to migrate to IPv6 networks with minimal or possibly no rewriting.

If you are working on IPv6 network infrastructure or are an early adopter of 6LoWPAN, you will have specific knowledge requirements that are beyond the current scope of this book.

MAC ADDRESSES

As well as an IP address, every network-connected device also has a MAC address, which is like the final address on a physical envelope in our analogy. It is used to differentiate different machines on the same physical network so that they can exchange packets. This relates to the lowest-level "link layer" of the TCP/IP stack. Though MAC addresses are globally unique, they don't typically get used outside of one Ethernet network (for example, beyond your home router). So, when an IP message is routed, it hops from node to node, and when it finally reaches a node which knows where the *physical* machine is, that node passes the message to the device associated with that MAC address.

MAC stands for *Media Access Control*. It is a 48-bit number, usually written as six groups of hexadecimal digits, separated by colons—for example:

```
01:23:45:67:89:ab
```

Most devices, such as your laptop, come with the MAC address burned into their Ethernet chips. Some chips, such as the Arduino Ethernet's WizNet, don't have a hard-coded MAC address, though. This is for production reasons: if the chips are mass produced, they are, of course, *identical*. So they can't, physically, contain a distinctive address. The address could be stored in the chip's firmware, but this would then require every chip to be built with custom code compiled in the firmware. Alternatively, one could provide a simple data chip which stores just the MAC address and have the WizNet chip read that. Obviously, most consumer devices use some similar process to ensure that the machine always starts up with the same unique MAC address. The Arduino board, as a low-cost prototyping platform for developers, doesn't bother with that nicety, to save time and cost. Yet it does come with a sticker with a MAC address printed on it. Although this might seem a bit odd, there is a good reason for it: that MAC address is reserved and therefore is guaranteed unique if you want to use it. For development purposes, you can simply choose a MAC address that is known not to exist in your network.

WizNet is a Korean manufacturer which specialises in networking chips for embedded devices. Many popular microcontrollers which we look at in Chapter 5 use these chips.

TCP AND UDP PORTS

A messenger with a formal invitation for a wealthy family of the Italian Renaissance would go straight to the front entrance to deliver it. A grocer delivering a crate of the first artichokes of the season would go instead to a service entrance, where the crate could be taken quickly to the kitchen without getting in the way of the masters. The following engraving, by John Gilbert, is taken from Shakespeare's *Romeo and Juliet*. This reminds us that the house of the Capulets has at least one other entrance—on Juliet's balcony. If Romeo wants to see his beloved, that is the only way to go. If he climbs up the wrong balcony, he'll either wait outside (the nurse is fast asleep and can't hear his knocks) or get chased away by the angry father.

Similarly, when you send a TCP/IP message over the Internet, you have to send it to the right port. TCP ports, unlike entrances to the Capulet house, are referred to by numbers (from 0 to 65535).

Romeo and Juliet, Act I, Scene 2, by John Gilbert, before 1873.
Public domain http://en.wikipedia.org/wiki/File:Scene_2.jpg.

AN EXAMPLE: HTTP PORTS

If your browser requests an HTTP page, it usually sends that request to port 80. The web server is "listening" to that port and therefore replies to it. If you send an HTTP message to a different port, one of several things will happen:

- Nothing is listening to that port, and the machine replies with an "RST" packet (a control sequence resetting the TCP/IP connection) to complain about this.

- Nothing is listening to that port, but the firewall lets the request simply hang instead of replying. The purpose of this (lack of) response is to discourage attackers from trying to find information about the machine by scanning every port. (Imagine Romeo knocking on the sleeping nurse's window.)

- The client has decided that trying to send a message to that port is a bad idea and refuses to do it. Google Chrome does this for a fairly arbitrary list of "restricted ports".
- The message arrives at a port that is expecting something other than an HTTP message. The server reads the client's response, decides that it is garbage, and then terminates the connection (or, worse, does a nonsensical operation based on the message).

Ports 0–1023 are "well-known ports", and only a system process or an administrator can connect to them.

Ports 1024–49151 are "registered", so that common applications can have a usual port number. However, most services are able to bind any port number in this range.

The Internet Assigned Numbers Authority (IANA) is responsible for registering the numbers in these ranges. People can and do abuse them, especially in the range 1024–49151, but unless you know what you're doing, you are better off using either the correct assigned port or (for an entirely custom application) a port above 49151.

You see custom port numbers if a machine has more than one web server; for example, in development you might have another server, bound to port 8080:

```
http://www.example.com:8080
```

Or if you are developing a website locally, you may be able to test it with a built-in test web server which connects to a free port. For example, Jekyll (the lightweight blog engine we are using for this book's website) has a test server that runs on port 4000:

```
http://localhost:4000
```

The secure (encrypted) HTTPS usually runs on port 443. So these two URLs are equivalent:

```
https://www.example.com
https://www.example.com:443
```

OTHER COMMON PORTS

Even if you will rarely need a complete catalogue of all port numbers for services, you can rapidly start to memorize port numbers for the common services that you use daily. For example, you will very likely come across the following ports regularly:

- 80 HTTP
- 8080 HTTP (for testing servers)
- 443 HTTPS
- 22 SSH (Secure Shell)
- 23 Telnet
- 25 SMTP (outbound email)
- 110 POP3 (inbound email)
- 220 IMAP (inbound email)

All of these services are in fact application layer protocols.

APPLICATION LAYER PROTOCOLS

We have seen examples of protocols at the different layers of the TCP/IP stack, from the low-level communication across wired Ethernet, the low-level IP communication, and the TCP transport layer. Now we come to the highest layer of the stack, the application layer. This is the layer you are most likely to interact with while prototyping an Internet of Things project (and we look at this in greater detail in Chapter 7). It is useful here to pause and flesh out the definition of the word "protocol".

A *protocol* is a set of rules for communication between computers. It includes rules about how to initiate the conversation and what format the messages should be in. It determines what inputs are understood and what output is transmitted. It also specifies how the messages are sent and authenticated and how to handle (and maybe correct) errors caused by transmission.

Bearing this definition in mind, we are ready to look in more detail at some application layer protocols, starting with HTTP.

HTTP

The Internet is much more than just "the web", but inevitably web services carried over HTTP hold a large part of our attention when looking at the Internet of Things.

HTTP is, at its core, a simple protocol. The client requests a resource by sending a command to a URL, with some headers. We use the current version of HTTP, 1.1, in these examples. Let's try to get a simple document at http://book.roomofthings.com/hello.txt. You can see the result if you open the URL in your web browser.

A browser showing "Hello World!"

But let's look at what the browser is actually sending to the server to do this. The basic structure of the request would look like this:

```
GET /hello.txt HTTP/1.1
Host: book.roomofthings.com
```

Notice how the message is written in plain text, in a human-readable way (this might sound obvious, but not all protocols are; the messages could be encoded into bytes in a binary protocol, for example).

We specified the GET method because we're simply getting the page. We go into much more detail about the other methods in Chapter 7, "Prototyping Online Components". We then tell the server which resource we want (/hello.txt) and what version of the protocol we're using.

Then on the following lines, we write the headers, which give additional information about the request. The Host header is the only required header in HTTP 1.1. It is used to let a web server that serves multiple virtual hosts point the request to the right place.

Well-written clients, such as your web browser, pass other headers. For example, my browser sends the following request:

```
GET /hello.txt HTTP/1.1
Host: book.roomofthings.com
Accept: text/html,application/xhtml+xml,application/
   xml;q=0.9,*/*;q=0.8
Accept-Charset: UTF-8,*;q=0.5
Accept-Encoding: gzip,deflate,sdch
Accept-Language :en-US,en;q=0.8
Cache-Control: max-age=0
Connection: keep-alive
If-Modified-Since: Tue, 21 Aug 2012 21:41:47 GMT
If-None-Match: "8a25e-d-4c7cd7e3d1cc0"
User-Agent: Mozilla/5.0 (Macintosh; Intel Mac OS X 10_6_8)
   AppleWebKit/537.1
(KHTML, like Gecko) Chrome/21.0.1180.77 Safari/537.1
```

The `Accept-` headers tell the server what kind of content the client is willing to receive and are part of "Content negotiation". For example, if I had passed

```
Accept-Language: it,en-US,en;q=0.8
```

the server might agree to give me the Italian version of the site instead, reverting to English only if it doesn't have that page in Italian.

The other fields give the server more information about the client (for statistics and for working around known bugs) and manage caching and so on.

Finally, the server sends back its response. We already saw what that looked like in the browser, but now let's look at what the full request/response looks like if we speak the HTTP protocol directly. (Obviously, you rarely have to do this in real life. Even if you are programming an Internet of Things device, you usually have access to code libraries that make the request, and reading of the response, easier.)

```
                                    6. bash
eschew:~ hakim$ telnet book.roomofthings.com 80
Trying 80.68.93.60...
Connected to book.roomofthings.com.
Escape character is '^]'.
GET /hello.txt http/1.1
Host: book.roomofthings.com

HTTP/1.1 200 OK
Date: Wed, 22 Aug 2012 06:33:38 GMT
Server: Apache
Last-Modified: Tue, 21 Aug 2012 21:41:47 GMT
ETag: "8a25e-d-4c7cd7e3d1cc0"
Accept-Ranges: bytes
Content-Length: 13
Content-Type: text/plain

Hello World!
Connection closed by foreign host.
eschew:~ hakim$ []
```

The request/response cycle.

Notice how we connect using the `telnet` command to access port 80 directly. Now that we can see the full request, it looks at first sight as if we're repeating some information: the hostname `book.roomofthings.com`. But remember that DNS will resolve the name to an IP address. All the server sees is the *request;* it doesn't know that the command that started the request was `telnet book.roomofthings.com 80`. If the DNS name `foo.example.com` also pointed at the same machine, the web server might want to be able to respond in a different way to `http://foo.example.com/hello.txt`.

The server replies, giving us a `200` status code (which it summarizes as "OK"; that is, the request was successful). It also identifies itself as an Apache server, tells us the type of content is `text/plain`, and returns information to help the client cache the content to make future access to the resource more efficient.

You may be wondering where the *Hypertext* part of the protocol is. All we've had back so far is text, so shouldn't we be talking HTML to the server? Of course, HTML documents are text documents too, and they're just as easy to request.

Notice how, for the server, replying with a text file or an HTML document is exactly the same process! The only difference is that the Content-Type is now `text/html`. It's up to the client to read that markup and display it appropriately.

```
                                    6. bash
eschew:~ hakim$ telnet book.roomofthings.com 80
Trying 80.68.93.60...
Connected to book.roomofthings.com.
Escape character is '^]'.
GET /hello.html http/1.1
Host: book.roomofthings.com

HTTP/1.1 200 OK
Date: Wed, 22 Aug 2012 06:42:25 GMT
Server: Apache
Last-Modified: Tue, 21 Aug 2012 21:43:06 GMT
ETag: "8a25f-a6-4c7cd82f28e80"
Accept-Ranges: bytes
Content-Length: 166
Content-Type: text/html

<!DOCTYPE html PUBLIC "-//W3C//DTD HTML 4.01//EN">
<html>
  <head>
    <title> Hello World! </title>
  </head>
  <body>
    <h1> Hello World! </h1>
  </body>
</html>
Connection closed by foreign host.
eschew:~ hakim$ []
```

The request/response cycle with HTML.

We look at more features of HTTP over the course of this book, but everything is based around this simple request/response cycle! In Chapter 7, we look at web APIs (which are, arguably, even higher-level protocols that just happen to sit on top of HTTP) while deepening our understanding of HTTP.

HTTPS: ENCRYPTED HTTP

We have seen how the request and response are created in a simple text format. If someone eavesdropped your connection (easy to do with tools such as Wireshark if you have access to the network at either end), that person can easily read the conversation. In fact, it isn't the *format* of the protocol that is the problem: even if the conversation happened in binary, an attacker could write a tool to translate the format into something readable. Rather, the problem is that the conversation isn't encrypted.

The HTTPS protocol is actually just a mix-up of plain old HTTP over the Secure Socket Layer (SSL) protocol. An HTTPS server listens to a different port (usually 443) and on connection sets up a secure, encrypted connection with the client (using some fascinating mathematics and clever tricks such as the "Diffie–Hellman key exchange"). When that's established, both sides just speak HTTP to each other as before!

*Published by Whitfield Diffie and Martin Hellman in 1976,
Diffie–Hellman (D-H) key exchange is a way for two people to
exchange cryptographic keys in public, without an eavesdropper
being able to decode their subsequent conversation. This is done
by each side performing mathematical calculations which are
simple to do but not to undo. For example multiplying two prime
numbers together is easily done, but if they are sufficiently large
numbers, an attacker cannot factor the result back into the
original primes given current computing power. Neither side ever
sends their own secret key unencrypted, but only the result of
multiplying it with a shared piece of information. By performing
the calculation again on the key sent to them over the network,
both parties end up with a "shared secret". The Khan Academy
provides a good walkthrough of this process, at Academy*
`https://www.khanacademy.org/math/applied-`
`math/cryptography/modern-crypt/v/`
`diffie-hellman-key-exchange--part-2`*.*

This means that a network snooper can find out only the IP address and port number of the request (because both of these are public information in the envelope of the underlying TCP message, there's no way around that). After that, all it can see is that packets of data are being sent in a request and packets are returned for the response.

OTHER APPLICATION LAYER PROTOCOLS

All protocols work in a roughly similar way. Some cases involve more than just a two-way request and response. For example, when sending email using SMTP, you first need to do the "HELO handshake" where the client introduces itself with a cheery "hello" (SMTP commands are all four letters long, so it actually says "HELO") and receives a response like "250 Hello example. org pleased to meet you!" In all cases, it is worth spending a little time researching the protocol on Google and Wikipedia to understand in overview how it works. You can usually find a library that abstracts the details of the communication process, and we recommend using that wherever possible. Bad implementations of network protocols will create problems for you and the servers you connect to and may result in bugs or your clients getting banned from useful services. So, it is generally better to use a well-written, well-debugged implementation that is used by many other developers. In general, the only valid reasons for you, the programmer, to ever speak to any application layer protocol directly (that is, without using a library) are

- There is no implementation of the protocol for your platform (or the implementation is inefficient, incomplete, or broken).
- You want to try implementing it from scratch, for fun.
- You are testing, or learning, and want to make a particular request easily.

SUMMARY

The TCP/IP protocol suite is the foundation of data communication over the Internet. Each layer represents a set of rules for how to communicate, and every higher layer builds on the lower ones, offering a higher level of abstraction. Most development on the Internet, then, will involve the very highest layers of abstraction—the application layer, which includes the HTTP protocol which enables the world wide web, as well as the APIs that we explore in Chapter 7. To really understand how communication works, and to make the best technological choices, it is important to understand the lower levels, too.

TCP offers great reliability on the transport layer; however, sometimes you may decide that the lightweight UDP protocol suits your needs better.

IP addresses, an important concept from the Internet layer, are key for accessing devices across the Internet. The next generation of this protocol, IPv6, is used heavily in infrastructure and will be critical in preventing the exhaustion of addresses which is coming, hastened by the massive growth in mobile telephony, tablet computing, and the Internet of Things.

At the lowest level, the link layer, devices are identified not by IP addresses (as this isn't defined until the layer above) but rather by MAC addresses. This layer includes common types of local network, such as wired Ethernet and WiFi, as well as new personal area network (PAN) protocols, such as the 802.15.4 standard.

In the next chapter, we take a first look at prototyping a connected device, from the physical Thing itself, to its embedded electronics and the online software platform which will turn it into an enchanted object.

4

THINKING ABOUT PROTOTYPING

NOW THAT WE'VE looked at the principles of design and the fundamentals of Internet communications, we hope you are itching to create an Internet of Things device! It's possible that you want a single device that is Just For You. But perhaps you have a fantastic idea and are planning to churn out millions of the products. In both cases, the most sensible approach is to start by making one Thing first: a prototype.

Making a prototype first has many benefits. You will inevitably come across problems in your design that you need to change and iterate. Doing this with a single object is trivial compared to modifying hundreds or thousands of products. With the Internet of Things, we are always looking at building three things in parallel: the physical Thing; the electronics to make the Thing smart; and the Internet service that we'll connect to. The last of these is relatively cheap and easy to change. You cannot change the physical object and its silicon controller unless you recall every item.

The prototype, therefore, is optimized for ease and speed of development and also the ability to change and modify it. Many Internet of Things projects start with a prototyping microcontroller, connected by wires to components on a prototyping board, such as a "breadboard", and housed in some kind of container (perhaps an old tin or a laser-cut box). This proto-type is relatively inexpensive, but you will most likely end up with something that is serviceable rather than polished and that will cost more than someone would be willing to pay for it in a shop.

At the end of this stage, you'll have an object that works. It may be useful for you already. It may be a talking point to show your friends. And if you are planning to move to production, it's a *demonstrable* product that you can use to convince yourself, your business partners, and your investors that your idea has legs and is worth trying to sell.

Finally, the process of manufacture will iron out issues of scaling up and polish. You might substitute prototyping microcontrollers and wires with smaller chips on a printed circuit board (PCB), and pieces improvised out of 3D-printed plastic with ones commercially injection-moulded in their thousands. The final product will be cheaper per unit and more professional, but will be much more expensive to change.

In the next few chapters, we look at aspects of prototyping in detail:

- Chapter 5: Choosing a specific microcontroller for prototyping
- Chapter 6: Designing a housing, any moving parts, and so on for the physical object that is Good Enough for the prototype
- Chapter 7: Developing the web service that the device will speak to

In this chapter, we discuss some more theoretical issues about the approach to choosing a prototyping platform. We could easily give a pat answer like "Use an Arduino and develop your online service in Ruby on Rails" or "Use a Raspberry Pi", but determining the best choice of prototyping platform can't come from on high or from a book. For one thing, your project has its own goals and requirements. For another, new microcontrollers are constantly coming onto the market; best practice and popularity of server software stacks is ever changing; and rapid prototyping continues to evolve—so we feel it is worth giving some more general advice and back-ground information before digging deeper.

SKETCHING

There is a good chance that the first step you'll take when working on your prototype will be to jot down some ideas or draw out some design ideas with pen and paper. That is an important first step in exploring your idea and one we'd like to extend beyond the strict definition to also include sketching in hardware and software.

What we mean by that is the process of exploring the problem space: iterating through different approaches and ideas to work out what works and what doesn't. The focus isn't on fidelity of the prototype but rather on the ease and speed with which you can try things out.

For the physical design, that could mean digging out your childhood LEGO collection to prototype the mix of cogs and three-dimensional forms, or maybe attacking some foamcore or cardboard with a craft knife. We examine such techniques in more detail in Chapter 6, "Prototyping the Physical Design".

To show how you might approach "sketching" for the electronics and software, an example will help.

The Internet of Things design firm BERG invited me (Adrian) along to their inaugural Little Printer hackday in June 2012. They filled their office with a bunch of interesting techies and creatives and tasked them with seeing what they could do, in a day, with BERG's (at the time) soon-to-be-released cute Internet-connected diminutive printer. (For more on the Little Printer, see the case study in Chapter 10, "Moving to Manufacture".)

Most of the attendees focused on creating new publications for the Little Printer—a task that meant writing server code to wrangle data (working with the Google Calendar API, spotting meteors passing overhead, and so on) into shape and experimenting with ways of displaying that on a narrow strip of receipt paper. I (Adrian) decided that having a connected device as the output for the system wasn't enough and spent the day prototyping a custom-hardware input device, too. Called the *Printernet Fridge*, it was a nod to the age-old Internet of Things cliché, the Internet fridge—an exercise in seeing what a semi-automated shopping list would be like.

From the design constraints (mostly how the Little Printer publishing system works but also limited by the hardware that I had thrown into my bag to take to the event), it was clear early on that the problem could be broken into three broad areas: the graphic design of the printed publication; the physical hardware to easily add items to the shopping list; and some server software to tie the rest of the system together. Breaking the problem into these three parts meant that, initially at least, each could be addressed separately.

The first step was to pull together the scaffolding of the server software, which other parts of the system could be built on as they were developed.

As this was a prototype, rather than a system to be deployed to thousands of users, I used the simple framework Sinatra. Sinatra is a way to quickly build web services, much like the Dancer framework which we cover in Chapter 7, "Prototyping Online Components", but using the Ruby programming language.

Given that the prototype was going to be demonstrated only to a handful of people and didn't need to extend beyond a single user, I didn't waste any time including a login system for multiple users or setting up any security to encrypt the requests to and from the service. That provided enough infrastructure to interact with the Little Printer publication system and to allow the addition of API hooks for the input device to call when it was ready. I created a crude placeholder image for the publication's icon and dashed off the description text with a simple "prints shopping lists", to let the focus stay on the server software rather than get sidelined into the design and polish. Similarly, the publication itself was just the bare minimum static text which was delivered whenever the publication was requested.

At this point it was possible to subscribe to the publication and have it print a set, one-line document on a Little Printer. Collaborating with one of the designers at the hackday, we iterated through the look and layout of the shopping list by tweaking the HTML, CSS, and images in the Sinatra app that made up the publication.

The content was still static—you would always get a list asking for two bottles of milk and some fresh orange juice—but the header image and text were refined and decisions made about how to convey the information to the user. The simple bullets for each list item were replaced with numbers of each item required, which then moved to the end of the list item so the bullet could be reinstated but as an empty check box to allow you to tick items off as you found them in the shop.

All it needed now was some live data. The workflow for that needed to be as easy as possible; it shouldn't be a chore to add items. However, this wasn't to be some seamless vision of the future where the fridge would order things for you. (The ultimate agency of the user is important.) It is a tool rather than an autonomous decision maker.

With only an Arduino Ethernet board in my bag, the decision over hardware platform was already made. For a production unit, the Ethernet cable would complicate installation, and encrypting the data being sent would stretch the board's limits; however, for a quick prototype, the ease of wiring up different circuits and changing the onboard code easily outweighed the longer-term disadvantages.

Once a basic pushbutton was wired up to the Arduino, I could write some simple code to trigger whenever the button was pressed. The first step merely output some text to the serial port, which could be monitored immediately over the USB cable on my laptop.

Now that the basic physical interaction was working, the next step was to hook it into the web service. That required me to change the software on both the Arduino and the web service. I added a new API call to the Sinatra app which allows new items to be added to the list and tested it with a web browser (as that gives an easier view of what is happening if things go wrong).

For a more complex project, I would have chosen Rails over Sinatra as the web framework. Doing so would have let me pull in the RailsAdmin module to check things like whether the item had been added to the database correctly. Such helper modules let you focus on sketching out one feature, without having to divert to building chunks of additional infrastructure before you have decided that the feature is going to stay. In this case, I could easily switch the static shopping list over to use the live data, which served as both feature development and debugging aid.

Then I pulled in some sample code to make a web request from the Arduino and modified it to call the newly written API on the web service. With that written, it was possible to push a button and have "milk" added to your shopping list. Success!

The next step was to add more buttons, as only being able to order more milk isn't the most useful of shopping list applications. Two more buttons were added and connected up to allow "cheese" and "orange juice" to also be ordered.

A quick round of user testing (or showing it off to fellow hackday attendees, as it is also known in this case) highlighted a problem with the design as it stood. Although recording a new selection to the server took less than a second, it was still long enough for subsequent button presses to be missed if you were running through them quickly.

Given that the end of the day was looming large, and as I would be able to talk around the issue in the demonstration, I chose expediency over the larger amount of coding required to decouple the user interface of buttons from the network communication. A "busy" LED was added to the breadboard and illuminated whenever the Arduino was talking to the network.

The work on the hardware and software left little time for developing a case for the input device, which is just as well because I hadn't room for any construction materials in my bag. Improvising with some sticky notes at least made the interface more self-explanatory. It also allowed room to hint at ways in which the prototype could be further extended, with "Add barcode scanner here" written on a note below the buttons. That was a result of further thinking through how the device might work in practice. You would want a number of buttons, with a web interface to let you reconfigure them for your set of non-packaged fridge goods, and then a barcode reader would allow scanning of anything that was in packaging.

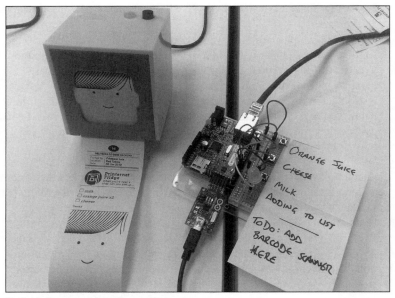

The finished prototype of the Printernet Fridge.

FAMILIARITY

Another option to consider is familiarity. If you can already program like a whiz in Python, for example, maybe picking a platform such as Raspberry Pi, which lets you write the code in a language you already know, would be better than having to learn Arduino from scratch.

The same applies to the server software, obviously. When creating the Printernet Fridge prototype, Adrian hadn't used Sinatra before but chose it because he was looking for a simple web framework and was already familiar with Ruby from writing a number of Ruby on Rails applications in the past.

And if you're already adept at fashioning sheets of foamcore into three-dimensional structures, we're not going to argue that you should ignore that expertise in favour of learning all about laser cutting.

COSTS VERSUS EASE OF PROTOTYPING

Although familiarity with a platform may be attractive in terms of ease of prototyping, it is also worth considering the relationship between the costs (of prototyping and mass producing) of a platform against the development effort that the platform demands. This trade-off is not hard and fast, but it is beneficial if you can choose a prototyping platform in a performance/capabilities bracket similar to a final production solution. That way, you will be less likely to encounter any surprises over the cost, or even the wholesale viability of your project, down the line.

For example, the cheapest possible way of creating an electronic device might currently be an AVR microcontroller chip, which you can purchase from a component supplier for about £3. This amount is just for the chip, so you would have to sweat the details of how to connect the pins to other components and how to flash the chip with new code. For many people, this platform would not be viable for an initial prototype.

Stepping upwards to the approximately £20 mark, you could look at an Arduino or similar. It would have exactly the same chip, but it would be laid out on a board with labelled headers to help you wire up components more easily, have a USB port where you could plug in a computer, and have a well-supported IDE to help make programming it easier. But, of course, you are still programming in C++, for reasons of performance and memory.

For more money again, approximately £30, you could look at the BeagleBone, which runs Linux and has enough processing power and RAM to be able to run a high-level programming language: libraries are provided within the concurrent programming toolkit Node.js for JavaScript to manipulate the input/output pins of the board.

If you choose not to use an embedded platform, you could think about using a smartphone instead. Smartphones might cost about £300, and although they are a very different beast, they have many of the same features that make the cheaper platforms attractive: connection to the Internet (usually by wireless or 3G phone connection rather than Ethernet), input capabilities (touchscreen, button presses, camera, rather than electronics components), and output capabilities (sound, screen display, vibration). You can often program them in a choice of languages of high or low level, from Objective C and Java, to Python or HTML and JavaScript.

Finally, a common or garden PC might be an option for a prototype. These PCs cost from £100 to £1000 and again have a host of Internet connection and I/O possibilities. You can program them in whatever language you already know how to use. Most importantly, you probably already have one lying around.

For the first prototype, the cost is probably not the most important issue: the smartphone or computer options are particularly convenient if you already have one available, at which point they are effectively zero-cost. Although prototyping a "thing" using a piece of general computing equipment might seem like a sideways step, depending on your circumstances, it may be exactly the right thing to do to show whether the concept works and get people interested in the project, to collaborate on it, or to fund it.

At this stage, you can readily argue that doing the easiest thing that could possibly work is entirely sensible. The most powerful platform that you can afford might make sense for now.

Of course, if your device has physical interactions (blowing bubbles, turning a clock's hands, taking input from a dial), you will find that a PC is not optimized for this kind of work. It doesn't expose GPIO pins (although people have previously kludged this using parallel ports). An electronics prototyping board, unsurprisingly, *is* better suited to this kind of work. We come back to combining both of these options shortly.

An important factor to be aware of is that the hardware and programming choices you make will depend on your skill set, which leads us to the obvious criticism of the idea of "ease of prototyping", namely "ease... for *whom*?"

For many beginners to hardware development, the Arduino toolkit is a surprisingly good choice. Yes, the input/output choices are basic and require an ability to follow wiring diagrams and, ideally, a basic knowledge of electronics. Yet the interaction from a programming point of view is essentially simple—writing and reading values to and from the GPIO pins. Yes, the language is C++, which in the early twenty-first century is few people's idea of the best language for beginners. Yet the Arduino toolkit abstracts the calls you make into a `setup()` function and a `loop()` function. Even more importantly, the IDE pushes the compiled code onto the device where it just runs, automatically, until you unplug it. The lack of capabilities of the board presents an advantage in the fact that the interaction with it is also streamlined.

Case Study: Bubblino

Let's look in some more detail at Bubblino, to see how the process of prototyping played out for a real project.

Bubblino has, from the start, targeted the Arduino hardware, in part because its original purpose was precisely to demonstrate "how to use Arduino to do Internet of Things stuff". So the original hardware connected an Arduino to the motor for an off-the-shelf bubble machine. The original prototype had a Bluetooth-enabled Arduino, which was meant to connect to Adrian's Nokia phone, which was programmed with Python for Series 60. The phone did the hard work of connecting to the Internet and simply sent the Arduino a number, being the number of recent tweets. Bubblino responded by blowing bubbles for that many seconds.

Although Python is a scripting language, with a reputation for being easy to learn, at the time the Series 60 port wasn't so mature and using it turned out more difficult than expected. For the next version, Adrian fell back to using a Perl script on his laptop which worked in exactly the same way, for example, sending a number to the Arduino. This approach worked by opening and writing to a COM port that represented the Bluetooth connection. The same technique could have been used with the current basic USB Arduino. Of course, in both cases, this limits Bubblino to working either within Bluetooth range or with a physical USB connection.

Although it's perfectly reasonable to have a laptop open to drive the device for a demo, Bubblino has now scaled up a little: you can now commission one, which will be hand-built within a few weeks. Although this isn't mass production, the process still requires some streamlining to be cost and time effective. So the current devices are based on an Arduino Ethernet. This means that the Twitter search and XML processing are done on the device, so it can run completely independently of any computer, as long as it has an Ethernet connection.

The original Perl version could use a full-featured XML parser because a wealth of them are available in Perl's collection of libraries, the CPAN (as there will be for any popular modern language). Such libraries do, of course, exist for C++ too. However, due to the memory limitations of the Arduino, loading and processing a large chunk of XML isn't the most appropriate thing to do. Instead, when Bubblino downloads the Atom XML feed for its Twitter search, it simply scans the returned XML looking for the `<published>` tags and the date fields within them. Normally, and with justification, programmers are advised against parsing XML by simple scanning or regular expressions. However, for a limited device, this solution may be acceptable.

In a final twist, the concept of Bubblino has been released as an iPhone app, "Bubblino and Friends", which simply searches Twitter for defined keywords and plays an animation and tune based either on the original Bubblino or on one of his friends (new characters invented for the app, such as a pirate's parrot).

Compare this with developing using a computer: if you already know how to develop an application in C#, in Python, or in JavaScript, you have a great place to start. But if you don't know, you first have to evaluate and choose a language and then work out how to write it, get it going, and make it start automatically. Any one of these tasks may be, strictly speaking, *easier* than any of the more opaque interactions with an odd-looking circuit board, but the freedom of choice adds its own complexities.

Another option is to marry the capabilities of a microcontroller to connect to low-level components such as dials, LEDs, and motors while running the hard processing on a computer or phone. A kit such as an Arduino easily connects to a computer via USB, and you can speak to it via the serial port in a standard way in any programming language.

Some phones also have this capability. However, because phones, like an Arduino, are "devices", in theory they can't act as the computer "host" to control the Arduino. (The side of the USB connection usually in charge of things.) The interesting hack used by the Android development kit (ADK), for example, is for the Arduino to have a USB host shield—that is, it pretends to be the computer end of the connection and so in theory controls the phone. In reality, the phone does the complicated processing and communication with the Internet and so on.

As always, there is no single "right answer" but a set of trade-offs. Don't let this put you off starting a prototype, though. There are really no "wrong answers" either for that; the prototype is something that will get you started, and the experience of making it will teach you much more about the final best platform for your device than any book, even this one, can.

PROTOTYPES AND PRODUCTION

Although ease of prototyping is a major factor, perhaps *the* biggest obstacle to getting a project started—scaling up to building more than one device, perhaps many thousands of them—brings a whole new set of challenges and questions.

CHANGING EMBEDDED PLATFORM

When you scale up, you may well have to think about moving to a different platform, for cost or size reasons. If you've started with a free-form, powerful programming platform, you may find that porting the code to a more restricted, cheaper, and smaller device will bring many challenges. This issue is something to be aware of. If the first prototype you built on a PC, iPhone,

BeagleBone, or whatever has helped you get investment or collaborators, you may be well placed to go about replicating that compelling functionality on your final target.

Of course, if you've used a constrained platform in prototyping, you may find that you have to make choices and limitations in your code. Dynamic memory allocation on the 2K that the Arduino provides may not be especially efficient, so how should that make you think about using strings or complex data structures? If you port to a more powerful platform, you may be able to rewrite your code in a more modern, high-level way or simply take advantage of faster processor speed and more RAM. But will the new platform have the same I/O capabilities? And you have to consider the ramping-up time to learn new technologies and languages.

In practice, you will often find that you don't need to change platforms. Instead, you might look at, for example, replacing an Arduino prototyping microcontroller with an AVR chip (the same chip that powers the Arduino) and just those components that you actually need, connected on a custom PCB. We look at this issue in much more detail in Chapter 10.

PHYSICAL PROTOTYPES AND MASS PERSONALISATION

Chances are that the production techniques that you use for the physical side of your device won't translate directly to mass production. However, while the technique might change—injection moulding in place of 3D printing, for example—in most cases, it won't change what is possible.

An aspect that may be of interest is in the way that digital fabrication tools can allow each item to be slightly different, letting you personalise each device in some way. There are challenges in scaling this to production, as you will need to keep producing the changeable parts in quantities of one, but *mass personalisation*, as the approach is called, means you can offer something unique with the accompanying potential to charge a premium.

CLIMBING INTO THE CLOUD

The server software is the easiest component to take from prototype into production. As we saw earlier, it might involve switching from a basic web framework to something more involved (particularly if you need to add user accounts and the like), but you will be able to find an equivalent for whichever language you have chosen. That means most of the business logic will move across with minimal changes.

Beyond that, scaling up in the early days will involve buying a more powerful server. If you are running on a cloud computing platform, such as Amazon Web Services, you can even have the service dynamically expand and contract, as demand dictates.

Case Study: DoES Liverpool

Some of the reasons to think about production techniques may actually simply be about having a more beautiful device, even for your own use. In later chapters we see some methods that can be used to clad and house an Internet of Things prototype device. But there may well be a progression from unhoused electronics to something in a box made from LEGO or using a repurposed casing to a device in a custom-made box (laser-cut, 3D printed) or even one machined commercially.

In our office and makespace, DoES Liverpool, the central heating system has been hooked up to the Internet. YAHMS, as the system is named, consists of a collection of sensors to measure temperature in the office and outside, an actuator to turn the heating on or off, and some server software to manage timer control and provide a web-based interface to the system. Like many non-Internet-connected heating systems, there is a timer-based programme which ensures a basic level of comfort automatically. However, users can log on to the YAHMS website to find out what the temperature is and decide to turn the heating on or off to override the programme. As it is web-based, it works equally well if you're sitting in the office at the time or if you're at home getting ready to head into work on a cold winter Saturday.

The temperature sensors have been left as unhoused Arduino boards. They are managed only by John, whose project it is. However, the cabling to the boiler itself is neatly installed, and the electronics are hidden away. The actual interface that people use every day, however, is well styled with a minimal interface and works equally well on a desktop browser or a smartphone. Mimicking the hobbyist-consumer scale that we saw for hardware, the software also has a similar scale: some tasks don't currently expose their functionality through the UI and require manual tweaking with database commands. Clearly, the whole system isn't currently suitable for mass sale, but it is serviceable, it fits into the ethos of tinkering and "interesting tech" in the location where it is installed, and the most common tasks that it carries out are well packaged.

Another example from DoES is the DoorBot. It originally consisted of a networked PC with a flat-screen monitor facing out towards the corridor through a conveniently located window. The DoorBot works as a kiosk device, showing webcam views of the office, a list of upcoming events (regularly pulled from Google Calendar), and a welcome message to any expected guests. Currently, its only input device is an RFID reader. Our members can register their RFID cards (Oyster, Walrus, DoES membership card, and so on). Finally, this device is also connected to speakers, so it can play a personalised tune or message when members check in or out. Developing this device was as simple as running software on a computer ever is: the trickiest cases are things such as turning the screen off and on after office hours and coping with losing or regaining power and network. Given how close the functionality is to that of a PC, it might seem crazy to think of any other solution. However, if we had to scale up—to cover more doors or to sell the idea to other companies—we suddenly have new trade-offs.

Just sticking a tower PC somewhere near the door may not be ideal for every office. A computer that fits neatly with an integrated screen might work, such as an iMac, a laptop, or a tablet. But these devices are much more expensive than the original commodity PC (effectively "free" when it was a one-off because it was lying around with nothing else to do). A small embedded computer, such as a Raspberry Pi, might be ideal because it costs relatively little, runs Linux, and has HDMI output.

Our co-workers, John and Ben, did eventually port the DoorBot to the Raspberry Pi, and this was a great learning experience with that platform. However, it was still an investment in time even though it was theoretically a simple change, as the Pi has similar capabilities to a Linux PC. The primary driver for investing the time to do this came from our expansion to a second and now third room— requiring three devices made finding a smaller, cheaper, more polished solution a requirement. We look at this process in greater detail in the next chapter.

For projects that aren't as clearly suited to being a computer and that do need to interface to electronics components, you are more likely to consider the continuum from basic microcontrollers (Arduino and others) to more powerful ones, such as the BeagleBone.

If you can already run on a smaller, cheaper platform, then if you suddenly have to start providing large numbers of devices, your costs will already be much more reasonable. You've already proved that your concept can run on a cheap, small, limited board. Of course, if your device is beating against the upper limits of the hardware capabilities, you may find that adding any new feature means you suddenly have to upgrade to a more powerful version of your chip or even change to a different platform. If you already have devices on the market, this would affect whether you can easily upgrade an existing device to a new version of firmware, which could be a disadvantage.

If you started with a more complex board, you may have reaped benefits from being able to be freer with dynamic memory allocation, libraries with nicely wrapped APIs, or other handy assumptions. But these assumptions may turn out to be painful if you do have to port the code to a more constrained device: you may be looking at a complete rewrite. Of course, rewriting is not necessarily a problem but has to be factored into your development costs.

OPEN SOURCE VERSUS CLOSED SOURCE

If you're so minded, you could spend a lifetime arguing about the definitions of "closed" and "open" source, and some people have, in fact, made a career out of it. Broadly, we're looking at two issues:

- Your assertion, as the creator, of your Intellectual Property rights
- Your users' rights to freely tinker with your creation

We imagine many of this book's readers will be creative in some sense, perhaps tinkerers, inventors, programmers, or designers. As a creative person, you may be torn between your own desire to learn how things work and modify and re-use them and the worry that if *other people* were to use that right on your own design/invention/software, you might not get the recognition and earnings that you expect from it.

In fact, this tension between the closed and open approaches is rather interesting, especially when applied to a mix of software and hardware, as we find with Internet of Things devices. While many may already have made up their minds, in one or the other direction, we suggest at least thinking about how you can use both approaches in your project.

The Open Source Hardware Association

Alongside the emergence of the Internet of Things, a similar, if slightly more advanced, rise of the Maker movement has occurred. This hands-on approach to playing around with technology encourages passionate amateurs and professionals alike to break out the soldering iron and their toolkit and create everything from robots and 3D printers to interactive artworks and games.

A heavy overlap exists between the Maker movement and hackspaces—the network of groups of like-minded individuals helping each other learn new skills and experiment with technology in novel ways. The democratic and open approach from hackspaces, along with that of the open source software community, has carried over into the Maker culture, resulting in a default stance of sharing designs and code.

As the community has grown and matured, this sharing has coalesced into the more formal form of open hardware.

In March 2010, at the Opening Hardware workshop, the participants started to define what open hardware is. Over the following 11 months, both online and at the first Open Hardware Summit, this definition was honed and refined into version 1.0 of the Open Source Hardware (OSHW) Statement of Principles and Definition (http://freedomdefined.org/OSHW), which was released in February 2011. Work on the definition is ongoing, and at the time of writing the draft for version 1.1 is a work in progress.

This definition is now accompanied by an Open Source Hardware logo, which designers can use on their products to indicate that the source files are available for learning, re-using, and extending into new products.

The Open Hardware Summit also established itself as a regular annual event, bringing together a huge number of hackers, makers, developers, and designers to discuss and celebrate open hardware each September.

Finally, in June 2012, the Open Source Hardware Association (`http://www.oshwa.org`) was formally incorporated. As we write, the organisation is still finding its feet and working out exactly how to undertake its aims of supporting the Open Hardware Summit and educating the wider public on all matters pertaining to open source hardware. Products which conform to the aims of open source hardware can use the logo.

The OSHWA logo.
`http://oshwlogo.com`

WHY CLOSED?

Asserting Intellectual Property rights is often the default approach, especially for larger companies. If you declared copyright on some source code or a design, someone who wants to market the same project cannot do so by simply reading your instructions and following them. That person would have to instead reverse-engineer the functionality of the hardware and software. In addition, simply copying the design slavishly would also infringe copyright. You might also be able to protect distinctive elements of the visual design with trademarks and of the software and hardware with patents.

Although getting good legal information on what to protect and how best to enforce those rights is hard and time-consuming, larger companies may well be geared up to take this route. If you are developing an Internet of Things device in such a context, working within the culture of the company may simply be easier, unless you are willing to try to persuade your management, marketing, and legal teams that they should try something different.

If you're working on your own or in a small company, you might simply trademark your distinctive brand and rely on copyright to protect everything else. Note that starting a project as closed source doesn't prevent you from later releasing it as open source (whereas after you've licensed something as open source, you can't simply revoke that licence).

You may have a strong emotional feeling about your Intellectual Property rights: especially if your creativity is what keeps you and your loved ones fed, this is entirely understandable. But it's worth bearing in mind that, as always, there is a trade-off between how much the rights actually help towards this important goal and what the benefits of being more open are.

WHY OPEN?

In the open source model, you release the sources that you use to create the project to the whole world. You might publish the software code to GitHub (http://github.com), the electronic schematics using Fritzing (http://fritzing.org) or SolderPad (http://solderpad.com), and the design of the housing/shell to Thingiverse (http://www.thingiverse.com).

If you're not used to this practice, it might seem crazy: why would you give away something that you care about, that you're working hard to accomplish? There are several reasons to give away your work:

- You may gain positive comments from people who liked it.
- It acts as a public showcase of your work, which may affect your reputation and lead to new opportunities.
- People who used your work may suggest or implement features or fix bugs.
- By generating early interest in your project, you may get support and mindshare of a quality that it would be hard to pay for.

Of course, this is also a gift *economy*: you can use other people's free and open source contributions within your own project. Forums and chat channels exist all over the Internet, with people more or less freely discussing their projects because doing so helps with one or more of the benefits mentioned here.

If you're simply "scratching an itch" with a project, releasing it as open source may be the best thing you could do with it. A few words of encouragement from someone who liked your design and your blog post about it may be invaluable to get you moving when you have a tricky moment on it. A bug fix from someone who tried using your code in a way you had never thought of may save you hours of unpleasant debugging later. And if you're very lucky, you might become known as "that bubble machine guy" or get invited to conferences to talk about your LED circuit.

If you have a serious work project, you may *still* find that open source is the right decision, at least for some of your work.

Disadvantages of Open Source

The obvious disadvantage of open source—"but people will steal my idea!"—may, in fact, be less of a problem than you might think. In general, if you talk to people about an idea, it's hard enough to get them to listen because they are waiting to tell you about *their* great idea (the selfish cads). If people do use your open source contribution, they will most likely be using it in a way that interests *them*. The universe of ideas is still, fortunately, very large.

However, deciding to release as open source may take more resources. As the saying goes: the shoemaker's children go barefoot. If you're designing for other people, you have to make something of a high standard, but for yourself, you often might be tempted to cut corners. When you have a working prototype, this should be a moment of celebration. Then having to go back and fix everything so that you can release it in a form that doesn't make you ashamed will take time and resources.

Of course, the right way to handle this process would be to start pushing everything to an open repository immediately and develop in public. This is much more the "open source way". It may take some time to get used to but may work for you.

After you release something as open source, you may still have a perceived duty to maintain and support it, or at least to answer questions about it via email, forums, and chatrooms. Although you may not have *paying* customers, your users are a community that you may want to maintain. It is true that, if you have volunteered your work and time, you are entirely responsible for choosing to limit that whenever you want. But abandoning something before you've built up a community around it to pass the reins to cannot be classed as a successful open source project.

Being a Good Citizen

The idea that there is a "true way" to do open source is worth thinking about. There is in some way a cachet to "doing open source" that may be worth having. Developers may be attracted to your project on that basis. If you're courting this goodwill, it's important to make sure that you do deserve it. If you say you have an open platform, releasing only a few libraries, months afterwards, with no documentation or documentation of poor quality could be considered rude. Also, your open source work should make some attempt to play with other open platforms. Making assumptions that lock in the project to a device you control, for example, would be fine for a driver library but isn't great for an allegedly open project.

In some ways, being a good citizen is a consideration to counterbalance the advantages of the gift economy idea. But, of course, it is natural that any economy has its rules of citizenship!

Open Source as a Competitive Advantage

Although you might be tempted to be very misty-eyed about open source as a community of good citizens and a gift economy, it's important to understand the possibility of using it to competitive advantage.

First, *using* open source work is often a no-risk way of getting software that has been tested, improved, and debugged by many eyes. As long as it isn't licensed with an extreme viral licence (such as the AGPL), you really have no reason not to use such work, even in a closed source project. Sure, you could build your own microcontroller from parts and write your own library to control servo motors, your own HTTP stack, and a web framework. Or you could use an Arduino, the Arduino servo libraries and Ethernet stack, and Ruby on Rails, for example. Commercial equivalents may be available for all these examples, but then you have to factor in the cost and rely on a single company's support forums instead of all the information available on the Internet.

Second, using open source aggressively gives your product the chance to gain mindshare. In this book we talk a lot about the Arduino—as you have seen in this chapter; one could easily argue that it isn't the most powerful platform ever and will surely be improved. It scores many points on grounds of cost but even more so on mindshare. The design is open; therefore, many other companies have produced clones of the board or components such as shields that are compatible with it. This has led to amusing things such as the Arduino header layout "bug" (http://forum.arduino.cc/index. php/topic,22737.0.html#subject_171839), which is the result of a design mistake that has nevertheless been replicated by other manufacturers to target the same community.

If an open source project is good enough and gets word out quickly and appealingly, it can much more easily gain the goodwill and enthusiasm to become a platform. The "geek" community often choose a product because, rather than being a commercial "black box", it, for example, exposes a Linux shell or can communicate using an open protocol such as XML. This community can be your biggest ally.

Open Source as a Strategic Weapon

One step further in the idea of open source used aggressively is the idea of businesses using open source strategically to further their interests (and undermine their competitors).

In "Commoditizing your complements" (http://www.joelonsoftware. com/articles/StrategyLetterV.html), software entrepreneur Joel Spolsky argues that many companies that invest heavily in open source projects are doing just that. In economics, the concept of *complements* defines products and services that are bought in conjunction with your product—for example, DVDs and DVD players.

If the price of one of those goods goes down, then demand for both goods is likely to rise. Companies can therefore use improvements in open source versions of complementary products to increase demand for their products. If you manufacture microcontrollers, for example, then improving the open source software frameworks that run on the microcontrollers can help you sell more chips.

Simon Wardley, a thought leader in the field of cloud computing, writes

> *For many, the words open source [conjure] up concepts of hippy idealism where geeks in a spirit of free love give away their work to others for nothing. For many, it's about as anti-capitalist as you can get. Those many are as gullible as the citizens of Ancient Troy.*
> *—http://blog.gardeviance.org/2012/04/*
> *be-wary-of-geeks-bearing-gifts.html*

While open sourcing your core business would be risky indeed, trying to standardise things that you use but which are core to *your competitor*'s business may, in fact, help to undermine that competitor. So Google releasing Android as open source could undermine Apple's iOS platform. Facebook releasing Open Compute, to help efficiently maintain large data centres, undermines Google's competitive advantage.

Facebook clearly needs efficient data centres. So to open source its code gives the company the opportunity to gain contributions from many clever open source programmers. But it gives nothing away about Facebook's core algorithms in social graphing.

This dynamic is fascinating with the Internet of Things because several components in different spaces interact to form the final product: the physical design, the electronic components, the microcontroller, the exchange with the Internet, and the back-end APIs and applications. This is one reason why many people are trying to become leaders in the middleware layers, such as Xively (free for developers, but not currently open source, though many non-core features are open).

While you are prototyping, these considerations are secondary, but being aware of these issues is worthwhile so that you understand the risks and opportunities involved.

MIXING OPEN AND CLOSED SOURCE

We've discussed open sourcing many of your libraries and keeping your core business closed. While many businesses can exist as purely one or the other, you shouldn't discount having both coexist. As long as you don't make unfounded assertions about how much you use open software, it's still possible to be a "good citizen" who contributes back to some projects whether by contributing work or simply by helping others in forums while also gaining many of the advantages of open source.

While both of us tend to be keen on the idea of open source, it's also true that not all our work is open source. We have undertaken some for commercial clients who wanted to retain IP. Some of the work was simply not polished enough to be worth the extra effort to make into a viable open release.

Adrian's project Bubblino has a mix of licences:

- Arduino code is open source.
- Schematics are available but not especially well advertised.
- Server code is closed source.

The server code was partly kept closed source because some details on the configuration of the Internet of Things device were possibly part of the commercial advantage.

CLOSED SOURCE FOR MASS MARKET PROJECTS

One edge case for preferring closed source when choosing a licence may be when you can realistically expect that a project might be not just successful but *huge*, that is, a mass market commodity. While "the community" of open source users is a great ally when you are growing a platform by word of mouth, if you could get an existing supply and distribution chain on your side, the advantage of being first to market and doing so cheaper may well be the most important thing.

Let's consider Nest, an intelligent thermostat: the area of smart energy metering and control is one in which many people are experimenting. The moment that an international power company chooses to roll out power monitors to all its customers, such a project would become instantaneously mass market. This would make it a very tempting proposition to copy, if you are a highly skilled, highly geared-up manufacturer in China, for example. If you also have the schematics and full source code, you can even skip the investment required to reverse-engineer the product.

The costs and effort required in moving to mass scale show how, for a physical device, the importance of supply chain can affect other considerations. In 2001, Paul Graham spoke compellingly about how the choice of programming language (in his case, Lisp) could leave competitors in the dirt because all of his competitors chose alternative languages with much slower speed of development (`www.paulgraham.com/avg.html`). Of course, the key factor wasn't so much about development platform as *time to market* versus your competitor's time to market. The tension between open and closed source informs this as well.

TAPPING INTO THE COMMUNITY

We talked about the "community" in the previous section, but it would be disingenuous to pretend that this is *exclusively* a feature of open source projects.

While thinking about which platform you want to build for, having a community to tap into may be vital or at least useful. Again, this is a major reason for our current support of the Arduino platform. If you have a problem with a component or a library, or a question about how to do something (for example, controlling a servo motor with a potentiometer dial), you could simply do a Google search on the words "arduino servo potentiometer" and find a YouTube video, a blog post, or some code.

Many other cute platforms, such as the Chumby Hacker Board, do have communities of aficionados, but perhaps smaller ones. If you are doing something more obscure or need more detailed technical assistance, finding someone who has already done exactly that thing may be difficult.

Mindshare may be important as you scale up, too—for example, if you want confidence that you can hire people with skills in the platform you've chosen. This issue may be less important for a small, focused team which has a lot of expertise in a new or obscure platform but still may be a consideration.

When you are an inexperienced maker, using a platform in which other people can mentor you is invaluable. If you have a local meeting for makers, such as Maker Night Liverpool, or equivalents in hackspaces around the world, you will very often find someone who is willing to take you through the basics in Arduino or another similar system. Perhaps that person is an expert on it or has simply gone through the basics (getting an LED flashing or playing "Mary had a little lamb" with a piezo speaker) at the last meeting. These meetings can be invaluable for both student and mentor.

Local meetings are also a great way to discuss your own project and learn about others. While to discuss your project is in some way being "open" about it, you are at all times in control of how much you say and whom you say it to. If you're not already open source minded, this approach can be much less intimidating than releasing your clever idea to the whole Internet at once.

The perceived danger of sharing an idea or an implementation or a question with other people is looking like an idiot in public. While many parts of many Internet communities are much more sympathetic to this fear than one might expect, the mask of anonymity on the Internet can seem to permit people to be less supportive or simply more rude than you might hope for. In general, face-to-face meetings at a hackspace may well be a friendlier and more supportive way to dip your toes into the idea of a "community" of Internet of Things makers.

One reason to be in touch with a (local or Internet) community of makers is that we are, in interaction designer and BERG hardware engineer Andy Huntington's words, at the stage of the "Geocities of things"—that is, at the frontier of the Internet of Things, just as Geocities was at the frontier of making websites and blogging. Sure, the design of some of the things may be clunky, the things might be pointless, and a lot of people may simply be doing something that they saw someone else do before. But from this outpouring of creativity will come the next generation of successful businesses and projects that actually change the world. This is a fascinating time to be getting involved in the Internet of Things.

SUMMARY

You now have a decent grounding in the wider issues around building your first Internet of Things prototype.

Prototyping is inherently a matter of balancing trade-offs between building something that allows you to learn more about the project you are looking to build and keeping an eye on how things scale up should your experiments prove you right.

In the next chapters we take each of the three main components of an Internet of Things device in turn: the embedded computing and electronics; the physical *Thing* itself; and the Internet service to which it talks. We look in more detail at how you would go about prototyping that aspect of your device.

You will be able to frame each element with concepts from this chapter to guide your choices—whether that is deciding to use Ruby on Rails for the server software due to its open source licence; plumping for a Raspberry Pi development board because you're an experienced Python programmer; or downloading a 3D design for a key component from Thingiverse to save having to design one from scratch.

5

PROTOTYPING
EMBEDDED DEVICES

YOU HAVE AN idea for a *thing*, and you know that it has some sort of interactive or electronic side to it. What is the first step in turning that from a vision in your head into something in the real world?

You likely can try out a number of different parts of the behaviour in isolation, and that's a good starting point for your initial prototype. After you do some research on the Internet to find similar projects or look through the catalogues of component retailers, such as RS (`www.rs-components.com/`) or Farnell (`www.farnell.com/`), you'll have a list of possible components and modules which might let you achieve your goal.

The more you dabble in electronics and microcontrollers, the bigger your collection of spare parts and leftovers from previous projects will grow. When you sit down to try out some of your ideas, either you'll have rooted through your collection for parts which are close enough to those you identified in your research, or you'll have an assortment of freshly purchased components. Usually, it's a combination of the two.

That's the typical decider when first trying out an idea: you use what's easily to hand, partly because it's generally something you're familiar with already but also because it helps keep the costs down. Even if you know that the board you're using won't be the ideal fit for a final version, if it lets you try out some of the functionality more quickly or more cheaply, that can mean it's the right choice for now.

One of the main areas where something vastly overpowered, and in theory much more expensive, can be the right choice for prototyping is using a mobile phone, laptop, or desktop computer to develop the initial software. If you already have a phone or computer which you can use, using it for your prototype isn't actually any more expensive.

However, if you haven't been playing around with electronics already and don't have a collection of development boards gathering dust in your desk drawer, how do you choose which one to buy? In this chapter, we explain some of the differences and features of a number of popular options. Over time the list will change, but you should still be able to work out how the same criteria we discussed in the preceding chapter apply to whichever boards you are considering.

This chapter starts with a look at electronics because whatever platform you end up choosing, the rest of the circuitry that you will build to connect it to will be pretty much the same. Then we choose four different platforms that you could use as a basis for your Internet of Things prototype. They aren't the only options, but they cover the breadth of options available. By the end of the chapter you will have a good feel for the trade-offs between the different options and enough knowledge of the example boards to make a choice on which to explore further.

ELECTRONICS

Before we get stuck into the ins and outs of microcontroller and embedded computer boards, let's address some of the electronics components that you might want to connect to them.

Don't worry if you're scared of things such as having to learn soldering. You are unlikely to need it for your initial experiments. Most of the prototyping can be done on what are called *solderless breadboards*. They enable you to build components together into a circuit with just a push-fit connection, which also means you can experiment with different options quickly and easily.

When it comes to thinking about the electronics, it's useful to split them into two main categories:

- **Sensors:** Sensors are the ways of getting information *into* your device, finding out things about your surroundings.
- **Actuators:** Actuators are the *outputs* for the device—the motors, lights, and so on, which let your device do something to the outside world.

Within both categories, the electronic components can talk to the computer in a number of ways.

The simplest is through digital I/O, which has only two states: a button can either be pressed or not; or an LED can be on or off. These states are usually connected via general-purpose input/output (GPIO) pins and map a digital 0 in the processor to 0 volts in the circuit and the digital 1 to a set voltage, usually the voltage that the processor is using to run (commonly 5V or 3.3V).

If you want a more nuanced connection than just on/off, you need an analogue signal. For example, if you wire up a potentiometer to let you read in the position of a rotary knob, you will get a varying voltage, depending on the knob's location. Similarly, if you want to run a motor at a speed other than off or full-speed, you need to feed it with a voltage somewhere between 0V and its maximum rating.

Because computers are purely digital devices, you need a way to translate between the analogue voltages in the real world and the digital of the computer.

An analogue-to-digital converter (ADC) lets you measure varying voltages. Microcontrollers often have a number of these converters built in. They will convert the voltage level between 0V and a predefined maximum (often the same 5V or 3.3V the processor is running at, but sometimes a fixed value such as 1V) into a number, depending on the accuracy of the ADC. The Arduino has 10-bit ADCs, which by default measure voltages between 0 and 5V. A voltage of 0 will give a reading of 0; a voltage of 5V would read 1023 (the maximum value that can be stored in a 10-bits); and voltages in between result in readings relative to the voltage. 1V would map to 205; a reading of 512 would mean the voltage was 2.5V; and so on.

The flipside of an ADC is a DAC, or digital-to-analogue converter. DACs let you generate varying voltages from a digital value but are less common as a standard feature of microcontrollers. This is due to a technique called *pulse-width modulation* (PWM), which gives an approximation to a DAC by rapidly turning a digital signal on and off so that the average value is the level you desire. PWM requires simpler circuitry, and for certain applications, such as fading an LED, it is actually the preferred option.

For more complicated sensors and modules, there are interfaces such as Serial Peripheral Interface (SPI) bus and Inter-Integrated Circuit (I2C). These standardised mechanisms allow modules to communicate, so sensors or things such as Ethernet modules or SD cards can interface to the microcontroller.

Naturally, we can't cover all the possible sensors and actuators available, but we list some of the more common ones here to give a flavour of what is possible.

SENSORS

Pushbuttons and switches, which are probably the simplest sensors, allow some user input. Potentiometers (both rotary and linear) and rotary encoders enable you to measure movement.

Sensing the environment is another easy option. Light-dependent resistors (LDRs) allow measurement of ambient light levels, thermistors and other temperature sensors allow you to know how warm it is, and sensors to measure humidity or moisture levels are easy to build.

Microphones obviously let you monitor sounds and audio, but piezo elements (used in certain types of microphones) can also be used to respond to vibration.

Distance-sensing modules, which work by bouncing either an infrared or ultrasonic signal off objects, are readily available and as easy to interface to as a potentiometer.

ACTUATORS

One of the simplest and yet most useful actuators is light, because it is easy to create electronically and gives an obvious output. Light-emitting diodes (LEDs) typically come in red and green but also white and other colours. RGB LEDs have a more complicated setup but allow you to mix the levels of red, green, and blue to make whatever colour of light you want. More complicated visual outputs also are available, such as LCD screens to display text or even simple graphics.

Piezo elements, as well as *responding* to vibration, can be used to *create* it, so you can use a piezo buzzer to create simple sounds and music. Alternatively, you can wire up outputs to speakers to create more complicated synthesised sounds.

Of course, for many tasks, you might also want to use components that *move* things in the real world. Solenoids can by used to create a single, sharp pushing motion, which could be useful for pushing a ball off a ledge or tapping a surface to make a musical sound.

More complicated again are motors. Stepper motors can be moved in *steps*, as the name implies. Usually, a fixed number of steps perform a full rotation. DC motors simply move at a given speed when told to. Both types of motor can be one-directional or move in both directions. Alternatively, if you want a motor that will turn to a given angle, you would need a servo. Although a servo is more controllable, it tends to have a shorter range of motion, often 180 or fewer degrees (whereas steppers and DC motors turn indefinitely). For all the kinds of motors that we've mentioned, you typically want to connect the motors to gears to alter the range of motion or convert circular movement to linear, and so on.

> *If you want to dig further into the ways of interfacing your computer or microcontroller with the real world, the "Interfacing with Hardware" page on the Arduino Playground website (*`http://playground.arduino.cc//Main/ InterfacingWithHardware`*) is a good place to start. Although Arduino-focused, most of the suggestions will translate to other platforms with minimal changes. For a more in-depth introduction to electronics, we recommend* Electronics For Dummies *(Wiley, 2009).*

SCALING UP THE ELECTRONICS

From the perspective of the electronics, the starting point for prototyping is usually a "breadboard". This lets you push-fit components and wires to make up circuits without requiring any soldering and therefore makes experimentation easy. When you're happy with how things are wired up, it's common to solder the components onto some protoboard, which may be sufficient to make the circuit more permanent and prevent wires from going astray.

Moving beyond the protoboard option tends to involve learning how to lay out a PCB. This task isn't as difficult as it sounds, for simple circuits at least, and mainly involves learning how to use a new piece of software and understanding some new terminology.

For small production runs, you'll likely use through-hole components, so called because the legs of the component go through holes in the PCB and tend to be soldered by hand. You will often create your designs as companion boards to an existing microcontroller platform—generally called *shields* in the Arduino community. This approach lets you bootstrap production without worrying about designing the entire system from scratch.

Journey to a Circuit Board

Let's look at the evolution of part of the Bubblino circuitry, from initial testing, through prototype, to finished PCB:

1. The first step in creating your circuit is generally to build it up on a breadboard. This way, you can easily reconfigure things as you decide exactly how it should be laid out.

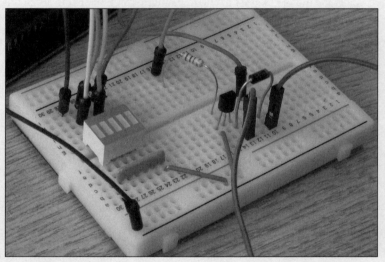

The breadboard.

2. When you are happy with how the circuit works, soldering it onto a stripboard will make the layout permanent. This means you can stop worrying about one of the wires coming loose, and if you're going to make only one copy of the circuit, that might be as far as you need take things.

The stripboard.

3. If you need to make many copies of the circuit, or if you want a professional finish, you can turn your circuit into a PCB. This makes it easier to build up the circuit because the position of each component will be labelled, there will be holes only where the components go, and there will be less chance of short circuits because the tracks between components will be protected by the solder resist.

The PCB.

When you want to scale things even further, moving to a combined board allows you to remove any unnecessary components from the microcontroller board, and switching to surface mount components—where the legs of the chips are soldered onto the same surface as the chip—eases the board's assembly with automated manufacturing lines.

PCB design and the options for manufacturing are covered in much greater detail in Chapter 10, "Moving to Manufacture".

EMBEDDED COMPUTING BASICS

The rest of this chapter examines a number of different embedded computing platforms, so it makes sense to first cover some of the concepts and terms that you will encounter along the way.

Providing background is especially important because many of you may have little or no idea about what a microcontroller is. Although we've been talking about computing power getting cheaper and more powerful, you cannot just throw a bunch of PC components into something and call it an Internet of Things product. If you've ever opened up a desktop PC, you've seen that it's a collection of discrete modules to provide different aspects of functionality. It has a main motherboard with its processor, one or two smaller circuit boards providing the RAM, and a hard disk to provide the long-term storage. So, it has a lot of components, which provide a variety of general-purpose functionality and which all take up a corresponding chunk of physical space.

MICROCONTROLLERS

Internet of Things devices take advantage of more tightly integrated and miniaturised solutions—from the most basic level of microcontrollers to more powerful system-on-chip (SoC) modules. These systems combine the processor, RAM, and storage onto a single chip, which means they are much more specialised, smaller than their PC equivalents, and also easier to build into a custom design.

These microcontrollers are the engines of countless sensors and automated factory machinery. They are the last bastions of 8-bit computing in a world that's long since moved to 32-bit and beyond. Microcontrollers are very limited in their capabilities—which is why 8-bit microcontrollers are still in use, although the price of 32-bit microcontrollers is now dropping to the level where they're starting to be edged out. Usually, they offer RAM capabilities measured in kilobytes and storage in the tens of kilobytes. However, they can still achieve a lot despite their limitations.

You'd be forgiven if the mention of 8-bit computing and RAM measured in kilobytes gives you flashbacks to the early home computers of the 1980s such as the Commodore 64 or the Sinclair ZX Spectrum. The 8-bit microcontrollers have the same sort of internal workings and similar levels of memory to work with. There have been some improvements in the intervening years, though—the modern chips are much smaller, require less power, and run about five times faster than their 1980s counterparts.

Unlike the market for desktop computer processors, which is dominated by two manufacturers (Intel and AMD), the microcontroller market consists of many manufacturers. A better comparison is with the automotive market. In the same way that there are many different car manufacturers, each with a range of models for different uses, so there are lots of microcontroller manufacturers (Atmel, Microchip, NXP, Texas Instruments, to name a few), each with a range of chips for different applications.

The ubiquitous Arduino platform is based around Atmel's AVR ATmega family of microcontroller chips. The on-board inclusion of an assortment of GPIO pins and ADC circuitry means that microcontrollers are easy to wire up to all manner of sensors, lights, and motors. Because the devices using them are focused on performing one task, they can dispense with most of what we would term an operating system, resulting in a simpler and much slimmer code footprint than that of a SoC or PC solution.

In these systems, functions which require greater resource levels are usually provided by additional single-purpose chips which at times are more powerful than their controlling microcontroller. For example, the WizNet Ethernet chip used by the Arduino Ethernet has eight times more RAM than the Arduino itself.

SYSTEM-ON-CHIPS

In between the low-end microcontroller and a full-blown PC sits the SoC (for example, the BeagleBone or the Raspberry Pi). Like the microcontroller, these SoCs combine a processor and a number of peripherals onto a single chip but usually have more capabilities. The processors usually range from a few hundred megahertz, nudging into the gigahertz for top-end solutions, and include RAM measured in megabytes rather than kilobytes. Storage for SoC modules tends not to be included on the chip, with SD cards being a popular solution.

The greater capabilities of SoC mean that they need some sort of operating system to marshal their resources. A wide selection of embedded operating systems, both closed and open source, is available and from both specialised embedded providers and the big OS players, such as Microsoft and Linux. Again, as the price falls for increased computing power, the popularity and familiarity of options such as Linux are driving its wider adoption.

CHOOSING YOUR PLATFORM

How to choose the *right* platform for your Internet of Things device is as easy a question to answer as working out the meaning of life. This isn't to say that it's an impossible question—more that there are almost as many answers as there are possible devices. The platform you choose depends on the particular blend of price, performance, and capabilities that suit what you're trying to achieve. And just because you settle on one solution, that doesn't mean somebody else wouldn't have chosen a completely different set of options to solve the same problem.

Start by choosing a platform to prototype in. The following sections discuss some of the factors that you need to weigh—and possibly play off against each other—when deciding how to build your device.

We cover the decisions that you need to make when scaling up both later in this chapter and in Chapter 10.

Processor Speed

The processor speed, or clock speed, of your processor tells you how fast it can process the individual instructions in the machine code for the program it's running. Naturally, a faster processor speed means that it can execute instructions more quickly.

The clock speed is still the simplest proxy for raw computing power, but it isn't the only one. You might also make a comparison based on millions of instructions per second (MIPS), depending on what numbers are being reported in the datasheet or specification for the platforms you are comparing.

Some processors may lack hardware support for floating-point calculations, so if the code involves a lot of complicated mathematics, a by-the-numbers slower processor with hardware floating-point support could be faster than a slightly higher performance processor without it.

Generally, you will use the processor speed as one of a number of factors when weighing up similar systems. Microcontrollers tend to be clocked at speeds in the tens of MHz, whereas SoCs run at hundreds of MHz or possibly low GHz.

If your project doesn't require heavyweight processing—for example, if it needs only networking and fairly basic sensing—then some sort of micro-controller will be fast enough. If your device will be crunching lots of data—for example, processing video in real time—then you'll be looking at a SoC platform.

RAM

RAM provides the working memory for the system. If you have more RAM, you may be able to do more things or have more flexibility over your choice of coding algorithm. If you're handling large datasets on the device, that could govern how much space you need. You can often find ways to work around memory limitations, either in code (see Chapter 8, "Techniques for Writing Embedded Code") or by handing off processing to an online service (see Chapter 7, "Prototyping Online Components").

It is difficult to give exact guidelines to the amount of RAM you will need, as it will vary from project to project. However, microcontrollers with less than 1KB of RAM are unlikely to be of interest, and if you want to run standard encryption protocols, you will need at least 4KB, and preferably more.

For SoC boards, particularly if you plan to run Linux as the operating system, we recommend at least 256MB.

Networking

How your device connects to the rest of the world is a key consideration for Internet of Things products. Wired Ethernet is often the simplest for the user—generally plug and play—and cheapest, but it requires a physical cable. Wireless solutions obviously avoid that requirement but introduce a more complicated configuration.

WiFi is the most widely deployed to provide an existing infrastructure for connections, but it can be more expensive and less optimized for power consumption than some of its competitors.

Other short-range wireless can offer better power-consumption profiles or costs than WiFi but usually with the trade-off of lower bandwidth. ZigBee is one such technology, aimed particularly at sensor networks and scenarios such as home automation. The recent Bluetooth LE protocol (also known as Bluetooth 4.0) has a very low power-consumption profile similar to ZigBee's and could see more rapid adoption due to its inclusion into standard Bluetooth chips included in phones and laptops. There is, of course, the existing Bluetooth standard as another possible choice. And at the boring-but-very-cheap end of the market sit long-established options such as RFM12B which operate in the 434 MHz radio spectrum, rather than the 2.4 GHz range of the other options we've discussed.

For remote or outdoor deployment, little beats simply using the mobile phone networks. For low-bandwidth, higher-latency communication, you could use something as basic as SMS; for higher data rates, you will use the same data connections, like 3G, as a smartphone.

USB

If your device can rely on a more powerful computer being nearby, tethering to it via USB can be an easy way to provide both power and networking. You can buy some of the microcontrollers in versions which include support for USB, so choosing one of them reduces the need for an extra chip in your circuit.

Instead of the microcontroller presenting itself as a device, some can also act as the USB "host". This configuration lets you connect items that would normally expect to be connected to a computer—devices such as phones, for example, using the Android ADK, additional storage capacity, or WiFi dongles.

Devices such as WiFi dongles often depend on additional software on the host system, such as networking stacks, and so are better suited to the more computer-like option of SoC.

Power Consumption

Faster processors are often more power hungry than slower ones. For devices which might be portable or rely on an unconventional power supply (batteries, solar power) depending on where they are installed, power consumption may be an issue. Even with access to mains electricity, the power consumption may be something to consider because lower consumption may be a desirable feature.

However, processors may have a minimal power-consumption sleep mode. This mode may allow you to use a faster processor to quickly perform operations and then return to low-power sleep. Therefore, a more powerful processor may *not* be a disadvantage even in a low-power embedded device.

Interfacing with Sensors and Other Circuitry

In addition to talking to the Internet, your device needs to interact with something else—either sensors to gather data about its environment; or motors, LEDs, screens, and so on, to provide output. You could connect to the circuitry through some sort of peripheral bus—SPI and I2C being common ones—or through ADC or DAC modules to read or write varying voltages; or through generic GPIO pins, which provide digital on/off inputs or outputs. Different microcontrollers or SoC solutions offer different mixtures of these interfaces in differing numbers.

Physical Size and Form Factor

The continual improvement in manufacturing techniques for silicon chips means that we've long passed the point where the limiting factor in the size of a chip is the amount of space required for all the transistors and other components that make up the circuitry on the silicon. Nowadays, the size is governed by the number of connections it needs to make to the surrounding components on the PCB.

With the traditional through-hole design, most commonly used for home-made circuits, the legs of the chip are usually spaced at 0.1" intervals. Even if your chip has relatively few connections to the surrounding circuit—16 pins is nothing for such a chip—you will end up with over 1.5" (~4cm) for the perimeter of your chip. More complex chips can easily run to over a hundred connections; finding room for a chip with a 10" (25cm) perimeter might be a bit tricky!

You can pack the legs closer together with surface-mount technology because it doesn't require holes to be drilled in the board for connections. Combining that with the trick of hiding some of the connections on the underside of the chip means that it is possible to use the complex designs without resorting to PCBs the size of a table.

The limit to the size that each connection can be reduced to is then governed by the capabilities and tolerances of your manufacturing process. Some surface-mount designs are big enough for home-etched PCBs and can be hand-soldered. Others require professionally produced PCBs and accurate pick-and-place machines to locate them correctly.

Due to these trade-offs in size versus manufacturing complexity, many chip designs are available in a number of different form factors, known as *packages*. This lets the circuit designer choose the form that best suits his particular application.

All three chips pictured in the following figure provide identical functionality because they are all AVR ATmega328 microcontrollers. The one on the left is the through-hole package, mounted here in a socket so that it can be swapped out without soldering. The two others are surface mount, in two different packages, showing the reduction in size but at the expense of ease of soldering.

Through-hole versus surface-mount ATmega328 chips.

Looking at the ATmega328 leads us nicely into comparing some specific embedded computing platforms. We can start with a look at one which so popularised the ATmega328 that a couple of years ago it led to a worldwide shortage of the chip in the through-hole package, as for a short period demand outstripped supply.

ARDUINO

Without a doubt, the poster child for the Internet of Things, and physical computing in general, is the Arduino.

These days the Arduino project covers a number of microcontroller boards, but its birth was in Ivrea in Northern Italy in 2005. A group from the Interaction Design Institute Ivrea (IDII) wanted a board for its design students to use to build interactive projects. An assortment of boards was around at that time, but they tended to be expensive, hard to use, or both.

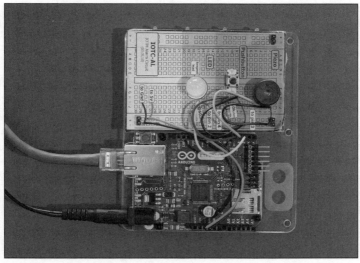

An Arduino Ethernet board, plugged in, wired up to a circuit and ready for use.

So, the team put together a board which was cheap to buy—around £20—and included an onboard serial connection to allow it to be easily programmed. Combined with an extension of the Wiring software environment, it made a huge impact on the world of physical computing.

Wiring: Sketching in Hardware

Another child of the IDII is the Wiring project. In the summer of 2003, Hernando Barragán started a project to make it easier to experiment with electronics and hardware. As the project website (http://wiring.org.co/about.html) puts it:

"The idea is to write a few lines of code, connect a few electronic components to the hardware of choice and observe how a light turns on when person approaches to it, write a few more lines add another sensor and see how this light changes when the illumination level in a room decreases.

This process is called sketching with hardware—a way to explore lots of ideas very quickly, by selecting the more interesting ones, refining them, and producing prototypes in an iterative process."

The Wiring platform provides an abstraction layer over the hardware, so the users need not worry about the exact way to, say, turn on a GPIO pin, and can focus on the problem they're trying to explore or solve.

That abstraction also enables the platform to run on a variety of hardware boards. There have been a number of Wiring boards since the project started, although they have been eclipsed by the runaway success of the project that took the Wiring platform and targeted a lower-end and cheaper AVR processor: the Arduino project.

A decision early on to make the code and schematics open source meant that the Arduino board could outlive the demise of the IDII and flourish. It also meant that people could adapt and extend the platform to suit their own needs.

As a result, an entire ecosystem of boards, add-ons, and related kits has flourished. The Arduino team's focus on simplicity rather than raw performance for the code has made the Arduino the board of choice in almost every beginner's physical computing project, and the open source ethos has encouraged the community to share circuit diagrams, parts lists, and source code. It's almost the case that whatever your project idea is, a quick search on Google for it, in combination with the word "Arduino", will throw up at least one project that can help bootstrap what you're trying to achieve. If you prefer learning from a book, we recommend picking up a copy of *Arduino For Dummies*, by John Nussey (Wiley, 2013).

The "standard" Arduino board has gone through a number of iterations: Arduino NG, Diecimila, Duemilanove, and Uno.

The Uno features an ATmega328 microcontroller and a USB socket for connection to a computer. It has 32KB of storage and 2KB of RAM, but don't let those meagre amounts of memory put you off; you can achieve a surprising amount despite the limitations.

The Uno also provides 14 GPIO pins (of which 6 can also provide PWM output) and 6 10-bit resolution ADC pins. The ATmega's serial port is made available through both the IO pins, and, via an additional chip, the USB connector.

If you need more space or a greater number of inputs or outputs, look at the Arduino Mega 2560. It marries a more powerful ATmega microcontroller to the same software environment, providing 256KB of Flash storage, 8KB of RAM, three more serial ports, a massive 54 GPIO pins (14 of those also capable of PWM) and 16 ADCs. Alternatively, the more recent Arduino Due has a 32-bit ARM core microcontroller and is the first of the Arduino boards to use this architecture. Its specs are similar to the Mega's, although it ups the RAM to 96KB.

DEVELOPING ON THE ARDUINO

More than just specs, the experience of working with a board may be the most important factor, at least at the prototyping stage. As previously mentioned, the Arduino is optimised for simplicity, and this is evident from the way it is packaged for use. Using a single USB cable, you can not only power the board but also push your code onto it, and (if needed) communicate with it—for example, for debugging or to use the computer to store data retrieved by the sensors connected to the Arduino.

Of course, although the Arduino was at the forefront of this drive for ease-of-use, most of the microcontrollers we look at in this chapter attempt the same, some less successfully than others.

Integrated Development Environment

You usually develop against the Arduino using the integrated development environment (IDE) that the team supply at `http://arduino.cc`. Although this is a fully functional IDE, based on the one used for the Processing language (`http://processing.org/`), it is very simple to use. Most Arduino projects consist of a single file of code, so you can think of the IDE mostly as a simple file editor. The controls that you use the most are those to check the code (by compiling it) or to push code to the board.

Pushing Code

Connecting to the board should be relatively straightforward via a USB cable. Sometimes you might have issues with the drivers (especially on some versions of Windows) or with permissions on the USB port (some Linux packages for drivers don't add you to the dialout group), but they are usually swiftly resolved once and for good. After this, you need to choose the correct serial port (which you can discover from system logs or select by trial and error) and the board type (from the appropriate menus, you may need to look carefully at the labelling on your board and its CPU to determine which option to select).

When your setup is correct, the process of pushing code is generally simple: first, the code is checked and compiled, with any compilation errors reported to you. If the code compiles successfully, it gets transferred to the Arduino and stored in its flash memory. At this point, the Arduino reboots and starts running the new code.

Operating System

The Arduino doesn't, by default, run an OS as such, only the bootloader, which simplifies the code-pushing process described previously. When you switch on the board, it simply runs the code that you have compiled until the board is switched off again (or the code crashes).

It is, however, possible to upload an OS to the Arduino, usually a lightweight real-time operating system (RTOS) such as FreeRTOS/DuinOS. The main advantage of one of these operating systems is their built-in support for multitasking. However, for many purposes, you can achieve reasonable results with a simpler task-dispatching library.

If you dislike the simple life, it is even possible to compile code without using the IDE but by using the toolset for the Arduino's chip—for example, for all the boards until the recent ARM-based Due, the `avr-gcc` toolset.

The `avr-gcc` toolset (`www.nongnu.org/avr-libc/`) is the collection of programs that let you compile code to run on the AVR chips used by the rest of the Arduino boards and flash the resultant executable to the chip. It is used by the Arduino IDE behind the scenes but can be used directly, as well.

Language

The language usually used for Arduino is a slightly modified dialect of C++ derived from the Wiring platform. It includes some libraries used to read and write data from the I/O pins provided on the Arduino and to do some basic handling for "interrupts" (a way of doing multitasking, at a very low level). This variant of C++ tries to be forgiving about the ordering of code; for example, it allows you to call functions before they are defined. This alteration is just a nicety, but it is useful to be able to order things in a way that the code is easy to read and maintain, given that it tends to be written in a single file.

The code needs to provide only two routines:

- `setup()`: This routine is run once when the board first boots. You could use it to set the modes of I/O pins to input or output or to prepare a data structure which will be used throughout the program.
- `loop()`: This routine is run repeatedly in a tight loop while the Arduino is switched on. Typically, you might check some input, do some calculation on it, and perhaps do some output in response.

To avoid getting into the details of programming languages in this chapter, we just compare a simple example across all the boards—blinking a single LED:

```
// Pin 13 has an LED connected on most Arduino boards.
// give it a name:
int led = 13;
```

```
// the setup routine runs once when you press reset:
void setup() {
  // initialize the digital pin as an output.
  pinMode(led, OUTPUT);
}

// the loop routine runs over and over again forever:
void loop() {
  digitalWrite(led, HIGH);    // turn the LED on
  delay(1000);                // wait for a second
  digitalWrite(led, LOW);     // turn the LED off
  delay(1000);                // wait for a second
}
```

Reading through this code, you'll see that the `setup()` function does very little; it just sets up that pin number 13 is the one we're going to control (because it is wired up to an LED).

Then, in `loop()`, the LED is turned on and then off, with a delay of a second between each flick of the (electronic) switch. With the way that the Arduino environment works, whenever it reaches the end of one cycle—on; wait a second; off; wait a second—and drops out of the `loop()` function, it simply calls `loop()` again to repeat the process.

Debugging

Because C++ is a compiled language, a fair number of errors, such as bad syntax or failure to declare variables, are caught at compilation time. Because this happens on your computer, you have ample opportunity to get detailed and possibly helpful information from the compiler about what the problem is.

Although you need some debugging experience to be able to identify certain compiler errors, others, like this one, are relatively easy to understand:

```
Blink.cpp: In function 'void loop()':Blink:21:
error:'digitalWritee' was not declared in this scope
```

On line 21, in the function `loop()`, we deliberately misspelled the call to `digitalWrite`.

When the code is pushed to the Arduino, the rules of the game change, however. Because the Arduino isn't generally connected to a screen, it is hard for it to tell you when something goes wrong. Even if the code compiled successfully, certain errors still happen. An error could be raised that can't be handled, such as a division by zero, or trying to access the tenth element of a 9-element list. Or perhaps your program leaks memory and eventually just stops working. Or (and worse) a programming error might make the code continue to work dutifully but give entirely the wrong results.

If Bubblino stops blowing bubbles, how can we distinguish between the following cases?

- Nobody has mentioned us on Twitter.
- The Twitter search API has stopped working.
- Bubblino can't connect to the Internet.
- Bubblino has crashed due to a programming error.
- Bubblino is working, but the motor of the bubble machine has failed.
- Bubblino is powered off.

Adrian likes to joke that he can debug many problems by looking at the flashing lights at Bubblino's Ethernet port, which flashes while Bubblino connects to DNS and again when it connects to Twitter's search API, and so on. (He also jokes that we can discount the "programming error" option and that the main reason the motor would fail is that Hakim has poured bubble mix into the wrong hole. Again.) But while this approach might help distinguish two of the preceding cases, it doesn't help with the others and isn't useful if you are releasing the product into a mass market!

The first commercially available version of the WhereDial has a bank of half a dozen LEDs specifically for consumer-level debugging. In the case of an error, the pattern of lights showing may help customers fix their problem or help flesh out details for a support request.

Runtime programming errors may be tricky to trap because although the C++ language has exception handling, the `avr-gcc` compiler doesn't support it (probably due to the relatively high memory "cost" of handling exceptions); so the Arduino platform doesn't let you use the usual `try...catch...` logic.

Effectively, this means that you need to check your data before using it: if a number might conceivably be zero, check that before trying to divide by it. Test that your indexes are within bounds. To avoid memory leaks, look at the tips on writing code for embedded devices in Chapter 8, "Techniques for Writing Embedded Code".

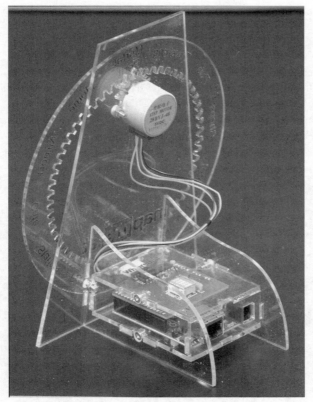

Rear view of a transparent WhereDial. The bank of LEDs can be seen in the middle of the green board, next to the red "error" LED.

But code isn't, in general, created perfect: in the meantime you need ways to identify where the errors are occurring so that you can bullet-proof them for next time. In the absence of a screen, the Arduino allows you to write information over the USB cable using `Serial.write()`. Although you can use the facility to communicate all kinds of data, debugging information can be particularly useful. The Arduino IDE provides a serial monitor which echoes the data that the Arduino has sent over the USB cable. This could include any textual information, such as logging information, comments, and details about the data that the Arduino is receiving and processing (to double-check that your calculations are doing the right thing).

SOME NOTES ON THE HARDWARE

The Arduino exposes a number of GPIO pins and is usually supplied with "headers" (plastic strips that sit on the pin holes, that provide a convenient solderless connection for wires, especially with a "jumper" connection). The headers are optimised for prototyping and for being able to change the purpose of the Arduino easily.

Each pin is clearly labelled on the controller board. The details of pins vary from the smaller boards such as the Nano, the classic form factor of the Uno, and the larger boards such as the Mega or the Due. In general, you have power outputs such as 5 volts or 3.3 volts (usually labelled 5V and 3V3, or perhaps just 3V), one or more electric ground connections (GND), numbered digital pins, and numbered analogue pins prefixed with an A.

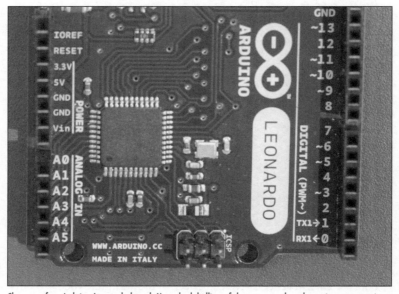

Close-up of an Arduino Leonardo board. Note the labelling of the power and analogue input connections.

You can power the Arduino using a USB connection from your computer. This capability is usually quite convenient during prototyping because you need the serial connection in any case to program the board. The Arduino also has a socket for an external power supply, which you might be more likely to use if you distribute the project. Either way should be capable of powering the microcontroller and the usual electronics that you might attach to it. (In the case of larger items, such as motors, you may have to attach external power and make that available selectively to the component using transistors.)

Outside of the standard boards, a number of them are focused on a particular niche application—for example, the Arduino Ethernet has an on-board Ethernet chip and trades the USB socket for an Ethernet one, making it easier to hook up to the Internet. This is obviously a strong contender for a useful board for Internet of Things projects.

The LilyPad has an entirely different specialism, as it has a flattened form (shaped, as the name suggests, like a flower with the I/O capabilities exposed on its "petals") and is designed to make it easy to wire up with conductive thread, and so a boon for wearable technology projects.

Choosing one of the specialist boards isn't the only way to extend the capabilities of your Arduino. Most of the boards share the same layout of the assorted GPIO, ADC, and power pins, and you are able to piggyback an additional circuit board on top of the Arduino which can contain all manner of componentry to give the Arduino extra capabilities.

In the Arduino world, these add-on boards are called *shields*, perhaps because they cover the actual board as if protecting it.

Some shields provide networking capabilities—Ethernet, WiFi, or Zigbee wireless, for example. Motor shields make it simple to connect motors and servos; there are shields to hook up mobile phone LCD screens; others to provide capacitive sensing; others to play MP3 files or WAV files from an SD card; and all manner of other possibilities—so much so that an entire website, `http://shieldlist.org/`, is dedicated to comparing and documenting them.

In terms of functionality, a standard Arduino with an Ethernet shield is equivalent to an Arduino Ethernet. However, the latter is thinner (because it has all the components laid out on a single board) but loses the convenient USB connection. (You can still connect to it to push code or communicate over the serial connection by using a supplied adaptor.)

OPENNESS

The Arduino project is completely open hardware and an open hardware success story.

The only part of the project protected is the Arduino trademark, so they can control the quality of any boards calling themselves an Arduino. In addition to the code being available to download freely, the circuit board schematics and even the EAGLE PCB design files are easily found on the Arduino website.

This culture of sharing has borne fruit in many derivative boards being produced by all manner of people. Some are merely minor variations on the main Arduino Uno, but many others introduce new features or form factors that the core Arduino team have overlooked.

In some cases, such as with the wireless-focused Arduino Fio board, what starts as a third-party board (it was originally the Funnel IO) is later adopted as an official Arduino-approved board.

Arduino Case Study: The Good Night Lamp

While at the IDII, Alexandra Deschamps-Sonsino came up with the idea of an Internet-connected table or bedside lamp. A simple, consumer device, this lamp would be paired with another lamp anywhere in the world, allowing it to switch the other lamp on and off, and vice versa. Because light is integrated into our daily routine, seeing when our loved ones turn, for example, their bedside lamp on or off gives us a calm and ambient view onto their lives.

This concept was ahead of its time in 2005, but the project has now been spun into its own company, the Good Night Lamp. The product consists of a "big lamp" which is paired with one or more "little lamps". The big lamp has its own switch and is designed to be used like a normal lamp. The little lamps, however, don't have switches but instead reflect the state of the big lamp.

Adrian was involved since the early stages as Chief Technology Officer. Adrian and the rest of the team's familiarity with Arduino led to it being an obvious choice as the prototyping platform. In addition, as the lamps are designed to be a consumer product rather than a technical product, and are targeted at a mass market, design, cost, and ease of use are also important. The Arduino platform is simple enough that it is possible to reduce costs and size substantially by choosing which components you need in the production version.

A key challenge in creating a mass-market connected device is finding a convenient way for consumers, some of whom are non-technical, to connect the device to the Internet. Even if the user has WiFi installed, entering authentication details for your home network on a device that has no keyboard or screen presents challenges. As well as looking into options for the best solution for this issue, the Good Night Lamp team are also building a version which connects over the mobile phone networks via GSM or 3G. This option fits in with the team's vision of connecting people via a "physical social network", even if they are not otherwise connected to the Internet.

Arduino Case Study: Botanicalls

Botanicalls (www.botanicalls.com/) is a collaboration between technologists and designers that consists of monitoring kits to place in plant pots. The Botanicalls kits then contact the owner if the plant's soil gets too dry. The project write-up humourously refers to this as "an effort to promote successful interspecies understanding" and as a way of translating between a plant's communication protocols (the colour and drooping of leaves) to human protocols, such as telephone, email, or Twitter.

The original project used stock Arduino controllers, although the kits available for sale today use the ATmega 168 microcontroller with a custom board, which remains Arduino-compatible, and the programming is all done using the Arduino IDE. To match the form factor of the leaf-shaped printed circuit board (PCB), the device uses a WizNet Ethernet chip instead of the larger Arduino Ethernet Shield. Future updates might well support WiFi instead.

Arduino Case Study: BakerTweet

The BakerTweet device (www.bakertweet.com/) is effectively a physical client for Twitter designed for use in a bakery. A baker may want to let customers know that a certain product has just come out of the ovens—fresh bread, hot muffins, cupcakes laden with icing—yet the environment he would want to tweet from contains hot ovens, flour dust, and sticky dough and batter, all of which would play havoc with the electronics, keyboard, and screen of a computer, tablet, or phone. Staff of design agency Poke in London wanted to know when their local bakery had just produced a fresh batch of their favourite bread and cake, so they designed a proof of concept to make it possible.

Because BakerTweet communicates using WiFi, bakeries, typically not built to accommodate Ethernet cables, can install it. BakerTweet exposes the functionality of Twitter in a "bakery-proof" box with more robust electronics than a general-purpose computer, and a simplified interface that can be used by fingers covered in flour and dough. It was designed with an Arduino, an Ethernet Shield, and a WiFi adapter. As well as the Arduino simply controlling a third-party service (Twitter), it is also hooked up to a custom service which allows the baker to configure the messages to be sent.

RASPBERRY PI

The Raspberry Pi, unlike the Arduino, wasn't designed for physical computing at all, but rather, for education. The vision of Eben Upton, trustee and cofounder of the Raspberry Pi Foundation, was to build a computer that was small and inexpensive and designed to be programmed and experimented with, like the ones he'd used as a child, rather than to passively consume games on. The Foundation gathered a group of teachers, programmers, and hardware experts to thrash out these ideas from 2006.

While working at Broadcom, Upton worked on the Broadcom BCM2835 system-on-chip, which featured an exceptionally powerful graphics processing unit (GPU), capable of high-definition video and fast graphics rendering. It also featured a low-power, cheap but serviceable 700 MHz ARM CPU, almost tacked on as an afterthought. Upton described the chip as "a GPU with ARM elements grafted on" (www.gamesindustry.biz/articles/digitalfoundry-inside-raspberry-pi).

A Raspberry Pi Model B board. The micro USB connector only provides power to the board; the USB connectivity is provided by the USB host connectors (centre-bottom and centre-right).

The project has always taken some inspiration from a previous attempt to improve computer literacy in the UK: the "BBC Micro" built by Acorn in the early 1980s. This computer was invented precisely because the BBC producers tasked with creating TV programmes about programming realised that there wasn't a single cheap yet powerful computer platform that was sufficiently widespread in UK schools to make it a sensible topic for their show. The model names of the Raspberry Pi, "Model A" and "Model B", hark back to the different versions of the BBC Micro. Many of the other trustees of the Raspberry Pi Foundation, officially founded in 2009, cut their teeth on the BBC Micro. Among them was David Braben, who wrote the seminal game of space exploration, Elite, with its cutting-edge 3D wireframe graphics.

Due in large part to its charitable status, even as a small group, the Foundation has been able to deal with large suppliers and push down the costs of the components. The final boards ended up costing around £25 for the more powerful Model B (with built-in Ethernet connection). This is around the same price point as an Arduino, yet the boards are really of entirely different specifications.

The following table compares the specs of the latest, most powerful Arduino model, the Due, with the top-end Raspberry Pi Model B:

	Arduino Due	Raspberry Pi Model B
CPU Speed	84 MHz	700 MHz ARM11
GPU	None	Broadcom Dual-Core VideoCore IV Media Co-Processor

	Arduino Due	**Raspberry Pi Model B**
RAM	96KB	512MB
Storage	512KB	SD card (4GB +)
OS	Bootloader	Various Linux distributions, other operating systems available
Connections	54 GPIO pins	8 GPIO pins
	12 PWM outputs	1 PWM output
	4 UARTs	1 UART
	SPI bus	SPI bus with two chip selects
	I²C bus	I²C bus
	USB 16U2 + native host	2 USB host sockets
	12 analogue inputs (ADC)	Ethernet
	2 analogue outputs (DAC)	HDMI out
		Component video and audio out

So, the Raspberry Pi is effectively a computer that can run a real, modern operating system, communicate with a keyboard and mouse, talk to the Internet, and drive a TV/monitor with high-resolution graphics. The Arduino has a fraction of the raw processing power, memory, and storage required for it to run a modern OS. Importantly, the Pi Model B has built-in Ethernet (as does the Arduino Ethernet, although not the Due) and can also use cheap and convenient USB WiFi dongles, rather than having to use an extension "shield".

Note that although the specifications of the Pi are in general more capable than even the top-of-the-range Arduino Due, we can't judge them as "better" without considering what the devices are for! To see where the Raspberry Pi fits into the Internet of Things ecosystem, we need to look at the process of interacting with it and getting it to do useful physical computing work as an Internet-connected "Thing", just as we did with the Arduino! We look at this next.

However, it is worth mentioning that a whole host of devices is available in the same target market as the Raspberry Pi: the Chumby Hacker Board, the BeagleBoard, and others, which are significantly more expensive. Yes, they may have slightly better specifications, but for the price difference, there may seem to be very few reasons to consider them above the Raspberry Pi. Even so, a project might be swayed by existing hardware, better tool support for a specific chipset, or ease-of-use considerations. In an upcoming section, we look at one such board, the BeagleBone, with regards to these issues.

CASES AND EXTENSION BOARDS

Still, due to the relative excitement in the mainstream UK media, as well as the usual hacker and maker echo chambers, the Raspberry Pi has had some real focus. Several ecosystems have built up around the device. Because the Pi can be useful as a general-purpose computer or media centre without requiring constant prototyping with electronic components, one of the first demands enthusiasts have had was for convenient and attractive cases for it. Many makers blogged about their own attempts and have contributed designs to Thingiverse, Instructables, and others. There have also been several commercial projects. The Foundation has deliberately not authorised an "official" one, to encourage as vibrant an ecosystem as possible, although staffers have blogged about an early, well-designed case created by Paul Beech, the designer of the Raspberry Pi logo (`http://shop.pimoroni.com/products/pibow`).

Beyond these largely aesthetic projects, extension boards and other accessories are already available for the Raspberry Pi. Obviously, in the early days of the Pi's existence post launch, there are fewer of these than for the Arduino; however, many interesting kits are in development, such as the Gertboard (`www.raspberrypi.org/archives/tag/gertboard`), designed for conveniently playing with the GPIO pins.

Whereas with the Arduino it often feels as though everything has been done already, in the early days of the Raspberry Pi, the situation is more encouraging. A lot of people are doing interesting things with their Pis, but as the platform is so much more high level and capable, the attention may be spread more thinly—from designing cases to porting operating systems to working on media centre plug-ins. Physical computing is just *one* of the aspects that attention may be paid to.

DEVELOPING ON THE RASPBERRY PI

Whereas the Arduino's limitations are in some ways its greatest feature, the number of variables on the Raspberry Pi are much greater, and there is much more of an emphasis on being able to do things in alternative ways. However, "best practices" are certainly developing. Following are some suggestions at time of writing. (It's worth checking on the Raspberry Pi websites, IRC channels, and so on, later to see how they will have evolved.)

If you want to seriously explore the Raspberry Pi, you would be well advised to pick up a copy of the Raspberry Pi User Guide, *by Eben Upton and Gareth Halfacree (Wiley, 2012).*

Operating System

Although many operating systems can run on the Pi, we recommend using a popular Linux distribution, such as

- **Raspbian:** Released by the Raspbian Pi Foundation, Raspbian is a distro based on Debian. This is the default "official" distribution and is certainly a good choice for general work with a Pi.
- **Occidentalis:** This is Adafruit's customised Raspbian. Unlike Raspbian, the distribution assumes that you will use it "headless"—not connected to keyboard and monitor—so you can connect to it remotely by default. (Raspbian requires a brief configuration stage first.)

For Internet of Things work, we recommend something such as the Adafruit distro. You're most probably not going to be running the device with a keyboard and display, so you can avoid the inconvenience of sourcing and setting those up in the first place. The main tweaks that interest us are that

- The sshd (SSH protocol daemon) is enabled by default, so you can connect to the console remotely.
- The device registers itself using zero-configuration networking (zero-conf) with the name `raspberrypi.local`, so you don't need to know or guess which IP address it picks up from the network in order to make a connection.

When we looked at the Arduino, we saw that perhaps the greatest win was the simplicity of the development environment. In the best case, you simply downloaded the IDE and plugged the device into the computer's USB. (Of course, this elides the odd problem with USB drivers and Internet connection when you are doing Internet of Things work.) With the Raspberry Pi, however, you've already had to make decisions about the distro and download it. Now that distro needs to be unpacked on the SD card, which you purchase separately. You should note that some SD cards don't work well with the Pi; apparently, "Class 10" cards work best. The class of the SD card isn't always clear from the packaging, but it is visible on the SD card with the number inside a larger circular "C".

At this point, the Pi may boot up, if you have enough power to it from the USB. Many laptop USB ports aren't powerful enough; so, although the "On" light displays, the device fails to boot. If you're in doubt, a powered USB hub seems to be the best bet.

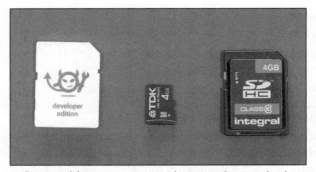

An Electric Imp (left), next to a micro SD card (centre), and an SD card (right).

After you boot up the Pi, you can communicate with it just as you'd communicate with any computer—that is, either with the keyboard and monitor that you've attached, or with the Adafruit distro, via ssh as mentioned previously. The following command, from a Linux or Mac command line, lets you log in to the Pi just as you would log in to a remote server:

```
$ ssh root@raspberrypi.local
```

From Windows, you can use an SSH client such as PuTTY (www.chiark. greenend.org.uk/~sgtatham/putty/). After you connect to the device, you can develop a software application for it as easily as you can for any Linux computer. How easy that turns out to be depends largely on how comfortable you are developing for Linux.

Programming Language

One choice to be made is which programming language and environment you want to use. Here, again, there is some guidance from the Foundation, which suggests Python as a good language for educational programming (and indeed the name "Pi" comes initially from Python).

Let's look at the "Hello World" of physical computing, the ubiquitous "blinking lights" example:

```
import RPi.GPIO as GPIO
from time import sleep

GPIO.setmode(GPIO.BOARD) # set the numbering scheme to be the
                         # same as on the board
GPIO.setup(8, GPIO.OUT)  # set the GPIO pin 8 to output mode

led = False
```

```
GPIO.output(8, led)  # initiate the LED to off

while 1:
    GPIO.output(8, led)
    led = not led # toggle the LED status on/off for the next
                  # iteration
    sleep(10)     # sleep for one second
```

As you can see, this example looks similar to the C++ code on an Arduino. The only real differences are the details of the modularization: the GPIO code and even the `sleep()` function have to be specified. However, when you go beyond this level of complexity, using a more expressive "high-level" language like Python will almost certainly make the following tasks easier:

- Handling strings of character data
- Completely avoiding having to handle memory management (and bugs related to it)
- Making calls to Internet services and parsing the data received
- Connecting to databases and more complex processing
- Abstracting common patterns or complex behaviours

Also, being able to take advantage of readily available libraries on PyPi (`https://pypi.python.org/pypi`) may well allow simple reuse of code that other people have written, used, and thoroughly tested.

So, what's the catch? As always, you have to be aware of a few trade-offs, related either to the Linux platform itself or to the use of a high-level programming language. Later, where we mention "Python", the same considerations apply to most higher-level languages, from Python's contemporaries Perl and Ruby, to the compiled VM languages such as Java and C#. We specifically contrast Python with C++, as the low-level language used for Arduino programming.

- **Python, as with most high-level languages, compiles to relatively large (in terms of memory usage) and slow code, compared to C++.** The former is unlikely to be an issue; the Pi has more than enough memory. The speed of execution may or may not be a problem: Python is likely to be "fast enough" for most tasks, and certainly for anything that involves talking to the Internet, the time taken to communicate over the network is the major slowdown. However, if the electronics of the sensors and actuators you are working with require split-second timing, Python *might* be too slow. This is by no means certain; if Bubblino starts blowing bubbles a millisecond later, or the DoorBot unlocks the office a millisecond after you scan your RFID card to authenticate, this delay may be acceptable and not even noticeable.

- **Python handles memory management automatically.** Because handling the precise details of memory allocation is notoriously fiddly, automatic memory management generally results in fewer bugs and performs adequately. However, this automatic work has to be scheduled in and takes some time to complete. Depending on the strategy for garbage collection, this may result in pauses in operation which might affect timing of subsequent events.

  Also, because the programmer isn't exposed to the gory details, there may well be cases in which Python quite reasonably holds onto more memory than you might have preferred had you been managing it by hand. In worse cases, the memory may never be released until the process terminates: this is a so-called *memory leak*. Because an Internet of Things device generally runs unattended for long periods of time, these leaks may build up and eventually end up with the device running out of memory and crashing. (In reality, it's more likely that such memory leaks happen as a result of programming error in manual memory management.)

- **Linux itself arguably has some issues for "real-time" use.** Due to its being a relatively large operating system, with many processes that may run simultaneously, precise timings may vary due to how much CPU priority is given to the Python runtime at any given moment. This hasn't stopped many embedded programmers from moving to Linux, but it may be a consideration for your case.

- **An Arduino runs only the one set of instructions, in a tight loop, until it is turned off or crashes.** The Pi constantly runs a number of processes. If one of these processes misbehaves, or two of them clash over resources (memory, CPU, access to a file or to a network port), they may cause problems that are entirely unrelated to your code. This is unlikely (many well-run Linux computers run without maintenance for years and run businesses as well as large parts of the Internet) but may result in occasional, possibly intermittent, issues which are hard to identify and debug.

We certainly don't want to put undue stress on the preceding issues! They are simply trade-offs that may or may not be important to you, or rather more or less important than the features of the Pi and the access to a high-level programming language.

The most important issue, again, is probably the ease of use of the environment. If you're comfortable with Linux, developing for a Pi is relatively simple. But it doesn't approach the simplicity of the Arduino IDE. For example, the Arduino starts your code the moment you switch it on. To get the same behaviour under Linux, you could use a number of mechanisms, such as an initialisation script in /etc/init.d.

First, you would create a wrapper script—for example, `/etc/init.d/`
`StartMyPythonCode`. This script would start your code if it's called with a
`start` argument, and stop it if called with `stop`. Then, you need to use the
`chmod` command to mark the script as something the system can run:
`chmod +x /etc/init.d/StartMyPythonCode`. Finally, you register
it to run when the machine is turned on by calling `sudo update-rc.d`
`StartMyPythonCode defaults`.

If you are familiar with Linux, you may be familiar with this mechanism for
automatically starting services (or indeed have a preferred alternative). If
not, you can find tutorials by Googling for "Raspberry Pi start program on
boot" or similar. Either way, although setting it up isn't *hard* per se, it's much
more involved than the Arduino way, if you aren't already working in the IT
field.

Debugging

While Python's compiler also catches a number of syntax errors and attempts
to use undeclared variables, it is also a relatively permissive language
(compared to C++) which performs a greater number of calculations at
runtime. This means that additional classes of programming errors won't
cause failure at compilation but will crash the program when it's running,
perhaps days or months later.

Whereas the Arduino had fairly limited debugging capabilities, mostly
involving outputting data via the serial port or using side effects like blinking
lights, Python code on Linux gives you the advantages of both the language
and the OS. You could step through the code using Python's integrated
debugger, attach to the process using the Linux `strace` command, view
logs, see how much memory is being used, and so on. As long as the device
itself hasn't crashed, you may be able to ssh into the Raspberry Pi and do
some of this debugging while your program has failed (or is running but
doing the wrong thing).

Because the Pi is a general-purpose computer, without the strict memory
limitations of the Arduino, you can simply use `try... catch...` logic so
that you can trap errors in your Python code and determine what to do with
them. For example, you would typically take the opportunity to log details of
the error (to help the debugging process) and see if the unexpected problem
can be dealt with so that you can continue running the code. In the worst
case, you might simply stop the script running and have it restart again afresh!

Python and other high-level languages also have mature testing tools which
allow you to assert expected behaviours of your routines and test that they

perform correctly. This kind of automated testing is useful when you're working out whether you've finished writing correct code, and also can be rerun after making other changes, to make sure that a fix in one part of the code hasn't caused a problem in another part that was working before.

SOME NOTES ON THE HARDWARE

The Raspberry Pi has 8 GPIO pins, which are exposed along with power and other interfaces in a 2-by-13 block of male header pins. Unlike those in the Arduino, the pins in the Raspberry Pi aren't individually labelled. This makes sense due to the greater number of components on the Pi and also because the expectation is that fewer people will use the GPIO pins and you are discouraged from soldering directly onto the board. The intention is rather that you will plug a cable (IDC or similar) onto the whole block, which leads to a "breakout board" where you do actual work with the GPIO.

Alternatively, you can connect individual pins using a female jumper lead onto a breadboard. The pins are documented on the schematics. A female-to-male would be easiest to connect from the "male" pin to the "female" breadboard. If you can find only female-to-female jumpers, you can simply place a header pin on the breadboard or make your own female-to-male jumper by connecting a male-to-male with a female-to-male! These jumpers are available from hobbyist suppliers such as Adafruit, Sparkfun, and Oomlout, as well as the larger component vendors such as Farnell.

The block of pins provides both 5V and 3.3V outputs. However, the GPIO pins themselves are only 3.3V tolerant. The Pi doesn't have any over-voltage protection, so you are at risk of breaking the board if you supply a 5V input! The alternatives are to either proceed with caution or to use an external breakout board that has this kind of protection. At the time of writing, we can't recommend any specific such board, although the Gertboard, which is mentioned on the official site, looks promising.

Note that the Raspberry Pi doesn't have any analogue inputs (ADC), which means that options to connect it to electronic sensors are limited, out of the box, to digital inputs (that is, on/off inputs such as buttons). To get readings from light-sensitive photocells, temperature sensors, potentiometers, and so on, you need to connect it to an external ADC via the SPI bus. You can find instructions on how to do this at, for example, `http://learn.adafruit.com/reading-a-analog-in-and-controlling-audio-volume-with-the-raspberry-pi/overview`.

We mentioned some frustrations with powering the Pi earlier: although it is powered by a standard USB cable, the voltage transmitted over USB from a laptop computer, a powered USB hub, or a USB charger varies greatly. If you're not able to power or to boot your Pi, check the power requirements and try another power source.

OPENNESS

Because one of the goals of the Raspberry Pi is to create something "hackable", it is no surprise that many of the components are indeed highly open: the customised Linux distributions such as "Raspbian" (based on Debian), the ARM VideoCore drivers, and so on. The core Broadcom chip itself is a proprietary piece of hardware, and they have released only a partial datasheet for the BCM2835 chipset. However, many of the Raspberry Pi core team are Broadcom employees and have been active in creating drivers and the like for it, which are themselves open source.

These team members have been able to publish certain materials, such as PDFs of the Raspberry Pi board schematics, and so on. However, the answer to the question "Is it open hardware?" is currently "Not yet" (`www.raspberrypi.org/archives/1090#comment-20585`).

Raspberry Pi Case Study: DoES Liverpool's DoorBot

When a group of friends and collaborators, including us, fell upon the idea of setting up a coworking and maker space, we soon discovered that keeping the space open required one of the keyholders to get in early enough and stay late enough to make it attractive to members. Between a big enough group of unpaid organisers, things work reasonably well, but after running for a year and a half, John and Ben extended the DoorBot, which we mentioned in Chapter 4, "Thinking About Prototyping", to managing door entry using a magnetically controlled lock.

Now running on a Raspberry Pi, three DoorBots each control one door (to the main space, or to the office and event spaces). They take input from an RFID pad and check it against a database of known IDs. On a successful entry, the DoorBot plays a piece of "entrance music" specific to that user, triggers a command to the magnetic door bolt to open for 3 seconds, and logs the user's entrance. This solution required fitting new locks with control wires and also drilling holes through the wall panel to feed the RFID reader through to the outside (the affordable reader we used isn't powerful to read through glass). The DoorBot also runs a screen which shows a calendar of events and some webcam feeds. The audio/visual requirements are the main reason that the Raspberry Pi was chosen to implement it. However, having a general-purpose Linux system has also been useful in general: in the case of the entry system code failing, it is possible to connect remotely over ssh to get the door open.

It is worth noting that the Broadcom chip is currently harder to source than either the widely available Atmel chips in the Arduino or the Texas Instruments chip in the BeagleBone. This could make it harder to spin up a prototype into a product.

BEAGLEBONE BLACK

The BeagleBone Black is the latest device to come from the BeagleBoard group. This group largely consists of employees of Texas Instruments, and although the products are not TI boards as such, they use many components with their employer's blessing. The relationship is thus similar to that of the Raspberry Pi Foundation with Broadcom. Similarly, the BeagleBoard team want to create "powerful, open, and embedded devices" with a goal of contributing to the open source community, including facilitating education in electronics. However, there is less of an emphasis on creating a general-purpose computer for education; these boards are very much designed with the expectation that they will be used for physical computing and experimentation in electronics.

The latest board from the BeagleBone family: the BeagleBone Black.

The BeagleBone Black is the smallest and cheapest of the team's boards, with a form factor comparable to that of the Raspberry Pi. Although the specs of the two are mostly comparable, there are some interesting trade-offs.

The original BeagleBone has no video or audio outputs built in, but it does have a far larger number of GPIO pins, extracted into two rows of female headers. It also has the crucial ADC pins for analogue input which the Raspberry Pi lacks. This shows the development team's focus on building something for working with electronics rather than as a general-purpose computer.

The BeagleBone was released before the Raspberry Pi, and its price reflects that. If you think of it as a more powerful embedded development board than any of the Arduino offerings, then a £63 price tag looks quite reasonable. When you compare it to a £25 Raspberry Pi, however, it makes less sense.

The influence of the Pi can be seen in the latest revision of the BeagleBone platform, the BeagleBone Black. Although still missing the analogue video and audio connectors, it adds a micro-HDMI connector to provide digital outputs for both audio and video. The price is also much closer at £31, and it retains the much better electronics interfacing capabilities of the original BeagleBone.

Let's compare the specs of the Raspberry Pi Model B with the new BeagleBone Black:

	BeagleBone Black	**Raspberry Pi Model B**
CPU Speed	1GHz ARM Cortex-A8	700 MHz ARM11
GPU	SGX530 3D	Broadcom Dual-Core VideoCore IV Media Co-Processor
RAM	512MB	512MB
Storage	2GB embedded MMC, plus uSD card	SD card (4GB +)
OS	Various Linux distributions, Android, other operating systems available	Various Linux distributions, other operating systems available
Connections	65 GPIO pins, of which 8 have PWM 4 UARTs SPI bus I²C bus USB client + host Ethernet Micro-HDMI out 7 analog inputs (ADC) CAN bus	8 GPIO pins, of which 1 has PWM 1 UART SPI bus with two chip selects I²C bus 2 USB host sockets Ethernet HDMI out Component video and audio out

Like the Raspberry Pi, the BeagleBone is a computer that mostly runs Linux but is capable of running a variety of other ported operating systems. Unlike the Pi, it isn't specified by default to communicate with a local user via a display and keyboard.

Importantly, for Internet of Things work, both boards come with Ethernet connectivity (assuming the Raspberry Pi Model B) and can take advantage of cheap USB WiFi dongle options if required.

If the actual advantages of the BeagleBone were limited to a slightly faster CPU and (in our opinion) a more aesthetically pleasing physical design, these might not be compelling reasons to dedicate a section of this book to the platform, never mind actually buy one, given its price.

Let's now look at the features of the BeagleBone that we think distinguish it, including both hardware features and the softer, usability-related ones.

CASES AND EXTENSION BOARDS

Although the BeagleBone hasn't had the same hype and media exposure as the Pi, a fair number of attractive cases are available, either sold commercially like the Adafruit BoneBox, or as freely available instructions and designs. In any case, given that the board is mostly designed to be used for open hardware, it is also likely that the specific project you are working on will require a custom casing to fit the form factor of the project.

Extension boards for the BeagleBone are known as "capes" rather than "shields" (the term for Arduino extension boards). This name comes from Underdog, the star of a 1960s US animation, a beagle who wore a superhero cape. Capes are available to add controllers for LCD displays and motors and various networking and sensor applications.

DEVELOPING ON THE BEAGLEBONE

We've already seen how the Arduino had one official way to do things, whereas the Raspberry Pi presented a blank slate and choices for operating system and programming language. Yes, you can skip the IDE entirely and use `avr-gcc` yourself and write code and build a toolchain to target the Arduino's AVR chip directly, rather than using the Arduino libraries; however, almost all users will at least start with the "official" development tools, and only a rare few will experiment beyond this. In contrast, although recommendations and best practices exist for the Raspberry Pi, you have to make an explicit decision which set of tools to use and even take a step to install them on the SD card. This flexibility makes some sense because the Pi's target audience is so wide (from education, general-purpose computing, programming, electronics, and home media).

Although the BeagleBone is capable of general-purpose computing, its target market is much more narrowly defined, and perhaps as a consequence, the team have been able to take a middle way: every board comes with the Ångström Linux distribution installed on it. Although several other operating systems have been ported to the platform, having a default installed with zero effort means that it is far simpler to get started and evaluate the board. If you enjoy tinkering, have a preferred embedded operating system, or have reached some insurmountable limitation of Ångström, by all means install another operating system! However, in this chapter we just look at the default.

The BeagleBone runs zeroconf networking by default and usually advertises itself as `beaglebone.local`. You can connect to it in a number of ways. Very usefully, you can connect to the excellent, interactive System Reference Manual and Hardware Documentation, which is generally at `http://beaglebone.local/README.htm`. You can also find this manual at `http://beagleboard.org/static/beaglebone/latest/README.htm`, although it is not usefully interactive in this case.

The manual is dynamically updated to give information about your BeagleBone and has pages where you can look at and change various settings, such as the outputs to GPIO pins. It also has links to the Cloud9 IDE, which is hosted on the board, and which is the simplest recommended way to write code for the device.

Cloud9 is an online programming environment—and a rather interesting idea. A hosted version of it is available at `https://c9.io`, where you can edit and code "in the cloud" (that is, as an Internet-hosted service). However, the primary component of the service is an open source application which can run locally on a given computer (`https://github.com/ajaxorg/cloud9/`). Because the BeagleBone is essentially a general-purpose computer, using the latter, stand-alone option makes more sense. This means that to develop on the BeagleBone, you can get started immediately, without needing to download any software at all, by connecting to the IDE at `http://beaglebone.local:3000`.

Although the online Cloud9 environment also supports Ruby and Python, the free component version supports only Node.js, a framework built on JavaScript. Here's what it says on the tin:

> *Node.js is a platform built on Chrome's JavaScript runtime for easily building fast, scalable network applications. Node.js uses an event-driven, non-blocking I/O model that makes it lightweight and efficient, perfect for data-intensive real-time applications that run across distributed devices.*
>
> —http://nodejs.org/

We've already addressed the trade-offs of "real-time" platforms compared to Python running on the Raspberry Pi. Many of the same factors apply to the Node.js platform, so let's just summarise those here:

- Although the Chrome JavaScript runtime is aggressively optimised, it is a virtual machine running a very high-level, dynamic language, with greater memory usage.
- Automated memory management has overheads which may affect timing.
- Linux itself is less suited to very precise timings than a true RTOS.

Another important trade-off when looking at real-time programming is the multitasking model. If more than one task needs to be done "at the same time" (or apparently at the same time), such as moving a motor, sensing whether a button has been pressed, and blinking multiple lights in different patterns, the runtime environment needs a strategy to choose when to switch between the "simultaneous" tasks. Node.js uses a cooperative model, whereby each action is run as appropriate by a coordinating central process. This process chooses the next action to run based on its schedule. But because only one action actually runs at a time, the coordinator has to wait until the previous action has completed before starting the next one. This means that there is no way to guarantee that a given task will start with millisecond precision.

The fact that the Node.js website mentions "real-time" code suggests that its developers believe their technology is perfectly capable of doing multitasking event scheduling. Although the specific definition of "real-time" may not match that used by some embedded programmers for applications requiring split-millisecond precision, it is "good enough" for most tasks. Besides which, the advantages of the high-level language and convenient development environment often are the overriding concern.

As mentioned previously, the Arduino has the benefit of a single-standard development toolchain, whereas the Raspberry Pi has the double-edged sword of an embarrassment of riches. The BeagleBone combines the best of these two extremes by having all the flexibility of the Pi but with a single standard toolchain installed.

For the rest of this section, we look mostly at the standard toolchain; rest assured, though, that if it doesn't quite live up to your requirements, you could substitute plenty of other options.

Operating System

The BeagleBone comes pre-installed with the Ångström Linux distribution. This operating system was developed specifically for running on embedded devices and can run with as little as 4MB of flash storage.

Much like Occidentalis for the Raspberry Pi, Ångström is configured to run "headless", without keyboard and monitor. There are convenient ways to access a command-line prompt, either over a serial connection with USB or using zeroconf and connecting to `beaglebone.local`.

One advantage of having a single *pre-installed* operating system is that you can start playing with the board the moment you open the box. Of course, the onboard instructions suggest updating the operating system as one of the first steps, if it's not already at the latest version; this is certainly good practice after you have briefly evaluated the board and are moving onto prototyping a project with it.

Programming Language

As with the Raspberry Pi, you can connect to BeagleBone via the terminal and develop a software application as you would for any other Linux computer. In the preceding section, we noted that this is a "simple" task if you already program for Linux, but it might seem a little overwhelming otherwise. In this section, we look at the Cloud9 IDE, which we mentioned earlier, in a little more detail.

As before, we start with the old, reliable "blinking lights" example. The `README.htm` presents code to do exactly this:

```
require('bonescript');

setup = function () {
    pinMode(bone.USR3, OUTPUT);     // Enable LED USR3 control
}

loop = function () {
    digitalWrite(bone.USR3, HIGH);  // Turn LED USR3 on
    delay(100);                     // Delay 100ms
    digitalWrite(bone.USR3, LOW);   // Turn LED USR3 off
    delay(100);                     // Delay 100ms
}
```

As always, the code is practically the same in concept: the details of the syntax vary, but you still have the usual two functions, `setup` and `loop`; have to set the mode of the pin to output; and alternate sending `HIGH` and `LOW` values to it with a pause in between.

Note that USR3 is actually connected to one of the status LEDs built into the board. If you want to connect a standard kit LED using the GPIO pins, you would simply substitute `USR3` with one of the standard pins, such as `P8_3`.

As with Python, JavaScript is a high-level language, so after you move beyond the physical input and output with electronic components, tasks dealing with text manipulation, talking to Internet services, and so on are far easier to handle than the relatively low-level C++ used in the Arduino.

And again, Node.js is a rich environment with a host of libraries available to integrate into the app. Currently, the convenient `npm` (Node Packaged Modules) utility isn't bundled with the IDE, but this is an item for a future version. In the meantime, online help and forums should get you over any possible stumbling blocks.

The code doesn't automatically start after a reboot, unlike the Arduino. However, once you have finished developing your application, copying it into the `autorun` subfolder will result in the system's picking it up on reboot and starting it automatically from then on.

Debugging

Just like Python, JavaScript is a permissive language compared to C++. Again, because the language is dynamic, the compiler does not catch several types of programming errors. Luckily, the IDE reports runtime errors quite usefully, so while you are running from that, you can get reasonable diagnostics with minimal effort.

When you move to running the Node.js code automatically as a service, you will probably want to enable logging to catch those errors that don't become evident until days or months later.

As with the Raspberry Pi, you have all the tools available on the Linux operating system to help debug. This is, of course, all the more necessary because Linux + Node.js is a more complicated platform than Arduino, but the flexibility and power are certainly appreciated!

Again, JavaScript has error handling, although it is extended and arguably complicated by Node.js's callback mechanisms. This feature can help handle and recover from unusual situations gracefully.

Node.js also has automated testing tools such as node-unit. Just because you are writing in a high-level language doesn't mean that all your code will be simpler. The fact that it is easier to write any given line often means that you write much more code and of greater complexity. Because Node.js is built on collaborative multitasking through callbacks, the execution path may be especially complicated: testing can allow you to make sure that all the expected paths through this code happen, in the right order.

SOME NOTES ON THE HARDWARE

For physical computing, the number of GPIO pins available is greatly superior to the Pi's, and a number of them have ADCs (allowing them to process analogue inputs, a capability which the Pi lacked), and others offer PWM capability (allowing the board to mimic analogue output). Although the pins are neatly laid along both long edges of the board, in two columns, the BeagleBone doesn't have enough space to label each pin, as the Arduino does. Instead, each set of headers has labels, and the documentation has a key for what each of the physical pins does. As with the Pi, each pin may have a number of different names, depending on which subsystem is accessing it, and this may feel unnecessarily complex if you are used to the simple, restricted naming (and labelling) conventions of the Arduino.

OPENNESS

One of the initial explicit goals of the BeagleBoard was to create an open platform for experimenting with embedded hardware. As such, the project has, to date, released more of its schematics as open source than has the Raspberry Pi Foundation. Specifically, "All hardware from BeagleBoard.org is open source, so you can download the design materials including schematics, bill-of-materials and PCB layout" (http://beagleboard.org/). The Ångström Linux distribution that is installed by default on the Beagle-Bone is also fully open source. Most of the nontechnical content of the site is also released under a Creative Commons licence. Although the Pi team also appear to be pro–open source, the explicit release of material under open source licence seems to be an issue that the BeagleBoard team are taking more seriously. This might be important to your project for philosophical reasons, but open schematics and code may potentially be critical at the stage of moving your project from prototype to product.

The BeagleBone web pages also link to proprietary operating systems and extension boards. As you may expect, we consider this to be a good thing, as the team are encouraging a good ecosystem around the product, both free and commercial.

BeagleBone Case Study: Ninja Blocks

Although the rise of the cheap microcontrollers we have been looking at brings Internet of Things applications such as home automation into the price range of an interested hobbyist, and the progressively simpler development environments put it within the reach of those with little or no programming experience, it is still true that developing useful prototypes with an Arduino, Raspberry Pi, BeagleBone, and the like does require getting your hands dirty with the awkward details of hardware and software. The Ninja Blocks (http://ninjablocks.com/) are one solution to this problem. Just as "If This Then That" offers simple rules-based programming for web applications—"If I am tagged in a picture on Facebook, Then upload that picture to Dropbox"—the Ninja Rules app extends this idea to Internet of Things devices: "If my washing machine has finished, Then send me an email".

The brains of a Ninja Block is a BeagleBone running Linux and packing an Arduino, too (presumably to take advantage of its connectivity, although in general the BeagleBone has equivalent connectivity options). It can be connected to other blocks to provide input and output. Input is provided by sensor blocks, such as motion and door contact sensors for security applications, and buttons and temperature sensors for general home monitoring. Outputs are provided by actuators, currently remote power controls. Although the Rules app provides the simplified use cases mentioned here, you also can program the blocks using a REST API or by using high-level code (such as Node.js) on the BeagleBone or, indeed, low-level C++ on the Arduino.

ELECTRIC IMP

Although we're featuring the Electric Imp here, it's a less mature and, in some ways, more problematic offering than the other boards we've discussed, and we can't tell, at the time of writing, if the platform will develop into a viable choice. But it is worth discussing in some detail, as a possible paradigm shift in the way that developers approach consumer electronics and physical computing.

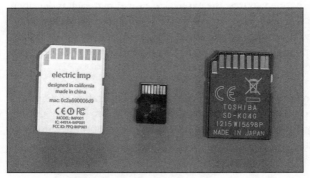

The rear of (from left to right): an Electric Imp, a micro SD card, an SD card.

Hugo Fiennes, formerly engineering manager on Apple's iPhone team, was attempting to connect LED lights to Google's share price. He evaluated various home automation options, like ZigBee, but realised that they were mostly single-vendor solutions, often using their own radio standards rather than based on open platforms (`www.eetimes.com/electronics-news/4373129/Former-Apple-Google-Facebook-engineers-launch-IoT-startup?pageNumber=2`). The Electric Imp uses a number of existing standards, such as WiFi, and the form factor of SD cards but ends up being very much less of an open platform than all the other devices that we've looked at in this chapter. Fiennes collaborated on the project with Kevin Fox, a former Gmail designer, and firmware engineer Peter Hartley. As you'll see, the startup feels as though it has much of the DNA (for good and bad) of the beautiful, technically polished walled gardens that are the iPhone and Gmail.

All the smarts of the Electric Imp, and also its WiFi connectivity, are located in an SD card–shaped microcontroller. It's important to note that the Imp isn't actually an SD card; it's just shaped like one. Using the same form factor means that producing the Imps is cheaper because the team can reuse existing cases and tooling, as well as existing component connectors for the *impee* (the name Electric Imp use for the rest of the circuit that the Imp plugs into). This last factor is important, as you see in the upcoming "Openness" section.

Although an SD card feels very robust, it is, on the outside, effectively a small, flat piece of plastic. It offers only one affordance to connect it to anything: namely, plug it into a device. Just as you would insert an SD card into a music player, computer, or printer, you insert an Imp into an impee. This host board provides power, GPIO connections to sensors and actuators, and an ID chip so that the Imp knows which device it's plugged into.

The Imp costs around £20, while an impee costs less than half that. Here, having used the standard SD form factor turns out to be a great choice for the prototyper. For prototyping a number of projects, you need only a single Imp, which can be reused across all the projects. You will see shortly that reconfiguring the Imp to run on a different impee is automatic, which is a very nice feature.

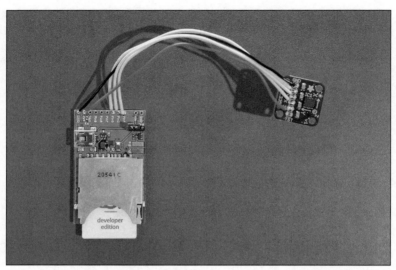

An Electric Imp inserted into an April impee development board and wired up to an accelerometer (the smaller circuit board).

DEVELOPING ON THE ELECTRIC IMP

We saw that the Electric Imp gets its power from the impee. Boards like the standard April impee have a connection that you can solder a battery to, but also have a USB connection, which is convenient while you're developing. But unlike the other boards we've looked at so far, the USB is *only* for power and not for communicating with the device. So you may be wondering how you would go about programming it.

In fact, the Imp is programmed and controlled over the Internet, so all it has to do is connect to your WiFi network with its built-in wireless connectivity. But, of course, you still have to tell it which wireless access point to connect to and most likely what password to use. This is obviously a tricky issue, until you already have a means of communicating with the board. The Electric Imp team have solved this bootstrapping problem using a very clever idea called *BlinkUp*. The Imp has a built-in light sensor (still contained in the tiny SD card format) which is activated whenever the Imp doesn't know how to access a WiFi connection. The Electric Imp smartphone apps currently available for iPhone and recent Android encode the WiFi connection data by simply changing the colour of the screen with an alternating pattern of white and black. You place the phone screen over the Imp to communicate with it, so you are quite literally "flashing" your microcontroller. If you don't have the appropriate kind of phone, you are slightly stuck (currently, you don't even have a way to encode the data using, say, your computer screen), but we assume that you can borrow a phone if required. Of course, the process of flashing the WiFi data across may fail: the Imp responds with a different pattern of blinking LEDs to help you diagnose this problem.

Writing Code

From the Electric Imp website, a sign-in link enables you to register for the site and then log in to your account (`https://plan.electricimp.com/`). This contains a list of all the device "nodes", which is empty at start. You can edit code in an IDE here.

The language used is *Squirrel*, which is a dynamic language with a C-like syntax. At present, Squirrel is poorly documented and poorly optimised. It is comparable to high-level embeddable scripting languages such as Lua, for which numerous published books are available, such as *Programming in Lua* (`www.lua.org/pil/`), currently in its third edition. Although Squirrel's relative obscurity may change, what will probably remain constant is that the name is overloaded. Unless your search engine, like Google, learns your habits and starts to concentrate on the appropriate articles, searches such as "squirrel performance", and "squirrel numbers" will give less than useful results. Including the term "language" or limiting searches to the `www.squirrel-lang.org/` domain may be useful.

After you write the code, pushing it to the device is one of the great strengths of the Electric Imp platform. When you signed in to the BlinkUp app, as well as giving your WiFi details, you also logged in to your electricimp.com account. This means that after you've flashed the Imp, it knows which account it is tied to. When you plug an Imp into an impee, that host device appears as a node in the planner application, which you access on the electricimp.com website. You can then associate it with one of the pieces of code that you've written. Now, whenever you plug the Imp into the impee, it connects to the web service and downloads the *latest* code onto the device. This means that after you have made a code change, you simply need to eject and reinsert the Imp to refresh the code.

Only at this point does the planner show you any error messages, which shows how dynamic the Squirrel language is; there are no compilation checks.

Although the deployment is very polished, the experience of using the editor and planner is still rather counterintuitive. Again, this issue will most likely improve as the platform matures. Let's see what the blinking light example looks like:

```
// Blink-O-Matic example code

local ledState = 0;

function blink()
{
    // Change state
    ledState = ledState?0:1;
    hardware.pin9.write(ledState);

    // Schedule the next state change in 100ms
    imp.wakeup(0.1, blink);
}

// Configure pin 9 as an open drain output with
// internal pull up
hardware.pin9.configure(DIGITAL_OUT_OD_PULLUP);

// Register with the server
imp.configure("Blink-O-Matic", [], []);

// Start blinking
blink();
```

The first point to note is that you don't have the usual obvious division of labour into `setup` and `loop`. All the setup functions are done within the body of the code, while the `blink` function is explicitly called and tells the Imp to call itself again in 100 milliseconds. Apart from this, most of the usual configuration of a hardware pin and writing alternately high and low values to it are familiar.

The `imp.configure()` call tells the planner details of the code. Here, the only parameter filled in is the descriptive name of the node, but as you can see, you have to supply two additional list parameters (in this case empty). We come back to this call shortly.

Debugging

As you saw, any error messages after deployment or during runtime are shown in the editor window. So are messages output from the Imp using the `server.show()` call. This feature is really handy, compared to the Arduino, for example, because it's easier to use than the serial console, and you also get useful automatic output from errors that occur while your code is running.

The output of `server.show()` is also sent to the planner screen, where it is shown on the "node" box for the impee. When you have only one impee running, this feature isn't especially impressive, but when you have a number of devices running, this box does provide a nice overview of all your devices' status. As you will now see, the planner screen is crucial to really getting the most out of the Imp.

Planner

Perhaps the most interesting feature of the platform is the way that the nodes can be *connected* to each other on the planner screen. Any node could have outputs, where some data is *output*, not just to be shown on the planner screen but to another node. This second node would then have a corresponding *input* which handles the data in some way. So, for example, one Imp might output the value of a switch, whereas another turns a light on or off in response to that switch. This feature works whether the second Imp is in another room (that is, sharing a WiFi network with the first) or on a different network, possibly in another country entirely. You could implement such a system with some code like this:

```
// NODE 1
local my_output = OutputPort("SwitchOut");
imp.configure("RemoteLightSwitch", [], [my_output]);
// later... switch the light on
my_output.set(1);

// NODE 2
class SwitchIn extends InputPort
{
    type = "integer"
    name = "switch_value"

    function set(value) {
        hardware.pin1.write(value)
    }
}
imp.configure("Light", [Servo()], []);
```

The Electric Imp platform has completely hidden all the details of how the two devices communicate with each other! All you have to focus on are the details of the message that gets passed between them and not the details of the HTTP or other protocol calls.

You may have spotted that the `imp.configure` calls in the preceding example have some values provided to the two list parameters that were empty when you last encountered it. This is how the network communication is wired together in the code. The first list shows any inputs (where information is sent from the Electric Imp server to this Imp), and the second list gives the outputs (where this Imp will send data out to the Electric Imp server). Once you have defined some inputs and outputs, you can wire them together in the planner to feed the output from one Imp into the input of another.

So, because communication between Imps doesn't require low-level details such as HTTP communication, the Imp doesn't have a way to make calls to the network. If this were the end of the story, it would obviously make it a terrible choice for any implementation of an Internet of Things product! The planner allows you to add nodes which make HTTP calls. They are run not on the Imp, but in the cloud, on the `plan.electricimp.com` servers. This makes a great deal of sense because the Imps themselves may be running in a network with restrictions on network traffic. Instead, the server application does the processing of the network call and passes JSON data (for example) to the next node.

So what would, in the world of Arduino, Raspberry Pi, or BeagleBone, be code on a single microcontroller, on the Electric Imp platform you would instead decompose the problem into a pipeline of several nodes. Let's look at a few examples of how to implement proof-of-concepts for some of the Internet of Things devices that Adrian and others in our workshop have worked on:

Bubblino:

1. The node which communicates with the Twitter servers would live on the Electric Imp server and periodically check for new tweets.
2. Whenever it found one, it would then communicate with the Imp, which triggers the bubble machine to blow bubbles.

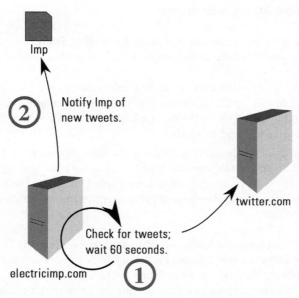

Network topology of an Electric Imp implementation of Bubblino.

Good Night Lamp:

This is effectively the example we gave in the preceding text. When the Big Lamp is switched on, its Imp would notify the Little Lamp's Imp, via the Electric Imp server.

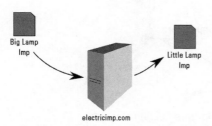

A single Big Lamp and Little Lamp for Good Night Lamp would be the simplest network example of Electric Imp.

Yet Another Home Management System:

This is the system we use to control the heating in our office. For more details on how it works, see the case study on DoES Liverpool in Chapter 4.

1. The office temperature monitor would be implemented as one Imp, the Monitoring Imp in the following diagram. That would regularly report the temperature to a node on the Electric Imp server, which would record the value to a feed on Xively.

2. Independently of the monitoring system, a control node on the Electric Imp server would poll the server at yahms.net to see if the heating should be on or off and notify another Imp, labelled the Control Imp in the diagram. That would then control the heating system and turn it on or off, accordingly.

These examples handwave over details of configuration and control. The planner allows parameters to be tweaked but is too flexible to make it into a commercial product. Of course, the Electric Imp's commercial offering to manufacturers offers more options for this than just this development planner.

Currently, only a handful of server nodes or "virtual impees" are available, but you can find documentation for writing your own server nodes (still in the Squirrel language), and you are encouraged to contact the Electric Imp team if you need access to this capability.

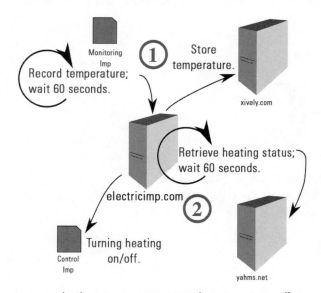

A more complex Electric Imp scenario, to monitor the temperature in an office and allow remote or automatic control of the heating.

Comments on Networking

This transparent networking, where you can join up server nodes with one or more Imps, possibly on multiple networks, is very appealing. But it does mean that you have a central point of communication, and therefore failure, on the Electric Imp team's servers. It also means that two Imps working together in the same room don't network together but via a round-trip to the Internet. This configuration makes the Imp unsuited to tasks in which faster mesh communication would be required and less appealing when you want to expand the communication beyond the reach of your WiFi network—for example, with a line-of-sight infrared or a longer-range radio communication.

Openness

Although you've seen how commercial ecosystems have grown up around the other microcontrollers described in this chapter, the Electric Imp is created not for hobbyists or for education but as a commercial system to be incorporated into products. As such, it isn't optimised for tinkering but rather for getting things done. And unsurprisingly, although the project does use open source elements, the two factors that make up its competitive advantage are, for the moment, resolutely closed source—namely, the innovative form factor and the online planner.

Form Factor

As a small microcontroller enclosed in the plastic casing of an SD card, the Imp doesn't lend itself to tinkering. It has no user-serviceable parts and provides no documentation on how to assemble your own.

Similarly, whatever operating system runs on the Imp is locked down. It runs BlinkUp, the diagnostic LEDs, the communication with the impee to find its ID, and the syncing of its code with the electricimp.com servers. Then it runs the code and communicates, as appropriate, with the server. There is no user-exposed way to change how this works.

Planner

The source code of the planner and the back-end infrastructure that connects Imps and virtual nodes are closed. This situation makes some sense because this is a commercial service; however, it means that when developing for the Imp, you are tied to a vendor to provide the service. You have to trust a third party to keep your code safe, backed up, and available. This isn't a great leap; it may make perfect sense to outsource parts of your business as an IT product, from hosting (Heroku), source control (GitHub), email sending (Postmark), and error logging (Sentry).

However, being reliant on a *single* vendor can be a real issue. The providers mentioned in the preceding paragraph may or may not be the best, long term, but each has viable alternatives. In the case of Electric Imp, which is to some extent blazing a trail, moving your code and devices to another provider if required may not be so simple. You need to be asking questions like these:

- If they close, will it be possible to reconfigure the Imps to point at another provider who can host the code?
- If the level of service is inadequate, what will you do?
- If you get big and want to configure the planning infrastructure in a direction that the Electric Imp team don't want to facilitate for their general customers, how will you proceed? Will they allow you to sponsor the development? Or to take on management of it yourself?

Programming Language

The Squirrel programming language is, in fact, developed under the MIT open source licence. Although it is a relatively new project, compared to other contenders such as Lua, it is possible for you to read the source of Squirrel, fix bugs, add features, and so on. However, as the Electric Imp team are wholly responsible for the version of Squirrel that runs on both the Imps and the virtual nodes, you have no guarantee that such changes will be applied in a timely fashion or indeed ever.

Impees

The reference designs for impees are placed in the public domain (`http://devwiki.electricimp.com/doku.php?id=boards:start`). Although, as a developer, you will probably want to start with the minimal "April" board, which exposes six pins and supplies power, you can easily create your own impee that fits the form factor of your project using the schematics, bill of materials, and Gerber files that the team provide. (And if none of those terms make any sense, fear not; you will find out more in Chapter 10 .)

Here, the decision to use the SD card form factor is also an excellent one. To interface with the Imp, you can buy readily available SD card slots, connect to a cheap Atmel cryptographic chip (to provide a unique ID for the impee) and a few other reasonably priced components, and you have a valid host for an Imp.

The ease of adding the Imp hardware makes real sense for one of the main target audiences of the Electric Imp: existing manufacturers of consumer electronics who want to find a convenient way to incorporate the Internet of Things technologies into it. Finding space for an SD card slot and an ID chip will be much simpler than trying to incorporate a larger board like the Arduino.

Electric Imp Case Study: Lockitron

Although the Raspberry Pi DoorBot solves a very specific problem for a fairly technical group of people, everyone uses doors and keys. Lockitron (https://lockitron.com/), from Apigy, is a consumer solution to the problem of granting visitors access to your home without getting more keys cut. As such, it doesn't require changing locks and drilling holes through walls. Rather, a device fits over your current deadbolt and can simply turn the existing lock. You then open the lock using an app on your mobile phone, rather than using RFID (although the Lockitron does also have optional support for NFC radio). This means that the device has to be constantly connected to the Internet: because many people do not have Ethernet cabling running to their front door, this makes wireless connectivity a requirement.

That's where the Electric Imp comes in: "Electric Imp's BlinkUp takes a notoriously difficult WiFi enrollment process and turns it into something simple and delightful. Electric Imp was incredibly straightforward to integrate, and we didn't need to worry about buying expensive toolkits to write our firmware" (http://blog.electricimp.com/post/45920501558/lockitron). Although the Imp is one of the simplest microcontrollers we've looked at, because of the specific use case of the Lockitron, it needs to interact only with the lock, sensing whether it has been opened and making it open or close. All the rest of the intelligence happens on the Internet, and is a perfect use case for the Electric Imp's model of division of labour between local impee and cloud nodes.

OTHER NOTABLE PLATFORMS

As we saw in the preceding chapter, any number of prototyping platforms are available, and in the future there will be many more. This chapter has presented our informed guesses on the likely contenders for choice of platform for an Internet of Things project for the next few years. Even if it turns out that we bet on the wrong platform, we hope that the analysis of specific pros and cons of these varied choices will remain useful.

However, we didn't go for several platforms which nevertheless are worth an honourable mention. Let us now briefly survey some of the more interesting options. We've traced a narrative from the low-level Arduino, via the highly capable but bafflingly flexible Raspberry Pi, to the better packaged and more "opinionated" BeagleBone, and finally the attractive but locked-down Electric Imp. We continue this progression by looking at some devices in which the hardware is entirely locked down: mobile phones and tablets, and plug computing.

There are still ways to get around this closed nature, however, as the explanation of the Android Development Kit (ADK) will demonstrate.

MOBILE PHONES AND TABLETS

Modern phones and tablets, whether they're running iOS (iPhone/iPad), Android, Blackberry, or even Windows, come bristling with sensors, from gyroscopes to thermometers, one or more cameras capable of capturing still images and video, microphones, GPS, WiFi, Bluetooth, USB, NFC (the same technology that runs your contactless bank card or travel pass), buttons, and a multitouch sensitive screen. Phones, of course, have always-on Internet connectivity, via WiFi or the phone network, and so do many tablets. These devices also have several appealing outputs: high-fidelity audio output, HD-quality video, and one or more vibrating elements. They also have processing power similar to the Raspberry Pi's (currently, they are probably faster for general processing but slower for graphics, due to the Pi's crazily powerful GPU.)

On the face of it, using a mobile device sounds like the perfect way to create an Internet of Things appliance. However, the temptation is always to fall back on the device's capabilities as a phone, at which point you are effectively creating an "app" for the device rather than a new "Thing". And although the inputs for a phone can be used remarkably creatively (using the camera to measure your pulse by analysing the changes in redness of your skin), there isn't an easy way to wire a phone up to additional circuits or inputs.

Finally, these devices are still rather large and expensive to be placed into arbitrary consumer devices.

Android Development Kit

Although the cost and size may not matter to you for a prototype, the inability to wire up additional sensors and actuators could stymie any serious use of a mobile device in the Internet of Things. The ADK deals with this problem by pairing an Android device with an ADK-compatible microcontroller (currently the ARM-based Arduino Due). We saw that mobile devices don't have great options for communicating to arbitrary electronics, but they *do* have a USB connection that is typically used to sync data to a computer.

USB connections traditionally distinguish between the Host (computer) and Device (phone and so on) roles. If you want to connect the Android device to the Arduino, the latter takes on the Host role. In reality, the Android device provides the Internet connection, input/output capabilities, and processing power. The Arduino itself simply offers dumb access to its GPIO pins.

With the cost and size implied by an Android device *and* Arduino Due, not to mention the current state of documentation, the ADK doesn't seem like a viable platform as yet. But the division of labour between an Internet-connected, multimedia-capable device and a physical computing platform is an appealing direction for the future.

PLUG COMPUTING: ALWAYS-ON INTERNET OF THINGS

No matter how small you make a computer, you still have to power it. Even the smallest board may have a power pack that is relatively chunky. The idea of a plug computer is to include the circuitry within the same enclosure as the plug and adaptor. This turns out to be a highly convenient form factor, for a number of reasons:

- You don't need to place the computer somewhere.
- It does not have a cable to get dislodged or pulled.
- Being plugged in, tight against a plug socket, the device is unobtrusive.

This last consideration has made the idea of plug computing appealing to, among other groups, security experts and attackers. The Pwn Plug (`http://pwnieexpress.com`) is an "enterprise-class penetration testing drop box" that can be plugged into a socket and test for classic security vulnerabilities. Although this product is advertised for "white-hat hackers" (that is, security consultants helping companies secure their data), similar products could be used for evil. Most employees wouldn't look twice at a new small white box plugged into the wall, if they noticed it at all.

This kind of device, of course, has perfectly legitimate uses. For example, the Freedom Box home office server (`http://p2pfoundation.net/Freedom_Box`) is a cheap and open source way of providing file sharing and email for small companies or your home.

One of the most popular plug computing platforms is the SheevaPlug (www.plugcomputer.org/), which typically runs a Debian distribution tailored for its ARM chip. It doesn't have many input/output capabilities, usually only an Ethernet socket and USB.

With the low power requirements of the boards that we've looked at, which can be powered by USB and a tiny adaptor, it should be simple enough to create a plug computer-style enclosure for the Raspberry Pi or BeagleBone which would, in addition, have superior access to GPIO pins. The SheevaPlug and others are attractive in terms of being *already available* consumer electronics rather than necessarily being the best solution for an Internet of Things product.

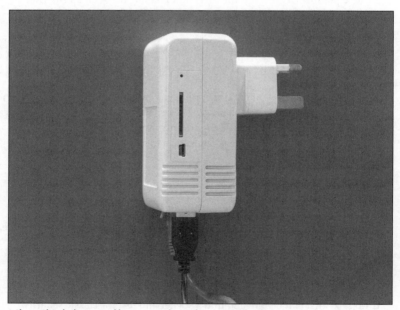

A SheevaPlug, looking more like a power adapter than a tiny computer.

SUMMARY

By now your ideas about the electronics and embedded software of your project should be starting to coalesce. If you're new to embedded development, don't worry too much about making the "wrong" choice. As you will see in later chapters, the road to a finished Internet of Things product involves some level of reworking of both the electronics and software, so focus on choosing the platform which is best for you *right now* rather than deliberating over a *perfect* choice.

The Electric Imp has great potential to find a niche that we weren't even aware existed: a hosted, walled garden, which is convenient to develop for, and where a commercial entity is responsible for making the right decisions on behalf of its users, who, in return for this capability, happily sacrifice control over some of the finer details. At the time of writing, the platform doesn't feel quite ready yet, but it is one of the more exciting developments, and it, or something like it, may well become the face of a swathe of Internet of Things development in the future.

The Arduino is the established and *de facto* choice, and for good reason. It is unrivalled in the wealth of support and documentation, and its open nature makes it easy to extend and incorporate into a finished product. The only downside to the Arduino is in its more limited capabilities. This simplicity is a boon in most physical computing scenarios, but with many Internet of Things applications requiring good security, the base Arduino Uno platform is looking a little stretched.

The Linux-based systems of the Raspberry Pi and BeagleBone will give you all the processing power and connectivity that you will need, but at the cost of additional complexity and, should you want to take the system into mass production, an additional cost per unit. There isn't much to choose between the Pi and tbe BeagleBone Black when it comes to cost for a prototype, so your choice is more likely to be down to other factors. The Raspberry Pi has a much higher profile, and better community around it, but its greater capability to interface to electronics and easier route to manufacture mean that, in our opinion, the BeagleBone Black has the edge.

With the electronics side covered, the next step is to look at the physical form into which the electronics will sit. The next chapter takes you through the design process, from initial sketches to the tools you can use to bring the design into the world, with a particular focus on the newer digital fabrication options, such as laser cutting and 3D printing.

6

PROTOTYPING THE PHYSICAL DESIGN

AS YOU SAW in the earlier chapters, one of the reasons that the Internet of Things is such an exciting area is that it cuts across so many different disciplines. It involves software, electronics, experience design, and product design.

It's this last field, product design, that seems to be the stumbling block for many a nascent Internet of Things project, judging by the number of technically brilliant creations gracing the pages of the Hackaday website or Kickstarter that are left as bare circuit boards or crammed into whatever box came to hand. If the Internet of Things is to succeed in reaching mass appeal, this lack of design is something we need to change. If you're a designer, give yourself a pat on the back; we need more people like you involved. If you're not a designer, don't worry; in this chapter we explore some of the techniques and tools to help get you started.

PREPARATION

To best prepare for design work, you should (in an ideal world) start long before you even have a particular problem to solve; developing an interest in design and having examples of design ideas you like are part of an ongoing process. Luckily, though, if you haven't already started this preparation, there's no better time than now. Even better, the process doesn't really look like work and might even become something that you class as fun!

All you need to do is develop an interest in the world around you and start paying attention to the wealth of objects and experiences that you encounter. This first step will help you work out what you like and what you don't like. Over time, you'll start to work out which qualities you particularly appreciate. Maybe you are attracted to the crisp, sleek lines of your Colnago road bike, or you admire the perfect balance of your 8-inch chef's knife, or you smile at the way your MacBook's MagSafe charger snaps into location. All such observations will help you work out what, for you, makes a good design.

Naturally, the more of the world you encounter, the more source material you'll have to work with. We're not suggesting that your accountant will let you get away with expensing your foreign holidays, but the exposure to different cultures and environments would help keep your critical faculties sharp. An easier sell, however, might be the occasional ticket to a gallery or museum, particularly those with a design slant or relevant exhibition. Who knew that *professional development* could be so enjoyable?

As you go, collect details about the items that inspire you. Take photos, jot down things in your notebook, or sketch them out. Paste them into an old-school scrapbook. Save them to Tumblr or Pinterest or your blog. Whatever works best for you. Over time you'll build up an archive of good design that will help you spark your creativity when designing things of your own.

The other side to a (very) basic design education is an understanding and appreciation of the tools available and the *materiality* of the processes involved in making things in the physical, rather than the digital, realm.

Items crafted in the digital world can focus exclusively on appearances and take on any form they like; in the real world, those pesky laws of physics and the limitations of the tools for fabrication come into play. That majestic overhang might look lovely in your 3D design package but would shift the centre of gravity of your chair such that it falls over when built. And those crisp 90-degree corners limit your options for making that housing—removing the former would be nearly impossible when trying vacuum forming, and it would complicate the injection moulding process.

A Note on Tools

Depending on how good (and for some of the tools how recent) your education was, you may not have any experience using some of the tools we've mentioned here. If you aren't an engineer, it's quite likely that you won't really know what they do or when to use them.

We'll cover laser cutters, 3D printers, and CNC mills later in the chapter, but we won't be looking at lathes or vacuum formers in detail.

Lathes tend to come in two main forms, depending on whether they're to be used for wood-work or metal-work. However, both types work in the same manner: the workpiece is held in a chuck which allows a motor to spin it along one axis. This then allows a cutter to be brought to bear on the spinning material, cutting it into the desired shape. As a result of this rotation around an axis, it produces good results for work that has a symmetry around an axis of rotation.

Another way to think of it is a bit like the inverse of a drill. Whereas drilling involves bringing a rotating tool to bear on a static workpiece, the lathe lets you bring a static tool into contact with a rotating workpiece.

Vacuum forming is an easy way to make thin plastic shells by sucking them onto a mould. A sheet of plastic is heated in a frame until it is very soft and pliable. Then the form or mould that provides the shape for the finished item is pushed into the softened plastic and a vacuum applied to help suck the plastic tight against the mould while it sets. It isn't suitable for particularly detailed or very deep moulding, but once the mould is created, pieces can be churned out quite quickly, even for manually operated machines.

As with most things, the more experience you gain with different materials and tools, the better your understanding will be when you come to design something. This is another great argument for seeking out and joining your local hackspace or makerspace. Most of them have tools that you wouldn't necessarily be able to afford on your own, such as laser cutters or 3D printers, and many have other machines, such as CNC mills, lathes, or vacuum formers. All of them have a wealth of expertise that you can tap into, in the form of the community of members.

So, whilst waiting for inspiration to strike, start playing around with the tools you've got to hand. Get involved in local (or not so local) hackdays; make things to give as gifts (or just to see what happens). By way of example, in the past month the members of DoES Liverpool (the makerspace that we helped found) have laser cut a (scaled down) woolly mammoth skeleton out of birch plywood, 3D-printed a replacement for a lost chess piece, and experimented with cutting some woollen felt into robot shapes in the laser cutter.

SKETCH, ITERATE, AND EXPLORE

Doing a lot of preparatory work doesn't mean that you won't do additional exploration and gathering of possible starting points when you do finally sit down with a specific project in mind. Arguably, in the early stages of a design, you can never do too much iterating through ideas and trying out different approaches to solving the problem.

Although a lot of this chapter is about the new digital fabrication tools— such as 3D printers and CNC machines—which let you produce small runs or one-offs that still look professional, we're going to start with a look at some much lower-tech solutions.

You might be tempted to fire up your 3D design package as soon as you sit down to design something. However, your first idea is unlikely to be the best, so you should be optimising for speed of iteration rather than quality of prototype. You could iterate through designs with a 3D printer, but doing so with a pen and paper is much quicker.

To begin with, you're looking for a broad search across the problem area. The objective is to get to grips with as many aspects of the design as possible, rather than drilling down into one specific possible result.

Pushing beyond the obvious solutions forces you to look at things differently and increases the likelihood that you'll have a good design among your options.

Use whatever tools make most sense to help with the idea generation and exploration. You might use a mood board—a whiteboard where you jot down thoughts and sketches over a few days—or a notebook that you doodle sketches in while sitting on a park bench watching the world pass by.

By now, some of you may be protesting, "That's all very well, but I can't draw!" This is much less of a problem than you might think. The sketches aren't for an art gallery; they're to help you work through your thinking. They only need to capture and convey your ideas. The more sketching you do, the better they will get. But ultimately, if the full extent of your abilities is stick men, just carry on drawing stick men and don't worry about it.

If the idea warrants it (and maybe even if it doesn't), don't be afraid to take your sketching into three dimensions. Mock up different designs with modelling clay or LEGO or some of the other methods we cover in this chapter. Try out different sizes and see how the changes in dimensions affect the feel or the look of the design.

Maybe even combine the approaches here with the things you learnt in Chapter 5 for prototyping the software and electronics and lash up a rough-and-ready prototype that you can try out properly. Then give it or show it to some of the people who might use the finished item to find out how they interact with it.

The key lesson is to use these techniques to experiment with different possibilities and learn which features of which designs are best. This approach allows you to synthesize the results into a coherent final design.

Consider, for example, the evolution of the design for the Good Night Lamp (which we featured in a case study in the last chapter). The original design was a more traditional lamp shape, but in a design workshop, the team batted around a range of ideas with the help of a purely functional prototype. They realised that a design echoing the shape of a house better conveyed the core concept of connecting loved ones in their homes.

The evolving design for the Good Night Lamp (from left to right): original design; functional mockup; redesign mockup; redesign functional prototypes (orange and wood/acrylic); revised size mockup; revised size functional prototype.

After the workshop, the new design was mocked up in laser-cut acrylic and plywood before functional prototypes were made in acrylic and veneered medium-density fibreboard (MDF) with a CNC milling machine.

After living with the redesign for a few weeks, they realised that the prototypes were a little bit large. More mockups followed, this time cut by hand in plywood, to try out different sizes. With the right size chosen, they milled out and assembled a new set of functional prototypes. The revised sizing has proven much better and forms the basis of the design for the first production run.

Now that we've covered some of the more general approaches to working through your design, we can dig deeper into some of the specific techniques to realise a prototype.

NONDIGITAL METHODS

We've already seen how pen and paper remain essential tools in the designer's arsenal, but they aren't the only ones to have survived the digital revolution. Many of what could be deemed more traditional craft techniques are just as valid for use when prototyping the physical form of your device.

One of the key advantages that these techniques have over the newer digital fabrication methods is their immediacy. Three-dimensional printing times are often measured in hours, and although laser cutting is much faster, performing a cut still takes minutes. And all this is without including the time taken to revise the design on the computer first.

Compare that to the speed with which you can reconfigure a model made from clay or from LEGO—and that isn't just down to the hours of practice you put in while you were growing up! Keeping the feedback loop as short as possible between having an idea and trying it out frees you up for more experimentation.

Let's look at some of the more common options here:

- **Modelling clay:** The most well-known brands are Play-Doh and Plasticine, but you can find a wealth of different versions with slightly different qualities. Some, like Play-Doh, have a tendency to dry out and crack if left exposed to the air. Plasticine doesn't suffer from this problem, but as it remains malleable, it isn't ideal for prototypes which are going to be handled. Modelling clay is best used for short-term explorations of form, rather than longer-term functional prototypes.
- **Epoxy putty:** You might have encountered this product as the brand Milliput; it is similar to modelling clay although usually available in fewer colours. It comes in two parts, one of which is a hardener. You mix equal parts together to activate the epoxy. You then mould it to the

desired shape, and in about an hour, it sets solid. If you like, you can then sand it or paint it for a better finish, so this product works well for more durable items.

- **Sugru:** Sugru is a mouldable silicone rubber. Like epoxy putty, it can be worked for only a short time before it sets (about 30 minutes, and then about a day to fully cure); but unlike epoxy, once cured, it remains flexible. It is also good at sticking to most other substances and gives a soft-touch grippy surface, which makes it a great addition to the designer's (and hacker's) toolkit.

- **Toy construction sets:** We've already mentioned the ubiquitous LEGO sets, but you might also consider Meccano (or Erector Sets in the United States) and plenty of others. If you're lucky, you already have some gathering dust in the attic or that you can borrow from your children. The other interesting feature of these sets is the availability of gears, hinges, and other pieces to let you add some movement to your model. You can purchase systems to control LEGO sets from a computer, but there's no requirement for you to use them. Many hackers combine an Arduino for sensing and control with LEGO for form and linkages, as this provides an excellent blend of flexibility and ease of construction.

- **Cardboard:** Cardboard is cheap and easy to shape with a craft knife or scissors, and available in all manner of colours and thicknesses. In its corrugated form, it provides a reasonable amount of structural integrity and works well for sketching out shapes that you'll later cut out of thin plywood or sheets of acrylic in a laser cutter (a topic we return to when we look at laser cutting later in the chapter).

- **Foamcore or foamboard:** This sheet material is made up of a layer of foam sandwiched by two sheets of card. It's readily available at art supplies shops and comes in 3mm or 5mm thicknesses in a range of sizes. Like cardboard, it is easily cut with a craft knife, although it is more rigid than corrugated cardboard. There are also specialist foamboard craft knives which allow easy 45-degree cuts for mitred edges and have two blades—spaced 3mm apart—which make it trivial to cut slots into which you can insert another sheet of foamboard to generate three-dimensional shapes. For an excellent primer in working with foamcore, see `http://www.paulos.net/teaching/2011/ BID/assignments/Foamcore_construction.pdf`.

- **Extruded polystyrene:** This product is similar to the *expanded* polystyrene that is used for packaging but is a much denser foam that is better suited to modelling purposes. It is often referred to as "blue foam", although it's the density rather than the colour which is important. Light yet durable, it can be easily worked: you can cut it with a craft knife, saw it, sand it, or, for the greatest ease in shaping it, buy a hot-wire cutter. Sheets of extruded polystyrene are much thicker than foamboard, usually between 25mm and 165mm. As a result, it is great for mocking up solid three-dimensional shapes. If you need something thicker than the sheet itself, you can easily glue a few layers together. The dust from sanding it and the fumes given off when cutting it with a hot-wire cutter aren't too nice, so make sure you wear a dust mask and keep the area ventilated when working with it.

Having reviewed the sorts of techniques which you learnt when your design education started, back in primary school, we can move on to looking at some of the newer tools. Like most aspects of modern life, computers have also swept through manufacturing, opening new possibilities in rapid prototyping. The combination of Moore's Law driving down the cost of computing and the expiration of the patents from the early developments in the 1980s has brought such technology within the reach of the hobbyist or small business.

LASER CUTTING

Although the laser cutter doesn't get the same press attention as the 3D printer, it is arguably an even more useful item to have in your workshop. Three-dimensional printers can produce more complicated parts, but the simpler design process (for many shapes, breaking it into a sequence of two-dimensional planes is easier than designing in three dimensions), greater range of materials which can be cut, and faster speed make the laser cutter a versatile piece of kit.

Laser cutters range from desktop models to industrial units which can take a full 8' by 4' sheet in one pass. Most commonly, though, they are floor-standing and about the same size as a large photocopier.

Most of the laser cutter is given over to the bed; this is a flat area that holds the material to be cut. The bed contains a two-axis mechanism with mirrors and a lens to direct the laser beam to the correct location and focus it onto the material being cut. It is similar to a flatbed plotter but one that burns things rather than drawing on them.

The computer controls the two-axis positioning mechanism and the power of the laser beam. This means that not only can the machine easily cut all manner of intricate patterns, but it can also lower the power of the laser so that it doesn't cut all the way through. At a sufficiently low power, this feature enables you to etch additional detail into the surface of the piece. You can also etch things at different power levels to achieve different depths of etching, but whilst the levels will be visibly different, it isn't precise enough to choose a set fraction of a millimetre depth.

CHOOSING A LASER CUTTER

When choosing a laser cutter, you should consider two main features:

- **The size of the bed:** This is the place where the sheet of material sits while it's being cut, so a larger bed can cut larger items. You don't need to think just about the biggest item you might create; a larger bed allows you to buy material in bigger sheets (which is more cost effective), and if you move to small-scale production, it would let you cut multiple units in one pass.
- **The power of the laser:** More powerful lasers can cut through thicker material. For example, the laser cutter at our workplace has a 40W laser, which can cut up to 10mm-thick acrylic. Moving a few models up in the same range, to one with a 60W laser, would allow us to cut 25mm-thick acrylic.

Depending on what you're trying to create, you can cut all sorts of different materials in a laser cutter. Whilst felt, leather, and other fabrics are easy to cut, for Internet of Things devices you will probably be looking at something more rigid. Card and, particularly, corrugated cardboard are good for quick tests and prototyping, but MDF, plywood, and acrylic (also commonly known by the brand name Perspex) are the most common choices.

Specialised materials are also available for specific purposes. For example, laserable rubber can be used to create ink stamps, and laminate acrylic provides a thin surface in one colour, laminated with a thicker layer in a contrasting colour so that you can etch through the thin layer for crisp, high-contrast detailing and text.

Whilst you are able to get laser cutters which can cut metal, they tend to be the more powerful and industrial units. The lower-powered models don't cut through the metal; and worse, as the shiny surface of many metals does an excellent job of reflecting the laser beam, you run a real risk of damaging the machine. The laser cutters can be used to etch metals, though, if you've carefully prepared the reflective surface beforehand with a ceramic coating compound, such as CerMark. Once coated, either from a spray-can or as tape, the laser will fuse the compound with the underlying metal to leave a permanent dark mark.

If you don't have a laser cutter of your own, there is a good chance that your local makerspace or hackspace will have one that you could use. You might even be able to obtain access to one at a local university or college. Failing that, laser-cutting bureau services somewhat like copy shops are becoming increasingly common. Architects often use these services to help them build architectural models, so that could provide a starting place for your search. If that approach proves fruitless, a number of online providers, such as Ponoko (`http://www.ponoko.com`), let you upload designs that they cut and then post back to you.

SOFTWARE

The file formats or software which you need to use to provide your design vary across machines and providers. Although some laser-cutting software will let you define an engraving pattern with a bitmap, typically you use some type of vector graphics format.

Vector formats capture the drawing as a series of lines and curves, which translate much better into instructions for moving the laser cutter than the grid-like representation of a bitmap. There's also no loss in fidelity as you resize the image. With a bitmap, as you might have seen if you've ever tried blowing up one small part of a digital photo, the details become jagged as you zoom in closely, whereas the vector format knows that it's still a single line and can redraw it with more detail.

CorelDRAW is a common choice for driving the laser cutters themselves, and you can use it to generate the designs too. Other popular options are Adobe Illustrator, as many designers already have a copy installed and are familiar with driving it, and Inkscape, largely because it's an open source alternative and therefore freely available. The *best* choice is the one you're most comfortable working with, or failing that, either the one your laser cutter uses or the one you can afford.

When creating your design, you use the stroke (or outline) of the shapes and lines rather than the filled area to define where the laser will cut and etch. The *kerf*, the width of the cut made by the laser, is about 0.2mm but isn't something you need to include in the design. A thinner stroke width is better, as it will stop the laser cutter from misinterpreting it as two cuts when you need only one.

Different types of operation—cut versus etch or even different levels of etching—can usually be included in the same design file just by marking them in different colours. Whoever is doing your cutting may have a set convention of colour scheme for different settings, so you should make sure that you follow this convention if that is the case.

HINGES AND JOINTS

Most of the mechanisms you use to construct items with the laser cutter aren't any different from those used in more general woodwork. A few lesser-known techniques, however, are either easier to achieve with the precision of the laser cutter or have found new popularity after being picked up by this new generation of makers.

Lattice (or Living) Hinges

If you're looking to introduce some curves into your design, one of these hinge patterns, reminiscent of the lattice pastry on top of a fruit pie, will do the trick. A series of closely laid-out cuts, perpendicular to the direction of the curve, allows the material to be bent after it has been cut. Varying the number of cuts and their separation affects the resulting flexibility of the hinge. Patrick Fenner has a lovely blog post (http://www. deferredprocrastination.co.uk/blog/2011/laser-cut-lattice-living-hinges/) where he digs into how the different parameters affect your results.

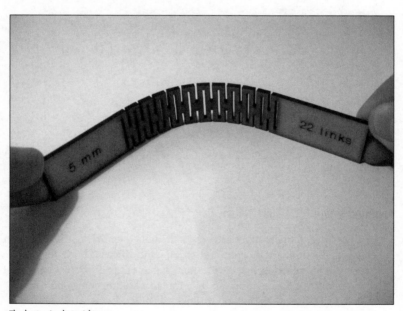

The lattice (or living) hinge.

Integrated Elastic Clips

This jointing technique is used in situations similar to a through mortise-and-tenon joint, when joining two sheets of material at 90 degrees. The tenon (tongue) is replaced with two hooks which protrude above and to the side of the mortise, thus holding the mortise sheet tight to the tenon sheet without any need for glue or additional fixings. To provide the required flexibility in the tenon to fit it through the mortise during assembly, additional, deeper cuts are made into the tenon side, as can be seen in the following image. This is another area Patrick Fenner has been exploring on his blog at `http://www.def-proc.co.uk/b/category/def-proc/laser-cut-elastic-clips/`.

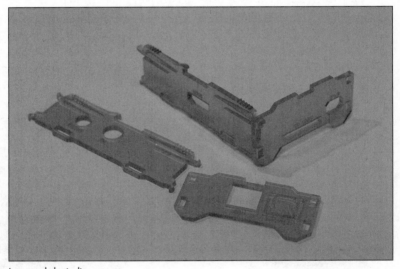

Integrated elastic clips.

Bolted Tenon (or T-Slot) Joints

An alternative to integrated elastic clips, the bolted tenon joint is a modified version of the standard mortise-and-tenon joint which adds a T- or cross-shaped slot to the tenon sheet, with the crossbar of the T or cross being just big enough to hold a nut. You can then thread a bolt through a hole in the mortise sheet, down the slot and through the nut.

Bolted tenon or T-slot joint.

Case Study: Nick O'Leary's Ambient Orb

In his spare time, IBM developer Nick O'Leary has been building a multichannel, multicoloured ambient orb to let him keep an eye on things such as his home energy usage.

The orb is controlled via the IBM-developed Message Queueing Telemetry Transport (MQTT) protocol, a way to easily connect outputs (subscribers) to data sources (publishers). Each of the three independently controllable RGB LEDs in the orb is mapped to a different subscription on the MQTT messaging system that he's using. So, for example, if he notices that one side of the orb sitting in his kitchen is glowing red, the reason could be that he's forgotten to turn off the fan heater in his office.

continued

continued

To produce something that would look nice in his home, Nick wanted a design better than a bare circuit board. For the diffuser, he repurposed one from a shop-bought lamp, but as the base needed to hold a completely different circuit board, he designed a new one himself.

He wanted the base to be built out of wood, which ruled out 3D printing and led him towards a laser-cut design with layers of birch plywood stacked on top of each other to achieve the desired height.

Because Nick didn't have immediate access to a laser cutter, his initial designs were done with corrugated cardboard cut out by hand with a craft knife. Using this technique let Nick work out how the layers needed to be laid out in order to accommodate the circuit boards, power connector, and so on, and to come up with a mechanism to bolt the base together. That means he can dismantle the base at a later date for any maintenance or future upgrades.

Ambient Orb bases.

When Nick was happy with the designs, he could get the laser cutting done elsewhere. You can see the cardboard prototype design on the right and two versions of the laser-cut plywood base. There was an additional round-trip in the design when it turned out there wasn't quite enough clearance to let the PCB fit easily, but Nick now has a lovely, professional finish to the design.

For more about the build process, including the source code and PCB design, see http://knolleary.net/orb/.

3D PRINTING

Additive manufacturing, or 3D printing as it's often called, is fast becoming one of the most popular forms in rapid prototyping—largely down to the ever-increasing number of personal 3D printers, available at ever-falling costs. Now a number of desktop models, available for less than £500, produce decent quality results.

The term *additive manufacturing* is used because all the various processes which can be used to produce the output start with nothing and *add* material to build up the resulting model. This is in contrast to *subtractive manufacturing* techniques such as laser cutting and CNC milling, where you start with more material and cut away the parts you don't need.

Various processes are used for building up the physical model, which affect what materials that printer can use, among other things. However, all of them take a three-dimensional computer model as the input. The software slices the computer model into many layers, each a fraction of a millimetre thick, and the physical version is built up layer by layer.

One of the great draws of 3D printing is how it can produce items which wouldn't be possible with traditional techniques. For example, because you can print interlocking rings without any joins, you are able to use the metal 3D printers to print entire sheets of chain-mail which come out of the printer already connected together. If only the medieval knights had had access to a metal laser-sintering machine, their armour would have been much easier to produce.

Another common trick with 3D printing is to print pieces which include moving parts: it is possible to print all the parts at the same time and print them ready-assembled. This effect is achieved with the use of what is called "support material". In some processes, such as the powder-based methods, this is a side effect of the printing technique; while the print is in progress, the raw powder takes up the space for what will become the air-gap. Afterwards, you can simply shake or blow the loose powder out of your solid print. Other processes, such as the extruded plastic techniques, require you to print a second material, which takes the supporting role. When the print is finished, this support material is either broken off or washed away. (The support material is specifically chosen to dissolve in water or another solution which doesn't affect the main printing material.)

TYPES OF 3D PRINTING

Lots of innovation is still happening in the world of additive manufacturing, but the following are some of the more common methods of 3D printing in use today:

- **Fused filament fabrication (FFF):** Also known as fused deposition modeling (FDM), this is the type of 3D printer you're most likely to see at a maker event. The RepRap and MakerBot designs both use this technique, as does the Stratasys at the industrial level. It works by extruding a fine filament of material (usually plastic) from a heated nozzle. The nozzle can be moved horizontally and vertically by the controlling computer, as can the flow of filament through the nozzle. The resulting models are quite robust, as they're made from standard plastic. However, the surface can have a visible ridging from the thickness of the filament.

- **Laser sintering:** This process is sometimes called selective laser sintering (SLS), electron beam melting (EBM), or direct metal laser sintering (DMLS). It is used in more industrial machines but can print any material which comes in powdered form and which can be melted by a laser. It provides a finer finish than FDM, but the models are just as robust, and they're even stronger when the printing medium is metal. This technique is used to print aluminium or titanium, although it can just as easily print nylon. MakieLab (discussed in Chapter 9, "Business Models") uses laser-sintered nylon to 3D print the physical versions of its dolls.

- **Powder bed:** Like laser sintering, the powder-bed printers start with a raw material in a powder form, but rather than fusing it together with a laser, the binder is more like a glue which is dispensed by a print head similar to one in an inkjet printer. The Z Corp. machines use this technique and use a print medium similar in texture to plaster. After the printing process, the models are quite brittle and so need post-processing where they are sprayed with a hardening solution. The great advantage of these printers is that when the binder is being applied, it can be mixed with some pigment; therefore, full-colour prints in different colours can be produced in one pass.

- **Laminated object manufacturing (LOM):** This is another method which can produce full-colour prints. LOM uses traditional paper printing as part of the process. Because it builds up the model by laminating many individual sheets of paper together, it can print whatever colours are required onto each layer before cutting them to shape and gluing them into place. The Mcor IRIS is an example of this sort of printer.

- **Stereolithography and digital light processing:** Stereolithography is possibly the oldest 3D printing technique and has a lot in common with digital light processing, which is enjoying a huge surge in popularity and experimentation at the time of this writing. Both approaches build their models from a vat of liquid polymer resin which is cured by exposure to ultraviolet light. Stereolithography uses a UV laser to trace the pattern for each layer, whereas digital light processing uses a DLP projector to cure an entire layer at a time. Whilst these approaches are limited to printing with resin, the resultant models are produced to a fine resolution. The combination of this with the relatively low cost of DLP projectors makes this a fertile area for development of more affordable high-resolution printers.

Deciding which 3D printer to use is likely to be governed mostly by what kind of machine you have ready access to. The industrial-level machines cost tens of thousands of pounds, so most of us don't have the luxury of buying one of them. If you do have that sort of budget, we're jealous; enjoy your shopping!

For the rest of us, a few options are available. If you live near to a fab lab or TechShop, they usually have a 3D printer that you are able to use. Similarly, local universities often have such facilities in their engineering or product design departments and might grant you access.

You may also find a local bureau service which will print your designs for you; these services are becoming increasingly common. Recently, Staples announced a service to deliver 3D prints for collection in its stores in the Netherlands.

The Staples announcement is just another, albeit well-known, entrant into the 3D-printing-by-post market. Shapeways (`http://www.shapeways.com/`), i.materialise (`http://i.materialise.com/`), and Ponoko (`https://www.ponoko.com/`) have all been offering similar services for a while now. You upload your design online, choose how you want it printed, and a few days later receive it in the post. Many of these services even facilitate your selling your designs, with them handling the fulfillment for you.

If you don't need the specialist materials or high resolution of the high-end machines, there's a good chance that your local hackspace or makerspace will have one of the lower-cost desktop machines; the pricing of these machines is such that buying one of your own is also an option. In fact, for most prototyping work, one can argue that the greater access and lower cost of materials in that approach far outweigh the disadvantages.

The following image shows some example prints from a few of the more common desktop machines, alongside one from a high-end Z Corp printer for comparison.

Some sample 3D prints: (l– r) MakerBot Replicator; Z Corp.; Ultimaker; RepRap Prusa Mendel.

A huge choice of desktop machines is available these days, thanks mostly to the RepRap project. This initiative was started by Adrian Bowyer back in 2004 with the aim of building a self-*rep*licating *rap*id prototyping machine. Whilst they haven't worked out how to get it to print motors and the like yet, it can print half its own parts. The remaining half are designed to be readily available from a hardware store or online.

The RepRap designs are fully open source, which means that users are free to make their own machines and modify the design to make it better or customise it to suit their particular needs. As a result, there has been a steady evolution in RepRap models—improving the quality of prints and ease of use and lowering the cost of the machines.

This project has also spawned a number of semi-related printers, which share some of the RepRap DNA but have abandoned the self-replicating goal to prioritise other qualities such as robustness or ease of assembly. The best known of these are the MakerBot and Ultimaker machines, which use a laser-cut plywood frame—or in the case of the latest MakerBot models, CNCed steel.

SOFTWARE

In much the same way as for laser cutting, no definitive software package is recommended for use when generating your 3D designs. If you are already familiar with one 3D design program, see whether it can export files in the correct format for the machine you'll use to print. If you are using a printing service, it will advise on which program it prefers you to use or what formats it accepts. Or failing that, choose one to suit your budget and that you find easiest to get to grips with.

Working out how to design items in three dimensions through a two-dimensional display isn't trivial, so it's more important than usual to work through the tutorials for the software you choose. This gives you the best grounding to manipulating objects, ensuring that the components which make up your design line up correctly to minimize the risk of artefacts in the finished print.

Tinkercad (`http://tinkercad.com`) and Autodesk's 123D Design Online (`http://www.123dapp.com/design`) are two options which just run in your web browser. So they let you start designing without having to install any additional software.

Autodesk also has a range of 123D apps available to download and install. You can find a desktop version of 123D Design and also of 123D Catch, a clever application which takes an array of photos of an object and automatically converts them into a 3D model. This inferred 3D model may then need subsequent refinement—for example, with 123D Design.

SolidWorks (`http://www.solidworks.com`) and Rhino (`http://www.rhino3d.com`) are the industry-standard commercial offerings, and SketchUp (`http://www.sketchup.com`), which was owned by Google for a while but in 2012 was sold to Trimble, is popular with hobbyists.

In the open source camp, the main contenders are OpenSCAD (`http://www.openscad.org`) , which has a rather unorthodox scripting workflow, and FreeCAD (`http://free-cad.sourceforge.net`). You also can use Blender (`http://www.blender.org`), but it has a steep learning curve and is better suited to 3D animation than computer-aided design.

When you have your design ready, you need a further piece of software to convert it into a set of instructions which will be fed to the printer. This is usually known as the *slicing algorithm* because its most important function is to carve the model into a series of layers and work out how to instruct the printer to build up each layer. In most cases the particular slicing software that you use is governed by the specific printer which is building your model, but with the open source designs such as RepRap, you might have a couple of options.

Skeinforge was the first slicing software used by the open source printers, but it has been largely overtaken by the newer and more user-friendly Slic3r. Both will let you tweak all manner of parameters to fine-tune your 3D prints, specifying options like the temperature to which the plastic should be heated, how densely to fill the solid objects, the speed at which the extruder head should move, etc.

Getting those settings right (or right enough) can be daunting for the beginner. With its configuration wizard, Slic3r does a much better job of guiding you through to a usable starting point. Running through some calibration tests will let you tailor the settings to your particular printer and the specific plastic that you're printing.

It can feel like a bit of a chore to be printing out 20mm cubes when you're itching to set it going with your great design, but taking some time to set things up when the issues are more easily spotted and remedied will pay back in better quality and more successful prints.

CNC MILLING

Computer Numerically Controlled (CNC) milling is similar to 3D printing but is a *subtractive* manufacturing process rather than *additive*. The CNC part just means that a computer controls the movement of the milling head, much like it does the extruder in an FDM 3D printer. However, rather than building up the desired model layer by layer from nothing, it starts with a block of material larger than the finished piece and cuts away the parts which aren't needed—much like a sculptor chips away at a block of stone to reveal the statue, except that milling uses a rotating cutting bit (similar to an electric drill) rather than a chisel.

Because cutting away material is easier, CNC mills can work with a much greater range of materials than 3D printers can. You still need an industrial-scale machine to work with hardened steel, but wax, wood, plastic, aluminium, and even mild steel can be readily milled with even desktop mills.

CNC mills can also be used for more specialised (but useful when prototyping electronic devices) tasks, such as creating custom printed circuit boards. Rather than sending away for your PCB design to be fabricated or etching it with acid, you can convert it into a form which your CNC mill can rout out; that is, the CNC mills away lines from the metal surface on the board, leaving the conductive paths. An advantage of milling over etching the board is that you can have the mill drill any holes for components or mounting at the same time, saving you from having to do it manually afterwards with your drill press.

A wide range of CNC mills is available, depending on the features you need and your budget.

Sizes range from small mills which will fit onto your desktop through to much larger machines with a bed size measured in metres. There are even CNC mills which fill an entire hangar, but they tend to be bespoke constructions for a very specific task, such as creating moulds for wind turbine blades.

Bigger is not always better, though; the challenges of accurately moving the carriage around increase with their size, so smaller mills are usually able to machine to higher tolerances. That said, the difference in resolution is only from high to extremely high. CNC mills can often achieve resolutions of the order of 0.001mm, which is a couple of orders of magnitude better than the current generation of low-end 3D printers.

Beyond size and accuracy, the other main attribute that varies among CNC mills is the number of axes of movement they have:

- **2.5 axis:** Whilst this type has three axes of movement—X, Y, and Z—it can move only any two at one time.

- **3 axis:** Like the 2.5-axis machine, this machine has a bed which can move in the X and Y axes, and a milling head that can move in the Z. However, it can move all three at the same time (if the machining instructions call for it).

- **4 axis:** This machine adds a rotary axis to the 3-axis mill to allow the piece being milled to be rotated around an extra axis, usually the X (this is known as the *A axis*). An indexed axis just allows the piece to be rotated to set points to allow a further milling pass to then be made, for example, to flip it over to mill the underside; and a fully controllable rotating axis allows the rotation to happen as part of the cutting instructions.

- **5 axis:** This machine adds a second rotary axis—normally around the Y—which is known as the *B axis.*

- **6 axis:** A third rotary axis—known as the *C axis* if it rotates around Z—completes the range of movement in this machine.

For prototyping work, you're unlikely to need anything beyond a 3-axis mill, although a fourth axis would give you some extra flexibility. The 5- and 6-axis machines tend to be the larger, more industrial units.

As with 3D printing, the software you use for CNC milling is split into two types:

- **CAD** (Computer-Aided Design) software lets you design the model.

- **CAM** (Computer-Aided Manufacture) software turns that into a suitable toolpath—a list of co-ordinates for the CNC machine to follow which will result in the model being revealed from the block of material.

The toolpaths are usually expressed in a quasi-standard called *G-code.* Whilst most of the movement instructions are common across machines, a wide variety exists in the codes for things such as initialising the machine. That said, a number of third-party CAM packages are available, so with luck you will have a choice of which to use. For a rundown of the possibilities, along with *lots* more information about getting started with CNC milling, see http://lcamtuf.coredump.cx/gcnc/.

REPURPOSING/RECYCLING

So far we've talked just about how you would go about creating a new object completely from scratch. Owning the designs of and knowing how to create all of the components of your device put you in a great position, but they aren't necessarily the overriding concerns in all prototyping scenarios.

As with the other elements of building your connected device, a complete continuum exists from buying-in the item or design through to doing-it-yourself. So, just as you wouldn't think about making your own nuts and bolts from some iron ore, sometimes you should consider reusing more complex mechanisms or components.

One reason to reuse mechanisms or components would be to piggyback onto someone else's economies of scale. If sections or entire subassemblies that you need are available in an existing product, buying those items can often be cheaper than making them in-house. That's definitely the case for your prototypes but may extend to production runs, too, depending on the volumes you'll be manufacturing. For example, the bubble machine used in Bubblino is an off-the-shelf unit from a children's game. In the batch production volumes that Bubblino is currently being built, it's cheaper to buy them, even at retail price, than it would be to manufacture the assorted gears, fans, bubble ring, and casing in-house.

Or perhaps you're making just a couple of units or maybe only one. In that scenario the labour involved in working out how to integrate the electronics, graft in newly fabricated parts, or work out how to disassemble the reused item for the bits you need might not matter, as you aren't going to be repeating it many, many times.

That's often the case with one-off items, when they are deliberately incorporated into existing, mass-produced products. When Russell Davies commissioned Adrian to build him a few minimal-interface WiFi sound boxes (http://russelldavies.typepad.com/planning/2011/07/secondary-attention-and-the-background-noise.html), he asked for two separate devices. One was made from scratch with all-new electronics and a laser-cut case, whereas the other was a reworked 1974 transistor radio. The radio circuits were removed to make space for a small ARM Linux board, but the original amplifier was retained and the wave band selector switches were reconfigured to act as the interface to the program. When everything was boxed up, it became a very familiar object but with very new capabilities.

We've drifted away from the idea of prototyping as a way to explore and develop your idea, but that is probably the most common case where reuse and repurposing of existing items are useful.

Given that the prototyping phase is all about rapid iteration through ideas, anything that helps speed up the construction period and gets you to where you can test your theories is useful. When you are thinking through the user interaction of a connected bedside table, for instance, gaffer taping an Arduino to your alarm clock would provide a good-enough approximation to let you try out different scenarios.

If the final design requires processes with massive up-front costs (such as tooling up for injection moulding the plastics) or the skills of a designer that you don't have the funds to hire right now, maybe a product already exists that is near enough to work as a proxy. That lets you get on with taking the project forwards, ending up at a point, one hopes, where making the bigger investment makes sense.

And, of course, it doesn't have to be a finished item that you reuse. The website Thingiverse (http://www.thingiverse.com) is a repository of all manner of designs, most of which are targeted at 3D printing or laser cutting, and all available under creative commons licenses which allow you to use the design as is or often allow you to amend or extend it to better suit your own needs.

Case Study: The Ackers Bell

It might be useful to look at a project that Adrian's company, MCQN Ltd., recently completed, especially as it pulls together a number of the themes we've explored in this chapter.

The Ackers Bell is an Internet-connected bell, which was commissioned by the big-data startup ScraperWiki (http://scraperwiki.com). It is connected to the company's online billing system and rings the bell whenever a new payment hits its bank account, giving the sales team further incentive to make more sales and everyone else a chance to celebrate every success.

That pretty much covers the project brief—now onto the design and implementation! Casting a bell from scratch was always going to be a stretch, so the first step was to investigate what bells could be sourced elsewhere and reused.

continued

continued

An initial discussion with a campanologist friend quickly found some very nice tuned bells, but sadly they were outside the available budget. After that, they looked at boxing-ring-style bells and at giving a new life to some vintage telephone bells. Both of these types appealed as they'd include both mechanical and electrical striking mechanisms. However, liaising with the customer on the choice led to their settling on a traditional brass ship's bell, which resonated more with ScraperWiki, due to its, and Adrian's, location in the port city of Liverpool.

With the bell procured, the next step was to work out how to mount it. The electronics were relatively easy to develop, given MCQN Ltd.'s experience, and an Arduino Ethernet board married to a solenoid was soon firing when triggered by events online. They just needed to devise a way to assemble the two parts: electronics and bell.

The following photo shows some of the initial sketches made in Adrian's Moleskine notebook, exploring possible ways to construct the housing and some detail of a possible joint design.

Early design ideas for the Ackers Bell.

They thought wood made the best choice of material to complement the brass of the bell but also wanted a darker wood than the stock birch ply we normally use in the laser cutter. In addition, the potential joint design would require wood a fair bit thicker than the 3mm ply, so they finally chose an 8mm thick oak from the range of hardwoods at the local timber merchant.

Unfortunately, some test cuts—or more accurately, test burns—showed that the oak was too hard for either of the readily available laser cutters to manage. Further experimentation was required.

For the choice of wood, they tried a variety of different veneers and also some stains and waxes on the birch ply. In the end, a dark beeswax on the birch ply gave a good colour with the added benefit of some protection and treatment for the wood.

As to how the wood would be used, that issue was solved by Ian Scott, a product design student from Liverpool University who was spending some time at the company on an internship. He came up with the idea of housing the bell inside a lattice framework of stock 3mm ply, shaped to echo the lines of the bell itself. That design meant that although the final form was a fairly complex three-dimensional design, it could be constructed from flat sheets of wood cut on the laser cutter.

In addition to providing a support to hang the bell, the laser-cut design included a platform to hold the Arduino board and a mounting point for the solenoid— cleverly hidden inside the bell to keep the external profile clean. However, the particular solenoid Adrian had chosen didn't have anything to arrest the travel of the striking pin when it is deactivated, so after the first firing, the return spring would cause it to fall out.

While they could no doubt have laser cut some sort of baffle, they decided that the 3D printer allowed them to fabricate a neater solution. Ian designed a relatively simple, L-shaped part which used the same mounting holes as the solenoid itself and provided a wall of black ABS plastic to keep the striking pin in check.

The final stage in the design work was positioning the solenoid so that it gave a clear and consistent chime from the bell. A bell which looks great but sounds awful is no use at all.

They had tested it earlier and included some room for adjustments in the mounting point, but when everything was assembled properly, it was apparent that they hadn't tested it well enough. Sometimes they'd get a crisp, resonating tone, but frequently the striker would either hardly strike the bell at all, or it would strike the bell with such force that the bell would swing back into the solenoid after firing and damp the sound.

This situation would have been much easier to remedy had they iterated through more options for mounting the solenoid when first designing the frame. Solving the problem this late in the build, when the scope for changes was smaller, meant lots of time was wasted trying things such as increasing the power supplied to the solenoid or working out how to alter the mounting point while keeping the existing one in place.

continued

continued

Eventually, they fashioned a shim which adjusted the angle at which the solenoid struck the bell, to make it perpendicular to the bell's surface at the point of impact. You'll have to take our word for it that it now sounds great, but at least we can show you how good it looks.

The Ackers Bell, ready for delivery to the customer.

SUMMARY

This chapter (and the previous one) provided you with a good grounding in building your Internet of Things device.

Some design iteration and exploration will have given you a better understanding of how the form and size of the design affect how it fits in with its use in people's lives, and that learning might well be evidenced in a succession of prototypes cluttering up your workshop.

In addition to showing the progression of the thinking behind the design, the prototypes will show a progression of refinement as you move from the foamcore or cardboard mockups through to sturdier and more polished versions created using some of the rapid prototyping tools like the laser cutter or 3D printer.

With the device side of your prototype covered, all that remains to complete your Internet of Things product is some online service for it to communicate with. The next chapter will take you through that, looking at how you can talk to existing online services or develop something completely new.

7

PROTOTYPING ONLINE COMPONENTS

YOU SAW IN Chapter 2, "Design Principles for Connected Devices", how Internet of Things devices are "magical" objects: a physical thing with an embedded controller and sensors that allow it to do clever things that a merely solid or mechanical object couldn't. Even with just these two components, you can already see some magical objects, such as air fresheners that pump fragrance into the room only when they sense that someone has walked past. But the phrase "Internet of Things" does suggest that the Internet is also part of the equation.

You can easily see that each component has a critical part to play. The physical, designed object ties into the design principles (as you saw in Chapter 2) of context, glanceability, and so on. The controller and associated electronics allow it to sense and act on the real world. The Internet adds a dimension of communication. The network allows the device to inform you or others about events or to gather data and let you act on it in real time. It lets you aggregate information from disparate locations and types of sensors. Similarly, it extends your reach, so you can control or activate things from afar, and it allows the online world to bleed out into the physical realm in new and interesting ways.

```
Physical Object
+
Controller, Sensor, and Actuators
+
Internet
=
Internet of Things
```

The key components of the Internet of Things.

So, sensor devices which record temperature might write that data to Xively. Notification devices like Bubblino blow bubbles in response to tweets on Twitter. In fact, although you have seen in Chapter 2 that one design principle is that Things should be "first class citizens" of the Internet, they do seem to be currently tied to particular websites or services. There is a good reason for this: unlike a general-purpose device, such as a computer, tablet, or phone, the physical object is designed for a purpose and doesn't necessarily have a keyboard and screen to let it easily change its configuration.

In the near future, devices will most likely use standardized protocols to speak to each other and to other apps and computers on your local or personal network. For now, though, in most of the examples we look at, each device is tied to a single web service. Although you've looked at existing services (Xively, Twitter), you might benefit from creating your own. For a personal project, creating such a service may not be important, but if you're developing a product to sell, you will want to be in control of the service—otherwise, you may have to recall every device to reprogram any time it is discontinued, changes terms and conditions, making your use of it abusive, or changes its API, making your code stop working. In fact, even Bubblino runs via a service at `http://bubblino.com` which allows users to customise their Bubblino to search for particular words and gives Adrian the flexibility to route all the Bubblini to a different service or API if anything changes.

GETTING STARTED WITH AN API

The most important part of a web service, with regards to an Internet of Things device, is the Application Programming Interface, or API. An API is a way of accessing a service that is targeted at machines rather than people. If you think about your experience of accessing an Internet service, you might follow a number of steps. For example, to look at a friend's photo on Flickr, you might do the following:

1. Launch Chrome, Safari, or Internet Explorer.
2. Search for the Flickr website in Google and click on the link.
3. Type in your username and password and click "Login".
4. Look at the page and click on the "Contacts" link.
5. Click on a few more links to page through the list of contacts till you see the one you want.
6. Scroll down the page, looking for the photo you want, and then click on it.

Although these actions are simple for a human, they involve a lot of looking, thinking, typing, and clicking. A computer can't look and think in the same way. The tricky and lengthy process of following a sequence of actions and responding to each page is likely to fail the moment that Flickr slightly changes its user interface. For example, if Flickr rewords "Login" to "Sign in", or "Contacts" to "Friends", a human being would very likely not even notice, but a typical computer program would completely fail. Instead, a computer can very happily call defined commands such as `login` or `get picture #142857`.

MASHING UP APIS

Perhaps the data you want is already available on the Internet but in a form that doesn't work for you? The idea of "mashing up" multiple APIs to get a result has taken off and can be used to powerful effect. For example:

- Using a mapping API to plot properties to rent or buy—for example, Google Maps to visualise properties to rent via Craigslist, or Foxtons in London showing its properties using Mapumental.
- Showing Twitter trends on a global map or in a timeline or a charting API.
- Fetching Flickr images that are related to the top headlines retrieved from *The Guardian* newspaper's API.

Do You Need a Full API?

For a personal project, you may be best off starting by targeting an existing service, such as Twitter or Xively, as mentioned already, or Transport for London's Rental Bike availability API, or mapme.at.

Perhaps, as with Bubblino, you will expand that service later to a simple configuration and wrapping API. But if the data you want to interact with doesn't yet exist, this may represent an opportunity to create a new service that could be generally useful.

Some of the more visible and easy-to-use APIs want to embed your data within them—for example, the Google Maps API. This means that they are ideal to use within a web browser, but you aren't in control of the final product, and there might be limited scope for accessing them from a microcontroller.

SCRAPING

In many cases, companies or institutions have access to fantastic data but don't want to or don't have the resources or knowledge to make them available as an API. While you saw in the Flickr example above that getting a computer to pretend to be a browser and navigate it by looking for UI elements was fragile, that doesn't mean that doing so is impossible. In general, we refer to this, perhaps a little pejoratively, as "screen-scraping". Here are a few examples:

- Adrian has scraped the Ship AIS system (www.shipais.com/, whose data is semi-manually plotted by shipping enthusiasts) to get data about ships on the river Mersey, and this information is then tweeted by the @merseyshipping account (www.mcqn.com/weblog/connecting_river_mersey_twitter). He says of the project that it is a way to "connect the river to the Internet", so although this doesn't have an Internet-connected "thing" as such, it arguably enters into the realm of the Internet of Things.

- The Public Whip website (www.publicwhip.org.uk/) is made possible by using a scraper to read the Hansard transcripts of UK government sessions (released as Word documents). With the resultant data, it can produce both human- and machine-readable feeds of how our elected representatives vote.

- As well as other tools for working with data online, the ScraperWiki site (https://scraperwiki.com) has an excellent platform for writing scrapers, in a number of dynamic programming languages, which collate data into database tables. Effectively, it provides infrastructure for "Mechanize" scripts that you could run on your own computer or server but allows you to outsource the boring, repetitive parts to ScraperWiki. Their CEO, Francis Irving, used this for an Internet of Things project of his own. He scrapes the Liverpool council website page to find out when his recycling bin is due to be collected. His Binduino device (https://github.com/frabcus/binduino), an Arduino plus custom electronics, checks the result regularly and illuminates some electroluminescent wire to make his recycling bin glow when he needs to take it out.

LEGALITIES

Screen-scraping may break the terms and conditions of a website. For example, Google doesn't allow you to screen-scrape its search pages but does provide an API. Even if you don't think about legal sanctions, breaking the terms and conditions for a company like Google might lead to its denying you its other services, which would be at the very least inconvenient.

Other data is protected by copyright or, for example, database rights. One project we discussed for the book would be a scraper that read football fixtures and moved a "compass" to point to the relative direction that your team was playing in. However, certainly in the UK, fixtures lists are copyrighted, and the English and Scottish football leagues have sued various operators for not paying them a licensing fee for that data (`http://www.out-law.com/page-10985`). For a personal pet project, creating such a scraper shouldn't be a huge issue but might reduce the viability of a commercial product (depending on whether the licensing costs are sensible business costs or prohibitive).

Alternative sources of information often are available. For example, you could use OpenStreetMap instead of Google Maps. The UK postcode database is under Crown Copyright, but there are other, perhaps partial, crowdsourced versions.

> *For additional discussions about the legal aspects of data, among other things, see Chapter 9, "Business Models".*

WRITING A NEW API

Assuming the data you want to play with isn't available or can't be easily mashed up or scraped using other existing tools and sources, perhaps you want to create an entirely new source of information or services. Perhaps you plan to assemble the data from free or licensed material you have and process it. Or perhaps your Internet-connected device can populate this data!

To take you through the process of building your own API, we use an example project, Clockodillo. This is an Internet of Things device that Hakim built to help him use the Pomodoro time management technique (`www.pomodorotechnique.com/`).

With the Pomodoro system you split your tasks into 25-minute chunks and use a kitchen-timer to help track how long the task takes you, and to encourage you to block out distractions during each 25-minute block.

Clockodillo explores how the Internet of Things might help with that: connecting the kitchen-timer to the Internet to make the tracking easier while keeping the simplicity of the physical twist-to-set timer for starting the clock and showing progress as it ticks down.

By the end of the chapter, you end up with the skeleton of an actual API that the timer device connects to.

Although the process of designing a web application to be used on a browser can mix up the actions that users will accomplish with the flows they will take to navigate through the application, writing the back-end API makes you think much more in terms of the data that you want to process.

As the legendary software engineer Frederick P. Brooks, Jr. wrote:

> *Show me your flowchart and conceal your tables, and I shall continue to be mystified. Show me your tables, and I won't usually need your flowchart; it'll be obvious.*
> —The Mythical Man-Month: Essays on Software Engineering
> *(Addison-Wesley, 1975)*

When you know what data you have, what actions can be taken on it, and what data will be returned, the flows of your application become simple. This is a great opportunity to think about programming without worrying (at first) about the user interface or interactions. Although this might sound very different from writing a web application, it is actually an ideal way to start: by separating the business problem from the front end, you decouple the model (core data structure) from the view (HTML/JavaScript) and controller (widgets, form interaction, and so on). If you've programmed in one of the popular MVC frameworks (Ruby on Rails, Django, Catalyst, and so on), you already know the advantage of this approach.

The best news is, if you start designing an API in this way, you can easily add a website afterwards, as you will see in the upcoming "Going Further" section.

CLOCKODILLO

As we saw earlier, Clockodillo is an Internet-connected task timer. The user can set a dial to a number of minutes, and the timer ticks down until completed. It also sends messages to an API server to let it know that a task has been started, completed, or cancelled.

A number of API interactions deal precisely with those features of the physical device:

- Start a new timer
- Change the duration of an existing timer
- Mark a timer completed
- Cancel a timer

Some interactions with a timer data structure are too complicated to be displayed on a device consisting mostly of a dial—for example, anything that might require a display or a keyboard! Those could be done through an app on your computer or phone instead.

- View and edit the timer's name/description

And, naturally, the user may want to be able to see historical data:

- Previous timers, in a list
  - Their name/description
  - Their total time and whether they were cancelled

Assuming you plan to build more than just one device, you need to have some form of identifying the device. We come back to this interesting topic when we look at scaling up to production in Chapter 10. For now, assume that each device will send some identifying token, such as a MAC address. (As you saw in Chapter 3, this is a unique code that every networked chip has.)

So the user will somehow identify himself with the server, after which all the preceding actions will relate just to a given user ID.

SECURITY

Does it look as though we're missing something? If you're jumping up and down shouting "What about security?" give yourself a pat on the back. How important security is depends a lot on how sensitive the information being passed is and whether it's in anyone's interest to compromise it. For Clocko-dillo, perhaps a boss might want to double-check that employees are using the timer. Or a competitor might want to check the descriptions of tasks to spy what your company is working on. Or a (more disreputable) competitor might want to disrupt and discredit the service by entering fake data.

If the service deals with health or financial information, it may be an even more attractive target. Location information is also sensitive; burglars might find it convenient to know when you are out of the house.

Security is a really important concern, so you need to bear it in mind while designing the API! But let's start off with an idea of what you want to do with it.

Task	Inputs	Outputs
1. Create a new timed task	User, Timer duration	Timer ID
2. Change duration of timed task	User, Timer ID, New duration	OK
3. Mark timer complete	User, Timer ID	OK
4. Cancel timer	User, Timer ID	OK
5. Describe the timed task	User, Timer ID, Description	OK
6. Get list of timers	User	List of Timer IDs
7. Get information about a timer	User, Timer ID	Description, Create time, Status

Obviously, the request has to pass details to identify the user, which is the problem of identity; that is, the application needs to know for which user to create the timer so that the user can retrieve information about it later.

But the application should also authenticate that request. A password is "good enough" authentication for something that isn't hypersensitive.

So, looking at the preceding list, you can see that tasks 1–4 could be requested by the physical timer device. To pass a description, display details about a list of timers, or get information about them would require more input and output capability than the timer will have!

But for tasks 1–4, how will the timer pass on the username and password? The user could configure them with a computer, via USB. But doing so is potentially complex and means that the device will need some persistent storage; this suggests more work, a more powerful microcontroller, and possibly an extra SD card storage reader for a lower-end controller.

One technique that is commonly used for microcontrollers is that they can send a physical ID, commonly their MAC address (this is a unique ID assigned to every networked device or rather to their network interface). As this is unique, it can be tied to a user.

Also, you have to consider the risks in sending the identification or authentication data over the Internet—whether that's a MAC address or username and password. If you think back to the description of Internet routing in Chapter 3, you know that the package with the request can be sent by all kinds of routes. If the username and password are in "clear text", they can be read by anyone who is packet sniffing. The two main cases here are as follows:

- **Someone who is targeting a specific user and has access to that person's wired or (unencrypted) wireless network.** This attacker could read the details and use them (to create fake timers or get information about the user).
- **Someone who has access to one of the intermediate nodes.** This person won't be targeting a specific device but may be looking to see what unencrypted data passes by, to see what will be a tempting target.

Of course, your Internet of Things device may not be a tempting target. We hope, though, that the word to add to the preceding sentence is "yet!" If your device becomes popular, it may have competitors who would be delighted to expose a security flaw. Although a software product can easily be updated to handle this situation, the logistics with upgrading a hardware project are much more complicated!

Even worse, if a software password is compromised, a website can easily provide a way of changing that password. But while a computer has a monitor and keyboard to make that task easy, an Internet-connected device may not. So you would need a way to configure the device to change its password—for example, a web control panel hosted on the server or on the device itself. This solution is trickier (and does require the machine to have local storage to write the new password to).

One obvious solution to the problem of sending cleartext passwords would be to encrypt the whole request, including the authentication details. For a web API, you can simply do this by targeting `https://` instead of `http://`. It doesn't require any further changes to your application code. It is easy to set up most web servers to serve HTTPS, and we do this in the sample code for this chapter.

Resolving this problem may be harder for the device. Encryption requires solving very large equations and takes CPU and memory. The current Arduino platform doesn't have an HTTPS library, for example. While more powerful microcontrollers, and no doubt future versions of Arduino will, you can easily imagine even smaller controllers in the future that have similar limitations.

If there is any chance that your connected device could be used maliciously by an attacker, then the ability to secure the communications should be a key factor in deciding on the platform to use. It is unlikely that an attacker could glean anything from the data being gathered by an air quality monitor, for example, but if the data is a reasonable proxy for occupancy of your house or if it can control items and so on, then you need to ensure that it is secure.

If you are defining your own API, there are cryptography libraries for Arduino, so there's scope for using them for a custom form of secure communications. You need to do so carefully and with the help of a security expert, if you take this approach.

The OAuth 1.0 protocol—used by services such as Twitter to allow third-party applications to access your account without requiring your password—is a good example of providing strong authentication without using HTTPS. The content of the API call is still sent in the clear, so an attacker sniffing the network traffic would still be able to see what was happening, but he wouldn't be able to modify or replay the requests. To add encryption—preventing people from watching what is going on—with OAuth 1.0, you would still have to run it over HTTPS. The OAuth 1.0 guide has a useful discussion of the issues it addresses, at `http://hueniverse.com/oauth/guide/security/`.

As a compromise, to save complicating discussion of the API, for this example we suggest insisting on username/password over HTTPS for any requests done over the web but allowing a MAC address over HTTP for requests 1-4 that will be sent by the timer.

Here's a revised table; we also added some requests to add and check the MAC address for a user and categorised the previous requests by the type of resource they affect.

Task	Auth	Inputs	Outputs
1. Create a new timed task	MAC or User/Pass	Timer duration	Timer ID
2. Change duration of timed task	MAC or User/Pass	Timer ID, New timer duration	OK
3. Mark timer complete	MAC or User/Pass	Timer ID	OK
4. Cancel timer	MAC or User/Pass	Timer ID	OK

Task	Auth	Inputs	Outputs
5. Describe the timed task	User/Pass	Timer ID, Description	OK
6. Get list of timers	User/Pass		List of Timer IDs
7. Get information about a timer	User/Pass	Timer ID	Info about Timer
8. Register a device to a user	User/Pass	MAC address	OK
9. Get details of the user's device	User/Pass		MAC address

As you can see, the first four options can be set by the device, but more methods relate to the clients (website or native) than the device itself. This is often the case: the device provides a number of functions that its inputs and outputs are particularly well suited for, but a whole host of other functions to support the data, control authentication, and present and edit it may require a richer input device (perhaps another Thing or a general-purpose device such as a computer or phone).

IMPLEMENTING THE API

An API defines the messages that are sent from client to server and from server to client. Ultimately, you can send data in whatever format you want, but it is almost always better to use an existing standard because convenient libraries will exist for both client and server to produce and understand the required messages.

Here are a few of the most common standards that you should consider:

- **Representational State Transfer (REST):** Access a set of web URLs like `http://timer.roomofthings.com/timers/` or `http::://timer.roomofthings.com/timers/1234` using HTTP methods such as `GET` and `POST`, but also `PUT` and `DELETE`. The result is often XML or JSON but can often depend on the HTTP content-type negotiation mechanisms.
- **JSON-RPC:** Access a single web URL like `http://timer.roomofthings.com/api/`, passing a JSON string such as `{'method':'update', 'params': [{'timer-id':1234, 'description':'Writing API chapter for book'}], 'id':12}`. The return value would also be in JSON, like `{'result':'OK', 'error':null, 'id':12}`.

- **XML-RPC:** This standard is just like JSON-RPC but uses XML instead of JSON.

- **Simple Object Access Protocol (SOAP):** This standard uses XML for transport like XML-RPC but provides additional layers of functionality, which may be useful for very complicated systems.

Jason and the Remote Procedure Calls

A brief word on some of the acronyms we're throwing at you here. None of them are vital to understand, but a brief description will no doubt help.

- JavaScript Object Notation (JSON), pronounced "Jason", is a way of formatting data so that it can be easily exchanged between different systems. As the name suggests, it grew from the JavaScript programming language but these days is just as easy to work with in other languages such as Ruby and Python.

  At its core it is a series of properties, in the form:

  ```
  "property name": "property value"
  ```

  The property values can be a string, a number, a Boolean value (true or false), or another JSON object or array (a sequence of objects).

  Individual properties are separated from each other with commas, and a set of different properties can be grouped into an object with { }. Arrays (a sequence of the same sort of object) are grouped with [ ].

  For example, an array of two objects — each with a name and an age — would look like this:

  ```
  [
      { "name": "Object 1", "age": 34 },
      { "name": "Second object", "age": 45 }
  ]
  ```

  For full details see the JSON website, http://json.org/.

- Remote Procedure Call (RPC) is a term to describe ways of calling programming code which isn't on the same computer as the code you are writing. The web APIs we have been discussing so far are a form of RPC. However, because the "web" part of that description better explains how the remote communication is done, the RPC moniker tends not to be used.

- Extensible Markup Language (XML), for the purposes we discuss in this book, can be thought of as an alternative to JSON. It uses < > to demark its elements and tends to be much more verbose than the equivalent JSON would be. As a result, it is less well suited for resource-constrained systems such as Internet of Things devices, so we recommend using JSON if you have the choice. XML has a common parentage with HTML, so if you're familiar with that, XML won't be unfamiliar. XML is defined by the World Wide Web Consortium (W3C), who also look after HTML, CSS, and other web standards. The XML section of their website (www.w3.org/standards/xml/) is a good starting point to learn more.

We recommend using REST, but you may have reasons to use another standard. For example, if you are trying to replicate the interface of another XML-RPC service, or you are already familiar with SOAP from other projects, that may well trump the other factors.

For this chapter, we use a REST API because it is popular, well supported, and simple to interact with for a limited microcontroller. The design considerations we describe mostly apply for all the standards, however.

REST has some disadvantages, too. For example, some of the HTTP methods aren't well supported by every client or, indeed, server. In particular, web browsers only natively support GET and POST, which can complicate things when interacting with REST from a web page.

There is also a lot of disagreement over best practices. REST experts may not always look at the most pragmatic solution favourably. This book isn't a resource on REST as such but aims to provide a flavour of how to use it; we try to point out where we're making a decision out of expediency.

In REST, you attach each resource to a URL and act on that. For example, to interact with a timer, you might speak to /timers/1234 for a timer with ID 1234. To create an entirely new timer, you would talk to /timers. As you can see, you can use different "methods" depending on whether you want to GET a resource, POST it onto the server in the first place, PUT an update to it, or DELETE it from the server.

Authorization and Session Management

In the previous table, we suggested passing username and password each time. That isn't really a good idea. If an attacker compromised the transaction, then she would have access to both. It is often a much better idea to perform a single login and then send some kind of token back with subsequent requests. This approach could be limited in terms of time or of session. In the case of REST, we are trying to use HTTP functionality as richly as possible. It turns out that "some kind of token" is a session cookie. Most servers and clients handle cookies automatically, so on subsequent requests only the cookie needs to be checked. Although that sounds like good news, at present, the Arduino HttpClient libraries don't support cookies. This issue will no doubt be resolved soon or worked around (by parsing and setting the HTTP headers manually). But for this timer example, you can continue to pass the MAC address for every request.

So the REST API will finally look like this:

Resource URL	Method	Auth	Parameters	Outputs
1. /timers	POST	MAC or Cookie	Timer duration	Timer ID
2. /timers/:id/ duration	PUT	MAC or Cookie	Timer duration	OK
3. /timers/:id/ complete	PUT	MAC or Cookie		OK
4. /timers/:id	DELETE	MAC or Cookie		OK
5. /timers/:id/ description	PUT	Cookie	Description	OK
6. /timers	GET	Cookie		List of Timer IDs
7. /timers/:id	GET	Cookie		Info about Timer
8. /user/device	PUT	Cookie	MAC address	OK
9. /user/device	GET	Cookie		MAC address
10. /login	POST	User/Pass	User/Pass	Cookie + OK
11. /user	POST		User/Pass	Cookie + OK

All the preceding work is vital to build an idea about how your Internet of Things device and service will interact. Actually, programming it is beyond the scope of this book, although we do present a rough partial implementation as an example. There is no single "best" solution for writing the code, and a lot of the choices will depend on your programming specializations, or if you are hiring a developer to do the back-end work, whether you can get someone who is good.

Following are some of the parameters you should consider when deciding on a platform for your web back end:

- What do you already know (if you are planning to develop the code yourself)?
- What is the local/Internet recruiting market like (if you are planning to outsource)?

- Is the language thriving? Is it actively developed? Does it have a healthy community (or commercial support)? Is there a rich ecosystem of libraries available?

We are deliberately not mentioning variables such as "power" or "speed". Almost any language that fulfils the most important criteria here is powerful enough to get the job done. When writing a web app, you probably care more about speed of development, robustness, and maintainability than power or speed. If you scale up enough that you have to rewrite your infrastructure in Erlang or critical subsystems in C++, that is a good problem to have!

If you are dipping your toes into web programming and don't have a firm idea about what platform to use already, you might want to consider a dynamic language, such as Ruby, Perl, Python, JavaScript (Node.js), or PHP. They are relatively simple to learn, well supported by web hosts, and have a host of libraries to help get the code written.

Those of you with experience of the Microsoft developer ecosystem may want to use C# or ASP.net. If you have skills with the JVM, Java or Scala would be a fine choice. If you're a functional programmer, Clojure, Erlang, or Haskell will get the job done.

Next, we look at an example of the back-end code in Perl, using the Dancer framework. This "lightweight" web framework uses a mindset similar to that of Ruby's Sinatra. We cover only the most interesting parts here, but you can look at the full example at `https://github.com/osfameron/aBookOfThings-examples/`, along with other code discussed in the book. (All the code on this site is open source, so feel free to fork it and make contributions, perhaps translations of the code, into your favourite programming language.)

Back-end Code in Perl

Perl has advantages and disadvantages just like all the other languages we mention. It is actively developed, has a great ecosystem of libraries on CPAN, and is powerful enough to serve large sites if the system is architected well. Its disadvantages (some areas have thorny syntax, the job market is patchy in some locations) are overweighed, in our case, by the fact that it's what Hakim knows best.

After a small amount of boilerplate, the code mostly consists of handlers for the different API calls. Each handler declares the HTTP verb (GET, POST, PUT, DELETE) and the route that it handles. Parameters can be passed within the route, marked by a colon (:id, for example), or as part of the HTTP request.

```
#1 Create a new timed task
post "/timers.:format" => sub {
    my $user = require_user;
        # 'require_user' wants a session cookie
        # OR a valid MAC address.

    my $duration = param 'duration'
        or return status_bad_request('No duration passed');

    my $timer = schema->resultset('Timer')->create({
        user_id  => $user->id,
        duration => $duration,
        status   => 'O', # open
    });
    return status_created({
        status=>'ok',
        id => $timer->id,
    });
};


#2 Change duration of timed task
put "/timers/:id/duration.:format" => {
    my $user = require_user;
    my $duration = param 'duration'
        or return update_complete;
    my $timer = require_open_timer;
        # a timer is open if it's in 'O' status

    ## NB: the following calculation has to extend the time
    ## as of now
    my $start_datetime = $timer->start_datetime;
    my $new_end_time = DateTime->now->add(
        minutes => $duration );
    my $total_duration = ($new_end_time - $start_datetime)
        ->in_units('minutes');

    $timer->update({ duration => $total_duration });

    return status_ok({
        ok => 1,
        message => 'Timer length updated',
```

```perl
    });
};


#3 Mark timer complete
put "/timers/:id/complete.:format" => sub {
    my $user = require_user;
    my $timer = require_open_timer;

    $timer->update({ status => 'C' });

    return status_ok({
        ok => 1,
        message => 'Timer marked complete',
    });
};


#4 Cancel timer
del "/timers/:id.:format" => sub {
    my $user = require_user;
    my $timer = require_timer;

    $timer->update({ status => 'D' });

    return status_ok({
        status => 'ok',
    });
};


#5 Describe the timed task
put "/timers/:id/description.:format" => sub {
    my $user = require_session;
        # 'require_user' demands a session cookie!
    my $timer = require_open_timer;
    my $description = param 'description';

    $timer->update({ description => $description });

    return status_ok({
        ok => 1,
        message => 'Description updated',
    });
};


#6 Get list of timers
get "/timers.:format" => sub {
    my $user = require_session;
```

```perl
    return status_ok({
        status => 'ok',
        timers => [ map $_->serialize, $user->timers ],
    });
};


#7 Get information about a timer
get "/timers/:id.:format" => sub {
    my $user = require_session;
    my $timer = require_timer;

    return status_ok({
        status => 'ok',
        timer => $timer->serialize,
    });
};


#8 TODO Set the user's device MAC address

#9 TODO Get the user's device MAC address

#10 Login
post "/login.:format" => sub {
    my $username = param 'user';
    my $password = param 'pass';

    my $user = schema->resultset('User')->find({
        email => $username });

    if ($user && $user->check_password($password)) {
        session user_id => $user->id;
        return status_ok({
            status=>'ok',
            message=>'Login OK',
        });
    }
    else {
        return status_bad_request("Bad username or password");
    }
};


#11 Register the user
post "/user.:format" => sub {
    my $username = param 'user';
    my $password = param 'pass';

    if (schema->resultset('User')->find({ email => $username }))
    {
```

```
            return status_bad_request("Duplicate user");
    }
    else {
        my $user = schema->resultset('User')->create({
            email    => $username,
            password => $password,
        });
        return status_created({
            status=>'ok',
            id => $user->id,
        });
    }
};
```

Note how all the requests end with `.:format`. This means that you could post to `http://api.roomofthings.com/timers.json` to get the result back from the server in JSON format or to `http://api.roomofthings.com/timers.txt` to get back a simple string, optimised for easy parsing by a microcontroller.

This code calls some functions defined by Dancer and Dancer::Plugin::REST, such as `status_ok` and `param`. The other things we had to write, omitted from the preceding listing, are as follows:

- The database definition (simply creating two tables, `users` and `timers`) and the code to connect them to Perl using `DBIx::Class` (an ORM layer, similar to ActiveRecord or LINQ)
- Some utility functions for user management: `require_user` and `require_session` (which distinguish between the "MAC or Cookie" and "Cookie" cases)
- Similar utility functions `require_timer` and `require_open_timer` to get the timer object from the database
- Basic configuration of Dancer/PSGI, to make the application easy to test and deploy

USING CURL TO TEST

While you're developing the API, and afterwards, to test it and show it off, you need to have a way to interact with it. You could create the client to interface with it at the same time (either an application on the web or computer, or the code to make your Internet of Things project connect to it). In this case, while we were developing Clockodillo, the API was ready long before the physical device. Luckily, many tools can interact with APIs, and one very useful one is curl, a command-line tool for transferring all kinds of data, including HTTP.

You can easily issue GET requests by simply calling `curl http://timer.roomofthings.com/timers.json`, for example. But, of course, the API is protected with logins. Luckily, curl takes this in its stride! Here is an example of interacting with it on a development server:

```
# the -F flag makes curl POST the request
$ curl http://localhost:3000/user.json \
      -F user=hakim -F pass=secret
{
    "status" : "ok",
    "id" : 2
}
```

curl simply makes an HTTP request and prints out the result to a terminal. Because the command line requests JSON, the result comes back in that format, with a dictionary of status and id values.

Here are some more examples:

```
# Check that login rejects a bad password
$ curl http://localhost:3000/login.json \
      -F user=hakim -F password=wrong
{
    "error" : "Bad username or password"
}

# save login session to our "cookie jar"
$ curl http://localhost:3000/login.json -c cookie.jar \
      -F user=hakim -F pass=secret
{
    "status" : "ok",
    "message" : "Login OK"
}

# use that cookie to login, and create a 25 minute timer
$ curl http://localhost:3000/timers.json -b cookie.jar \
      -F duration=25
{
    "status" : "ok",
    "id" : 1
}

# change the request to a PUT
$ curl http://localhost:3000/timer/1/duration.json \
      -X PUT -b cookie.jar -F duration=12
{
    "ok" : 1,
    "message" : "Timer length updated"
```

```
}

# GET the information about that timer

$ curl http://localhost:3000/timers/1.json -b cookie.jar
{
    "status" : "ok",
    "timer" : {
        "start_datetime" : "2012-05-21 19:30:40",
        "status" : "O",
        "id" : 1,
        "user_id" : 1,
        "duration" : 12,
        "description" : null,
        "end_datetime" : null
    }
}

# DELETE (cancel) it
$ curl http://localhost:3000/timer/1.json \
        -X DELETE -b cookie.jar
{
    "status" : "ok"
}

# GET it again (note how the status is now 'D' as it's deleted)
$ curl -b cookie.jar http://localhost:3000/timers/1.json
{
    "status" : "ok",
    "timer" : {
        "start_datetime" : "2012-05-21 19:30:40",
        "status" : "D",
        "id" : 1,
        "user_id" : 1,
        "duration" : 12,
        "description" : null,
        "end_datetime" : null
    }
}
```

Although the preceding examples may look a little arcane if you aren't familiar with code, we hope they are understandable enough for you to get a feel for what is happening. They exercise the main methods in the API and show the sorts of basic sanity tests that you would perform to make sure your code was functioning in the way you anticipated. That lets you go on to develop the device code knowing that the service it will be talking to has a reasonable foundation.

GOING FURTHER

The preceding sketch is missing a few tweaks before it can become a production-ready API. The timer duration changing is rudimentary. The code doesn't handle the case in which the timer should already have expired by the time the user tries to change it. Perhaps the data structure should also be expanded to store more history about a single timer (for example, if the user changes the time repeatedly, the server could store each change rather than only the total duration).

This example also has a number of architectural features that we didn't examine at all.

API Rate Limiting

If the service becomes popular, managing the number of connections to the site becomes critical. Setting a maximum number of calls per day or per hour or per minute might be useful. You could do this by setting a counter for each period that you want to limit. Then the authentication process could simply increment these counters and fail if the count is above a defined threshold. The counters could be reset to 0 in a scheduled cron job.

While a software application can easily warn users that their usage limit has been exceeded and they should try later, if a physical device suddenly fails, users might assume that it is broken! Solutions to this problem might include simply not applying the limit to calls made by a device.

OAuth for Authenticating with Other Services

While OAuth may not (currently) be the best solution for connecting with a microcontroller (at present, there are no accepted libraries for Arduino), there is no reason why the back-end service should not accept OAuth to allow hooks to services like Twitter, music discovery site last.fm, or the web automation of If This Then That.

Interaction via HTML

The API currently serialises the output only in JSON, XML, and Text formats. You might also want to connect from a web browser. When we first looked at the API design, we split up tasks into those that the device could do and then the rest. The latter could easily be done in a browser-based application. Of course, the users won't want to make raw API calls, and the flows taken to carry out an action may well be slightly different, but the basic data being manipulated is the same: The calls we've looked at would form the heart of the web application, just as they do the experience with the physical device.

Note that not every Internet of Things product needs a browser application. Perhaps the API is all you need, with maybe a static home page containing some documentation about how to call the API.

In the case of Clockodillo, however, we do want to have a set of web pages to interact with: Users should be able to look at their timers, assign descriptions, and so on.

It would be easy to set up specific route handlers just for the HTML application, for example:

```
post '/login.html' => sub { ... }
```

But a more elegant approach might be to use exactly the same code as before but with an HTML option. Instead of returning a JSON string, this code might inject the data into an HTML template. Simply calling, for example, /timers/1234.html instead of /timers/1234.json would then get a view of that data targeted at a human rather than a connected device.

Drawbacks

Although web browsers do speak HTTP, they don't commonly communicate in all the methods that we've discussed. In particular, they tend to support the following:

- GET: Used to open pages and click on links to other pages. You can link to http://timer.roomofthings.com/timers/1234.html and get the HTML version of the API call (using the "get_timer" template).
- POST: Used when submitting a form or to upload files. To post a timer, you could create a web form like the following:

```
<form method="POST" action="/timers.html">
    <input type="text" name="duration">
    <input type="submit" value="Create a new timer!">
</form>
```

This form calls the POST action and returns the appropriate HTML.

But what about the lovingly crafted PUT and DELETE methods? Web browsers don't commonly support those…but never fear! One option is to make these calls in JavaScript, which can indeed support them. Another is to "tunnel" the requests through a POST. There is a convention in Perl to use a field called x-tunneled-method, which you could implement like this:

```
<form method="POST"
    action="/timer.html?x-tunneled-method=DELETE">
    <input type="hidden" name="id" value="1234">
    <input type="submit" value="Cancel this timer!">
</form>
```

Now you just need to convince your web framework to accept this POST as if it were actually a DELETE. In the example app using Dancer, we use the module Plack::Middleware::MethodOverride to do this in a single line (https://metacpan.org/module/Plack::Middleware::MethodOverride). Other frameworks will have similar extensions.

Alternatively, you could write the web application in an entirely different code base and interact with the main service through the API. This can be a winning combination because it forces the human-facing code to use (and therefore exercise) the same API that the device uses, increasing the amount of testing it receives and preventing the device-facing code from being neglected. Whether you decide to follow that path would depend very much on your team's skill set.

Designing a Web Application for Humans

However you choose to implement it, as well as the text-based API we've spent most of the chapter working on, you can easily also have an elegant and well-designed application for humans to interact with.

Because numerous excellent books are available on designing a web application, we don't look at this topic in any great detail, but you might be interested in looking at some examples to think about the design process.

For example, the following figure shows a static login page, to be served by GET. The API didn't even specify a GET action, as it was superfluous for a computer. This page is entirely for the convenience of a human. All the labels like "Your email address" and the help text like "Remember your password is case sensitive" are purely there to guide the user. The logo, as well as proving that we are really not designers, is there as a branding and visual look and feel for the site.

The human-facing Clockodillo login page.

That's a simple example, but the following figure shows an even more extreme change. The list of timers, instead of being a JSON string containing a raw data structure, is highly formatted. The dates are formatted for humans. The duration of the timer and the status (in progress, completed, abandoned) are visualised with colours, progress bars, and a duration "badge". The page also links to other actions: The "Edit" button opens a page that allows access to the actions that change description, and so on. The menu bar at the top links to other functions to help users flow through the tasks they want to carry out.

The human-facing list of timers.

Finally, as we were preparing this mockup, we added a "Search for a specific timer" input. This hadn't even occurred to us when preparing the API (the timer device doesn't need it) but seemed obvious as soon as we thought about things from the viewpoint of a human user. Looking at your product from both contrasting perspectives (machine and human) will make it stronger and better designed.

REAL-TIME REACTIONS

We've looked at a traditional sort of API, where you make an HTTP request to the server and receive a response. This method has some disadvantages if you want a very responsive system. To establish an HTTP request requires several round-trips to the server. There is the TCP "three-step handshake" consisting of a SYN (synchronise) request from the client, a SYN-ACK from the server to "acknowledge" the request, and finally an ACK from the client. Although this process can be near instantaneous, it could also take a noticeable amount of time.

The time taken to establish the connection may or may not matter. Any of the most powerful boards is able to run the connection in the background and respond to it when it's completed. For a bare-bones board such as the Arduino, the current Ethernet/HTTP shields and libraries tend to block during the connection, which means that during that time, the microcontroller can't easily do any other processing (although it is possible to work around this issue using hardware interrupts, doing so poses certain restrictions and complications). Because the connection is usually made on a "breakout board" with its own processor, there is no reason that the connection couldn't happen in parallel, without blocking the main thread, so this restriction may well be lifted in future.

If you want to perform an action the instant that something happens on your board, you may have to factor in the connection time. If the server has to perform an action immediately, that "immediately" could be nearly a minute later, depending on the connection time. For example, with the task timer example, you might want to register the exact start time from when the user released the dial, but you would actually register that time plus the time of connection.

We look at two options here: polling and the so-called "Comet" technologies. And then, in the section on non-HTTP protocols, MQTT, XMPP, and CoAP offer alternative solutions.

POLLING

If you want the device or another client to respond immediately, how do you do that? You don't know when the event you want to respond to will happen, so you can't make the request to coincide with the data becoming available. Consider these two cases:

- The WhereDial should start to turn to "Work" the moment that the user has checked into his office.
- The moment that the task timer starts, the client on the user's computer should respond, offering the opportunity to type a description of the task.

The traditional way of handling this situation using HTTP API requests was to make requests at regular intervals. This is called *polling*. You might make a call every minute to check whether new data is available for you. However, this means that you can't start to respond until the poll returns. So this might mean a delay of (in this example) one minute plus the time to establish the HTTP connection. You could make this quicker, polling every 10 seconds, for example. But this would put load on the following:

- **The server:** If the device takes off, and there are thousands of devices, each of them polling regularly, you will have to scale up to that load.
- **The client:** This is especially important if, as per the earlier Arduino example, the microcontroller blocks during each connect!

COMET

Comet is an umbrella name for a set of technologies developed to get around the inefficiencies of polling. As with many technologies, many of them were developed before the "brand" of Comet was invented; however, having a name to express the ideas is useful to help discuss and exchange ideas and push the technology forward.

Long Polling (Unidirectional)

The first important development was "long polling", which starts off with the client making a polling request as usual. However, unlike a normal poll request, in which the server immediately responds with an answer, even if that answer is "nothing to report", the long poll waits until there is something to say. This means that the server must regularly send a keep-alive to the client to prevent the Internet of Things device or web page from concluding that the server has simply timed out.

Long polling would be ideal for the case of WhereDial: the dial requests to know when the next change of a user's location will be. As soon as WhereDial receives the request, it moves the dial and issues a new long poll request. Of course, if the connection drops (for example, if the server stops sending keep-alive messages), the client can also make a new request.

However, it isn't ideal for the task timer, with which you may want to send messages from the timer quickly, as well as receive them from the server. Although you can send a message, you have to establish a connection to do so. Hence, you can think of long polling as unidirectional.

Multipart XMLHttpRequest (MXHR) (Unidirectional)

When building web applications, it is common to use a JavaScript API called `XMLHttpRequest` to communicate with the web server without requiring a full new page load. From the web server's point of view, these requests are no different from any other HTTP request, but because the intended recipient is some client-side code, conventions and support libraries (both client- and server-side) have developed to address this method of interaction specifically.

Many browsers support a `multipart/x-mixed-replace` content type, which allows the server to send subsequent versions of a document via XHR. Note that XMLHttpRequest is a misnomer because there's no requirement to actually use XML at all. Using this content type is perhaps more sophisticated if you want to be able to receive multiple messages from the server.

It is perfectly possible to simply long poll and create a new request on breaking the old one, but this means that you might miss a message while you're establishing the connection. In the example of WhereDial, this is unlikely; you're unlikely to change location first to Home and then to Work in quick succession. However, for an Internet of Things device such as Adrian's Xively meter, which tries to show the state of a Xively feed in real time, being able to respond to changes from the server almost immediately is the essential purpose of the device.

HTML5 WebSockets (Bidirectional)

In Chapter 3 you saw how the HTTP protocol used in web services sits atop the TCP protocol. Traditionally, the API used to talk directly to the TCP layer is known as the *sockets API*. When the web community was looking to provide similar capabilities at the HTTP layer, they called the solution *WebSockets*.

Although WebSockets are currently a working draft in the HTML5 spec, they seem to have traction in modern browsers, servers, and other clients.

For example, there is a (partial) implementation for the Arduino platform
(`https://github.com/krohling/ArduinoWebsocketClient`).

WebSockets have the benefit of being bidirectional. You can consider them
like a full Unix socket handle that the client can write requests to and read
responses from.

This might well be the ideal technology for the task timer. After a socket is
established, the timer can simply send information down it about tasks being
started, modified, or cancelled, and can read information about changes
made in software, too.

*Because WebSockets are new and push the HTTP protocol in a
slightly unorthodox direction, they are known to have some issues
with proxy servers. This situation should change as the proxies
currently broken in this respect are fixed to be aware of WebSockets.
This may be an issue with your system's architecture; see the later
section on "Scaling".*

Implementations

The options described in the preceding section seemed to us to have most
traction currently; however, as a fast-changing area with no absolute
consensus as yet, the actual details of transports and limitations are bound to
change. It is worth paying attention to these transports as they develop. The
Wikipedia page on Comet (`http://en.wikipedia.org/wiki/
Comet_(programming)`) is a useful starting point for tracking the current
state of play.

Let's look at support for these techniques on the three main platforms that
you may need to consider for an Internet of Things application: the browser
web app (if applicable), the microcontroller itself, and the server application.

On the browser side, it is often possible to abstract the actual transport using
a library which chooses which method to connect to the server. For example,
it might use WebSockets if available; otherwise, it will fall back to MXHR or
long polling. This capability is useful because each web browser currently
has varying levels of support for the different techniques. There are well-
known Comet libraries for jQuery and for Dojo.

In addition, many web servers have abstractions to support Comet techniques. `Web::Hippie::Pipe` provides a unified bidirectional abstraction
for Perl web servers such as Twiggy, again using WebSockets if available,

otherwise MXHR or long polling. You can find similar abstractions for `node.js` (JavaScript), `Thin` (Rails), `jetty` (Java), and so on.

There are also libraries for the microcontroller; however, they tend to support only one scheme. For example, several dedicated WebSockets libraries are available for Arduino. In fact, the fallback to different methods of interchanging data aren't really needed on the Arduino. Unlike the case of a desktop web app, with Arduino you don't have to worry about the users having different browsers because you'll be providing the firmware for the device.

Scaling

An important consideration is that all these Comet techniques require the client to have a long-term connection with the server. For a single client, this is trivial. But if there are many clients, the server has to maintain a connection with each of them. If you run a server with multiple threads or processes, you effectively have an instance of the server for each client. As each thread or process will consume system resources, such as memory, this doesn't scale to many clients.

Instead, you might want to use an asynchronous web server, which looks at each client connection in turn and services it when there is new input or output. If the server can service each client quickly, this approach can scale up to tens of thousands of clients easily. There is a problem that each process on a typical Unix server has a maximum number of sockets, so you are restricted to that number of simultaneous clients. This, of course, is a good problem to have! When you hit that wall, you can look at load-balancing and other techniques that a good systems team will be able to apply to scale up the load.

You also might be able to let your front-end proxy (Varnish or similar) do some of the juggling of persistent client connections.

OTHER PROTOCOLS

As you have seen, although HTTP is an extremely popular protocol on the Internet, it isn't ideally suited to all situations. Rather than work around its limitations with one of the preceding solutions, another option—if you have control of both ends of the connection—is to use a different protocol completely.

There are plenty of protocols to choose from, but we will give a brief rundown of some of the options better suited to Internet of Things applications.

MQ TELEMETRY TRANSPORT

MQTT (`http://mqtt.org`) is a lightweight messaging protocol, designed specifically for scenarios where network bandwidth is limited or a small code footprint is desired. It was developed initially by IBM but has since been published as an open standard, and a number of implementations, both open and closed source, are available, together with libraries for many different languages.

Rather than the client/server model of HTTP, MQTT uses a publish/subscribe mechanism for exchanging messages via a *message broker*. Rather than send messages to a pre-defined set of recipients, senders publish messages to a specific *topic* on the message broker. Recipients subscribe to whichever topics interest them, and whenever a new message is published on that topic, the message broker delivers it to all interested recipients. This makes it much easier to do one-to-many messaging, and also breaks the tight coupling between the client and server that exists in HTTP.

A sister protocol, MQTT for Sensors (MQTT-S), is also available for extremely constrained platforms or networks where TCP isn't available, allowing MQTT's reach to extend to sensor networks such as ZigBee.

EXTENSIBLE MESSAGING AND PRESENCE PROTOCOL

Another messaging solution is the Extensible Messaging and Presence Protocol, or XMPP (`http://xmpp.org`). XMPP grew from the Jabber instant messaging system and so has broad support as a general protocol on the Internet. This is both a blessing and a curse: it is well understood and widely deployed, but because it wasn't designed explicitly for use in embedded applications, it uses XML to format the messages. This choice of XML makes the messaging relatively verbose, which could preclude it as an option for RAM-constrained microcontrollers.

CONSTRAINED APPLICATION PROTOCOL

The Constrained Application Protocol (CoAP) is designed to solve the same classes of problems as HTTP but, like MQTT-S, for networks without TCP. There are proposals for running CoAP over UDP, SMS mobile phone messaging, and integration with 6LoWPAN. CoAP draws many of its design features from HTTP and has a defined mechanism to proxies to allow mapping from one protocol to the other. At the time of this writing, the protocol is going through final stages of becoming a defined standard, with the work being coordinated by the Internet Engineering Task Force Constrained RESTful Environments Working Group.

SUMMARY

This chapter took a good look at the network side of the Internet of Things. We looked at how to interact with existing services, either through published APIs or via web scraping, and then worked through an example to see how to create something completely new if the need arose.

Together with the previous two chapters, you will now have a good feel for the breadth of work required to build an entire Internet of Things prototype. There is more work to do to take it into production, but you will see that in later chapters. If you are just planning to build something to make your own life easier or more fun, you should be well placed to get cracking.

The next chapter takes us back to the device side of the equation, with a more detailed exploration of the techniques you will need to write code for an embedded system. It explains some of the ways that embedded coding differs from standard desktop or server programming, with tips on how to approach it and how to investigate when things don't quite go to plan.

8

TECHNIQUES
FOR WRITING
EMBEDDED CODE

FOR THE MOST part, writing code for an embedded platform is no different to writing code for a desktop or server system. However, there are a few differences, and it is worth bearing them in mind as you write. In this chapter we explore what some of these issues are and outline ways that you can avoid or work around the problems.

As you saw in Chapter 5, "Prototyping Embedded Devices", one of the big differences between embedded systems and "normal" computing platforms is the lack of resources available. Whereas on laptops or servers you have gigabytes of memory and hundreds of gigabytes of storage, on a microcontroller the resources are typically measured in kilobytes. For example, your web browser will think nothing of slurping 330KB of HTML, CSS, JavaScript, and images into memory, and then copying it around to parse it and rework it into a better data structure for displaying just to show you the (relatively simple) home page of Google. That's 150 times the total memory available on an Arduino Uno, just for the download—before you start any processing of it.

Aside from resource constraints, connected devices are, by their nature, likely to be something that people turn on and then "forget about"—not literally, of course, because, one hopes, they provide a valuable service or brighten up people's lives. However, the owner of the device doesn't expect to have to regularly restart or maintain it. Consequently, your system should expect to run for months or years at a time without any user intervention.

The same goes for any configuration or tuning of the system. Although it's just about acceptable for server software to require an administrator to keep an eye on things and run through some maintenance procedure from time to time, this is not true for devices such as laptops and PCs. We've seen tasks such as disk defragmentation fading in importance as an explicit job for end users, for example. The aim with ubiquitous computing devices should be to take that idea of automated or *self*-maintenance further still.

MEMORY MANAGEMENT

When you don't have a lot of memory to play with, you need to be careful as to how you use it. This is especially the case when you have no way to indicate that message to the user. The computer user presented with one too many "low memory" warning dialog boxes will try rebooting, and so will the system administrator who spots the server thrashing its disk as it pages memory out to the hard drive to increase the amount of virtual memory. On the other hand, an embedded platform with no screen or other indicators will usually continue blindly until it runs out of memory completely—at which point it usually "indicates" this situation to the user by mysteriously ceasing to function.

Even while you are developing software for a constrained device, trying to debug these issues can be difficult. Something that worked perfectly a minute ago now stops inexplicably, and the only difference might be a hard-to-spot extra character of debug logging or, worse still, something subtler such as another couple of iterations through the execution loop.

TYPES OF MEMORY

Before we get into the specifics of how to make the most of the resources you have available, it's worth explaining the different types of memory you might encounter.

ROM

Read-only memory refers to memory where the information stored in the chips is hard-coded at the chips' creation and can only be read afterwards.

This memory type is the least flexible and is generally used to store only the executable program code and any data which is fixed and never changes. Originally, ROM was used because it was the cheapest way of creating memory, but these days it has no cost advantage over Flash chips, so their greater flexibility means that pure ROM chips are all but extinct.

Flash

Flash is a semi-permanent type of memory which provides all the advantages of ROM—namely, that it can store information without requiring any power, and so its contents can survive the circuit being unplugged—without the disadvantage of being unchangeable forever more. The contents of flash memory can be rewritten a maximum number of times, but in practice it is rare that you'll hit the limits. Reading from flash memory isn't much different in speed as from ROM or RAM. Writing, however, takes a few processor cycles, which means it's best suited to storing information that you want to hold on to, such as the program executable itself or important data that has been gathered.

RAM

Random-access memory trades persistence for speed of access. It requires power to retain its contents, but the speed of update is comparable with the time taken to read from it (particularly when compared to flash memory). As a result it is used as the working memory for the system—the place where things are stored while being processed.

Systems tend to have a lot more persistent storage than they do RAM, so it makes sense to keep as much in flash memory as is possible. Obviously, the program code itself lives in flash. You can also provide hints to the compiler (the program which turns your source code into the machine code that the processor understands) to help it place as much as possible of the running program into flash.

If you know that the contents of a variable won't ever change, it is better to define that variable as a constant instead. In the C and C++ programming languages (which are commonly used in embedded systems), you do this by using the `const` keyword. This keyword lets the compiler know that the variable doesn't need to live in RAM because it will never be written to—only read from. Using constants this way can be a big saving if you have any large lookup tables or other big data structures such as fonts or bitmaps. Even text strings for debugging purposes can take up a noticeable amount of space. It's much better to get this storage out of RAM and into flash.

For certain processor architectures—in the authors' experience, most notably the Harvard architecture of the Atmel chips used in Arduino—the data (RAM) and program (flash/ROM) memory spaces are separated, which means that they aren't trivially interchangeable. As a result, you may have to do a little additional work to copy the data from flash into RAM when you want to use it. You usually can find tried-and-tested methods to do this, but they involve a tiny bit more work than just making strings and other large variables constant. This issue is therefore something to be aware of when you are working on these platforms.

The Arduino platform, for example, provides an additional macro to let you specify that certain strings should be stored in flash memory rather than RAM. Wrapping the string in `F( . . .)` tells the system that this is a "flash" string rather than a "normal" one:

```
Serial.println("This string will be stored in RAM");
Serial.println(F("This one will be in flash"));
```

MAKING THE MOST OF YOUR RAM

Now that you've moved everything that you can out of RAM and into flash, all that remains is to work out ways to make better use of the free memory you have.

When you have only a few kilobytes or tens of kilobytes of RAM available, it is easier to fill up that memory, causing the device to misbehave or crash. Yet you may want to use as much of the memory as possible to provide more features. This consideration is important, and it's easier to make the best trade-off between maximising RAM usage and reliability if your memory usage is *deterministic*—that is, if you know the maximum amount of memory that will be used.

The way to achieve this result is to not allocate any memory dynamically, that is, while the program is running. To people coming from programming on larger systems, this concept is exotic; after all, when you're downloading some information from the Internet, for example, how could you possibly know beforehand exactly how large it is going to be? What happens if the web page you're retrieving has gained an extra paragraph or two since you wrote the code? Your algorithm has to take into account this possibility. The standard mechanism on desktop or server systems would be to allocate just enough memory at the time you're downloading things, *when* you know how much you'll need.

In a deterministic model, you need to take a different tack. Rather than allocate space for the entire page, you set aside space to store the important information that you're going to extract and also a buffer of memory that you can use as a working area whilst you download and process the page. Rather than download the entire page into memory at once, you download it in chunks—filling the buffer each time and then working through that chunk of data before moving on to the next one. In some cases you might need to remember some part of one chunk before moving to the next—if a key part of the page you're parsing spans the break between chunks, for example—but a well-crafted algorithm usually works around even that issue.

An upside of this approach is that you are able to process pages which are much larger than you could otherwise process; that is, you can handle datasets which are bigger than the entire available memory for the system! The code used for Bubblino, which runs on an Arduino board with only 2KB of RAM, can easily process the standard response XML from Twitter's search API, which is typically 10–15KB per download. Because Bubblino's code condenses all that text into a single number—the count of new tweets—it can discard a lot of the data as it goes. All it needs to track is whether or not each tweet is newer and the timestamp for the newest tweet it has seen (so it can pick up where it left off next time around).

The downside of this sort of single-pass parsing, however, is that you have no way to go back through the stream of data. After you discard the chunk you were working on, it's gone. If the format of the data you're consuming means that you know if something is needed only by the time you reach a later part of the file, you have to set aside space to save the potentially useful segment when you encounter it. Then when you reach the decision point, you still have it available to use and can discard it then if it's not required.

Using this type of parsing also means that you generally can't build up complex data structures to check that the data is correct or complete before you process it. Rather than a rigorous parsing of an XML file, for instance, you tend to be restricted to more basic sanity tests: that it's well formed (looks like an XML file) rather than whether it's valid (conforms to a given schema). If it's a vital feature of your system that you can do the additional complex checks, you need to consider alternative approaches. In these cases you could choose a system with more memory available in the first place. Alternatively, you might cache the download to an SD card or other area of flash memory, where it could be processed in multiple passes without needing to read it all into RAM at once.

Organising RAM: Stack versus Heap

When the system first boots up, it has all RAM available to store things in, but how does it decide what goes where and how to find it later? Two general concepts for arranging memory are used: the stack and the heap. Each has its advantages and disadvantages, and computers (including most embedded systems) tend to make use of both.

The stack is organised just as the name implies—like a stack of papers. New items which are added to the stack go on the top, and items can be removed only in strict reverse order, so the first thing to be removed is the last item that was placed onto the stack.

This arrangement makes it easy for the processor to keep track of where things are and how much space is being used because it has to track only the top of the stack. The downside to this approach is that if you're finished with a particular variable, you can release the memory used for it only when you can remove it from the stack, and you can do that only when everything added since it was allocated is removed from the stack, too.

Consequently, the stack is really only useful for

♦ Items that aren't going to survive for long periods of time

♦ Items that remain in constant use, from the beginning to the end of the program

Global variables, which are always available, are allocated first on the stack. After that, whenever the path of execution enters a function, variables declared within it are added. The parameters to the function get pushed onto the stack immediately, while the other variables are pushed as they are encountered. Because all the variables within a function are available only to code inside it, when you reach the end of that function, all those parameters and variables are ready to be discarded. So the stack gets unwound back to the same size it was just before control passed to the function.

The space on the stack is used up as the algorithm dives deeper into the nest of functions and released as execution winds back. For example, consider this pseudocode:

```
// global variables
function A {
    variable A1
    variable A2
    call B()
}
function B {
    variable B1
    variable B2
    variable B3
    call C()
    call D()
}
```

```
function C {
    variable C1
    // do some processing
}
function D {
    variable D1
    variable D2
    // do some other processing
}

// Main execution starts here
// Just call function A to do something...
call A()
...
```

Then, stack usage proceeds as follows:

1. Before function A is called, the stack looks like state (i).

2. As execution moves into function A, its variables are added to the stack (ii).

3. Function A then calls function B, resulting in its variables being added to the stack (iii).

4. Inside function B, first function C is called, resulting in its variables being added to the stack (iv).

5. When execution returns from function C, its variables are removed from the stack, taking you back to stack (iii).

6. Then function D is called, so its variables are pushed onto the stack instead (v).

7. Then execution returns to function B, with D's variables removed (iii).

8. And back to A, removing B's variables (ii).

9. And, finally, you leave function A, dropping back to just the global variables being defined (i).

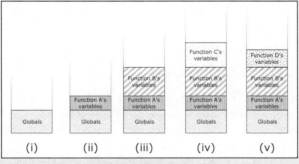

Stack usage at points during the example program execution.

continued

continued

As you can see, the maximum memory usage on the stack depends very much on the execution path that code can take through your code.

The heap, in comparison, enables you to allocate chunks of memory whenever you like and keep them around for as long as you like.

The heap is a bit like the seating area of a train where you fill up the seats strictly from the front and have to keep everyone who is travelling as a group in consecutive seats. To begin, all the seats are empty. As groups of people arrive, you direct them to the next available block of seats.

If, for example, a group of six people gets off at one stop, you are left with a block of six empty seats in the middle of the train. If the next group to get on is a group of three, those people can take up half of those empty seats, which leaves you with an empty block of three.

When a group of four people gets on at the following stop, they can't fit into the three empty seats because they have to sit together, so they sit towards the rear of the train where all the empty seats are.

This sort of behaviour continues happily, with people coming and going and filling up and vacating seats. But two possible problems exist. First, you might simply have more people to fit on the train than there are seats (this is the same problem as running out of memory). The second problem is more subtle: though you theoretically have enough free seats for the next group of passengers, those free seats are spread across the train and aren't available in a continuous block of free seats. This last situation is known as memory fragmentation.

Like we did with the stack, some pseudocode will help demonstrate normal usage of the heap:

```
create object A (size 20 bytes)
create object B (size 35 bytes)
create object C (size 50 bytes)
// do some work that needs object C
delete object C
create object D (size 18 bytes)
// do more work with objects B and D
delete object B
create object E (size 22 bytes)
```

Then, as execution flows through the code, the heap will evolve as follows:

1. At the start of execution, the heap will be empty (i).

2. Object A is added to the heap (ii), taking up 20 bytes of space.

3. Object B is added to the heap (iii), consuming a further 35 bytes straight after the space for object A.

4. Object C is added to the heap (iv), adding 50 bytes to the heap right after object B.

5. Object C is no longer needed and is deleted, releasing the space it consumed on the heap and taking us back to heap (iii).

6. Object D is created and takes up 18 bytes of the space just vacated by object C (v).

7. Now object B is finished with and deleted. As other code might be relying on the position of object D, we can't move it, so there's now a free space between objects A and D (vi).

8. Object E is created. It requires 22 bytes of space, which means it will fit in the hole left by object B (vii).

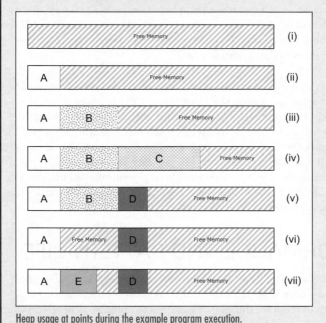

Heap usage at points during the example program execution.

What we've called *deterministic memory usage* boils down to avoiding placing things on the heap at all costs. That is, in systems with only a few kilobytes of RAM, we recommend exclusively using the stack to store variables. But strictly speaking, it is still possible to run out of memory when just using the stack. This situation is called *stack overflow*. On some processors this situation occurs because the stack is a fixed block partitioned off in memory: if your program has used more of the stack at some point during its execution (for example, in a deeply nested recursive routine), it could outgrow this fixed space. However, even on architectures where the stack can automatically grow to use all available RAM, some path through your algorithm may use more than is available.

One way to reduce the chance of this situation occurring is to keep the number of global variables to a minimum. Global variables are attractive, particularly to newcomers to coding because they're available everywhere. You don't have to worry about how to pass them from function to function or work out why the compiler is complaining that variable such-and-such hasn't been defined despite it being plainly obvious to you...just there...in that *other* function.... However, because they are always allocated (as you can see from the example in the preceding sidebar), any global variables take up valuable RAM at all times. In comparison, local variables exist only during the function in which they're declared (assuming you don't use modifiers such as `static` to make them persistent) and so take up space only when they're needed. If you can move more of your variables inside the functions where they're actually used, you can free up more space for use during other parts of the execution path.

The other way to keep down your stack usage, or at least within well-defined bounds, is to avoid using recursive algorithms. Although they are elegant and can make your code easier to understand, the stack grows with each recursion. If you know how many times a given function will recurse for the expected inputs, this may not be a problem. But if you cannot be certain that the algorithm won't recurse so many times that it blows your stack, it may be better, in an embedded system, to rework your algorithm as an iterative one. An iterative algorithm has a known stack footprint, whereas a recursive one adds to the stack with each level of recursion.

PERFORMANCE AND BATTERY LIFE

When it comes to writing code, performance and battery life tend to go hand in hand—what is good for one is usually good for the other. Whether either or both of these are things that you need to optimise depends on your application. A device which is tethered to one place and powered by an AC adaptor plugged into the wall isn't as reliant on energy conservation, for example. However, consuming less energy is something to which all devices should aspire.

Similarly, if you're building something which doesn't have to react instantly— maybe an ambient notifier for a weather forecast, which doesn't have any ill effect if it updates a few seconds later—or if it doesn't have an interactive user interface which needs to respond promptly to the user's actions, maximising performance might not be of much concern.

For items which run from a battery or which are powered by a solar cell, and those which need to react instantaneously when the user pushes a button, it makes sense to pay some attention to performance or power consumption. Although there is a lot of truth in the Donald Knuth (or was it Edsger Dijkstra, opinion seems divided (http://hans.gerwitz.com/2004/08/12/ premature-optimization-is-the-root-of-all-evil.html) quote that "premature optimization is the root of all evil", it is useful to know some of the techniques which can be applied. An awareness can help you default to more efficient algorithms when there is an otherwise arbitrary choice to be made. (However, we firmly believe that understandable, maintainable code trumps the efficient if the latter is more obtuse—at least until you profile your code to work out where the optimizations are needed.)

A lot of the biggest power-consumption gains come from the hardware design. In particular, if your device can turn off modules of the system when they're not in use or put the entire processor into a low-power sleep mode when the code is finished or waiting for something to happen, you have already made a quick win. That said, it is still important to optimize the software, too! After all, the quicker the main code finishes running, the sooner the hardware can go to sleep.

One of the easiest ways to make your code more efficient is to move to an event-driven model rather than polling for changes. The reason for this is to allow your device to sit in a low power state for longer and leap into action when required, instead of having to regularly do busywork to check whether things have changed and it has real work to do. Setting up this model is trickier to do with the networking code if you are acting as a client, rather than waiting as a server. The techniques such as long polling that you saw in Chapter 7, "Prototyping Online Components", or protocols like Message Queue Telemetry Transport (MQTT) or basic socket connections enable you to work around this situation.

On the hardware side, look to use processor features such as comparators or hardware interrupts to wake up the processor and invoke your processing code only when the relevant sensor conditions are met. If your code needs to pause for a given amount of time to allow some effect to occur before continuing, use calls which allow the processor to sleep rather than wait in a busy-loop.

If you can reduce the amount of data that you're processing, that helps too. The service API that you're talking to might have options which reduce how much information it sends you. When you're downloading tweets from a certain account on Twitter, for example, you can ask for only tweets after a specified ID. The first time you call the API, you have to deal with all the tweets it sends, but on subsequent calls, you can ask just for tweets since the ID of the most recent one that you already processed.

This optimization works only if the API that you're connecting to offers that sort of feature. For many operations, restricting things is a concept that simply doesn't make sense. If it would make sense to restrict the data, but the existing API doesn't provide that possibility, you always have the option of writing a service of your own to sit between the device and the proper API (known as a *shim service*). The shim service has all the processing power and storage available to a web server and so can do most of the heavy lifting. After this, it just sends the minimum amount of data across to be processed in your embedded system.

For instance, Bubblino talks directly to Twitter and downloads a full set of search results as XML each time it checks for new messages. All this data is processed and finally reduced down to a single number—how many new tweets it finds. In theory, an optimised intermediary service could perform the searches and just transmit a single number to the Bubblino device. The downside to that is you would need to write another service and maintain infrastructure to support it. Also, as the product scales, it would funnel more and more requests over the Internet route between the "Bubblino Server" and the Twitter servers. In this case, it is better to have that traffic distributed across the globe wherever the Bubblino devices themselves live.

When it comes to raw performance of your coding algorithm itself, nothing beats profiling to work out where the speed bottlenecks are. That said, following are a few habits that, if they become ingrained, help make your code generally more efficient:

- When you are writing if/else constructs to choose between two possible paths of execution, try to place the more likely code into the first branch— the *if* rather than the *else* part—as follows:

```
if something is true
    The more likely to happen code goes here
else
    The less likely path of execution should go here
```

This allows the pre-fetch and lookahead pipelining of instructions to work in the more common cases, rather than requiring the lookahead instructions to be discarded and the pipeline refilled. Having to re-prime the pipeline takes only a few extra processor cycles, but every bit helps.

- You saw in the "Memory Management" section that declaring data as constant where it is known never to change can help the compiler to place it into flash memory or ROM, but it can also help the compiler to know how to optimise the code. In some scenarios it is quicker to insert a value into the code as a plain number rather than to load that value from a variable's location in memory somewhere, and if the compiler knows what the variable's value is always going to be, it can make that substitution.

■ Avoid copying memory around. Moving big chunks of data from place to place in memory can be a real performance killer. In an ideal world, your code would look only at the data it needed to and read it only once. In practice, achieving this result is difficult but is a good way to help challenge your assumptions on how to write code. This is particularly an issue in protocol work, where data is initially read into a packet buffer for the Ethernet layer, say, and then passed up to the IP layer, then the TCP layer, followed by the HTTP code, and finally the application layer. A naive approach would copy the data at each step, as you unpack the relevant protocol headers. This approach could result in all the application data being copied five times as it travelled up the stack. A better approach would be to have a pointer or a reference to the initial buffer passed from layer to layer instead. In addition to the length of the data, you may need to store an offset into the buffer to show where the relevant data starts, but that's a small increment in complexity to greatly reduce how much data is copied around.

■ Related to the previous point, when you do need to copy data around, the system's memory copying and moving routines (such as memcpy and memmove) usually do a more efficient job than you could, so use them. Where possible, and this is particularly the case on 32-bit processors such as the ARM family, they use processor instructions that copy more than one byte in a single operation, thus considerably speeding up the process.

LIBRARIES

These days, when developing software for server or desktop machines, you are accustomed to having a huge array of possible libraries and frameworks available to make your life easier. Need to parse a chunk of RSS XML? No problem. Just pull in the RSS parsing library for your language of choice. Want to send an email? Don't worry; there's a module for that, too. And so on and so on.

In the embedded world, tasks are often a little trickier. It's getting better with the rise of the system-on-chip offerings and their use of embedded Linux, where most of the server packages can be incorporated in the same way as you would on "normal" Linux. The trickiest part is likely to be working out how to recompile a library for your target processor if a prebuilt version isn't readily available for your system—for example, for ARM.

On the other hand, microcontrollers are still too resource-constrained to just pull in mainstream-operating system libraries and code. You might be able to use the code as a starting point for writing your own version, but if it does lots of memory allocations or extensive processing, you probably are better off starting from scratch or finding one that's already written with microcontroller limitations in mind.

We don't have space here to cover all the possible libraries that are available, and we're by no means aware of everything that's available. However, here are a few which might be of interest:

- **lwIP:** lwIP, or LightWeight IP (http://savannah.nongnu.org/projects/lwip/), is a full TCP/IP stack which runs in low-resource conditions. It requires only tens of kilobytes of RAM and around 40KB of ROM/flash. The official Arduino WiFi shield uses a version of this library.

- **uIP:** uIP, or micro IP (http://en.wikipedia.org/wiki/UIP_%28micro_IP%29), is a TCP/IP stack targeted at the smallest possible systems. It can even run on systems with only a couple of kilobytes of RAM. It does this by not using any buffers to store incoming packets or outgoing packets which haven't been acknowledged. This means that some of the retransmission logic for the TCP layer bleeds into the application code, making your code more tightly coupled and more complex. It's quite common on Arduino systems which don't use the standard Ethernet shield and library, such as the Nanode board, using the Ethercard port for AVR (https://github.com/jcw/ethercard).

- **uClibc:** uClibc (http://www.uclibc.org/) is a version of the standard GNU C library (glibc) targeted at embedded Linux systems. It requires far fewer resources than glibc and should be an almost drop-in replacement. Changing code to use it normally just involves recompiling the source code.

- **Atomthreads:** Atomthreads (http://atomthreads.com/) is a lightweight real-time scheduler for embedded systems. You can use it when your code gets complicated enough that you need to have more than one thing happening at the same time (not quite literally, but the scheduler switches between the tasks quickly enough that it looks that way, just like the multitasking on your PC).

- **BusyBox:** Although not really a library, BusyBox (http://www.busybox.net/) is a collection of a host of useful UNIX utilities into a single, small executable and a common and useful package to provide a simple shell environment and commands on your system.

DEBUGGING

One of the most frustrating parts of writing software is knowing your code has a bug, but it's not at all obvious where that bug is. In embedded systems, this situation can be doubly frustrating because there tend to be fewer ways to inspect what is going on so that you can track down the issue.

Building devices for the Internet of Things complicates matters further by introducing both custom electronic circuits (which could be misbehaving or incorrectly designed) and communication with servers across a network. Troubleshooting electronic circuits is outside the scope of this book, but we'll cover some ways to debug the network communication.

Modern desktop integrated development environments (often shortened to IDEs) have excellent support for digging into what is going on while your code is running. You can set breakpoints which stop execution when a predefined set of conditions is met, at which point you can poke around in memory to see what it contains, evaluate expressions to see whether your assumptions are correct, and then step through the code line by line to watch what happens. You can even modify the contents of memory or variables on the fly to influence the rest of the code execution and in the more advanced systems rewrite the code while the program is stopped.

The debugging environment for embedded systems is usually more primitive. If your embedded platform is running a more fully featured operating system such as Linux, you are better placed than if you're developing on a tiny microcontroller.

Systems such as embedded Linux usually have support for remote debugging with utilities such as `gdb`, the GNU debugger (`www.gnu.org/software/gdb/`). This utility allows you to attach the debugger from your desktop system to the embedded board, usually over a serial connection but sometimes also over an Ethernet or similar network link. Once it is attached, you then have access to a range of capabilities similar to desktop debugging—the ability to set breakpoints, single-step through code, and inspect variables and memory contents.

Another way to get access to desktop-grade debugging tools is to emulate your target platform on the desktop. Because you are then running the code on your desktop machine, you have access to the same capabilities as you would with a desktop application. The downside of this approach is that you aren't running it on the exact hardware that it will operate on in the wild.

Although it is a useful way to flush out initial bugs and get things mostly working, there's likely to be the odd problem that you don't catch this way and that reveals itself only when you run it on the final hardware.

Emulation is a good approach if the software is particularly involved and/or complex because that's the scenario in which you need the most development and debugging time. However, the further the target hardware is from a desktop PC—particularly when it comes to having specialised sensors or actuators—the harder it is to write software subsystems for the emulator which accurately reflect the behaviour of the electronics.

If you need on-the-hardware debugging and your platform doesn't allow you to use gdb (or if the serial port is in use for another part of the system), JTAG access might give you the capabilities you need. JTAG is named after the industry group which came up with the standard: the Joint Test Action Group. Initially, it was devised to provide a means for circuit boards to be tested after they had been populated, and this is still an important use.

However, since its inception, JTAG has been extended to provide more advanced debugging features. Of particular interest from a software perspective are those features available when connected to some software on a separate PC called an *in-circuit emulator* (ICE). These allow you to use the additional computer to set breakpoints, single-step through the code running on the target processor, and often access registers and RAM too. Some systems even allow you to trigger the debugger from complex hardware events, which gives you even better control and access than debuggers such as gdb.

If you don't have access to any of these tools, you have to fall back on some of the simpler, yet tried-and-tested techniques.

The most obvious, and most common, poor-man's debugging technique is to write strings out to a logging system. This approach is something that almost all software does, and it enables you to include whatever information you deem useful. That could be the value of certain variables at key points in the code. Or if you suspect the system is running out of RAM, writing out the amount of free space at startup and then at various points throughout the code can help you work out whether that is the case. And if your code appears to hang during execution, something as simple as some "reached line X" debug output can let you narrow in on the offending point with a binary chop approach.

If you have access to a writable file system, for example, on an SD card, you can write the output to a file there, but it is more common to write the information to a serial port. This approach enables you to attach a serial monitor, such as HyperTerminal on Windows, to the other end of the connection and see what is being written in (pretty much) real time.

You should be aware of a couple of gotchas, though, but in many cases you won't encounter them. The first is obviously the amount of space needed for any logging information: all the strings and code to do the logging have to fit into the embedded system along with your code.

The second gotcha is alluded to in the "pretty much" modifier to the previous real-time line. As the serial communication runs at a strict tempo, typically a small buffer is used to store the outgoing data while it is being transmitted. If your code hangs or crashes very soon after your logging output, there's a chance that it won't be written out over the serial connection before the system halts. So, if you are printing out "got here" messages to work out how far through your program things got before encountering the bug, there's a chance that it actually got a tiny bit further than your serial log would suggest. This isn't just an issue for serial logging; the file system tends to have a buffer for writing out data to the file too, so a log file may have the same problem.

Because most Internet of Things devices have a persistent connection to the network, you could add a debugging service to the network interface. This way, you can create a simple service which lets you connect using something as basic as telnet and find out more about what is happening in real time. At its simplest, this service could output the logging data which would otherwise be directed to the serial port, or it might understand a number of simple programmer-defined commands to query parts of the system status or trigger functionality or test code. Obviously, one warning with this approach is to take care that you don't inadvertently open a backdoor security hole. We don't recommend leaving such a system in place in the production models.

Actually, even without a dedicated debug interface on the network, you can use the fact that your device has network connectivity to help figure out what has gone wrong.

TCP/IP stacks generally offer basic capabilities such as responding to ICMP ping requests, even if the higher-level code isn't doing what you expect. If you know the IP address of the device and it responds when you query it with the `ping` network utility, you can infer that at least some part of the system is still functioning.

Taking that thinking further, if you can connect a computer somewhere on the network path between the device and the service it communicates with, running a *packet sniffer* enables you to see what is happening at the network level. (Wireshark, http://www.wireshark.org/, is the authors' usual choice here.) Usually, you monitor the network at one end of the connection or the other—with a computer connected to the same LAN as the device or running the packet sniffer software on the remote server.

Unless the network has very little traffic, you need to use the filtering options to reduce the amount of information flowing down to something manageable. Filtering on the MAC address of the device is a good approach if you're at the device end; otherwise, use its IP address to restrict the display just to traffic to and from the device. This approach enables you to see whether it's registering with the network (if there's DHCP traffic) and if it's succeeding in connecting to the remote service and sending out the relevant data and getting the correct response—all of which, we hope, helps you narrow down where the problem lies.

At a slightly higher level, you can also use the logging and software on the server to gather information about the device's activity. If the transport between the device and the server is a standard protocol, such as the HTTP communication with a web server, there is a good likelihood that any requests were recorded in the server log file. If you can modify the server API too, you can add analytics to keep track of the time the client last accessed the service, for example, or the count of API accesses.

If all else fails, the debugging tool of (often not-so-) last resort is a variation on what was probably your first step in building hardware: flashing an LED. As long as you have one GPIO pin free, you should be able to connect an LED and have your code turn it on at a given point. As with the string logging approach, you can use this technique to narrow in on a problem area if the system hangs or possibly use different patterns of flashing to indicate different conditions.

You also are able to reuse an LED that's normally used elsewhere in the system, during debugging at least, as long as the different uses can be distinguished from each other. Adrian remembers using this method when debugging the network stack on a mobile phone web browser; the only means of indicating the activity lower down was to flash the (fortunately) two-colour status LED one colour for incoming packets and the other colour for packets heading out.

SUMMARY

Although this chapter by no means provides a comprehensive list of ways to improve your embedded coding, we hope it provides some useful tips and pointers. To make it easier to refer to and refresh your memory, revisit the main points here:

- Move as much data and so forth as possible into flash memory or ROM rather than RAM because the latter tends to be in shorter supply.

- If items aren't going to change, make them constant. This makes it easier to move them into flash/ROM and lets the compiler optimise the code better.

- If you have only tiny amounts of memory, favour use of the stack over the heap.

- Choose your algorithm carefully. A single-pass algorithm enables you to process much more data than reading it all into memory, and iterative rather than recursive options make memory use deterministic.

- For best power usage, spend as much time as possible asleep.

- If you aren't using it (whatever "it" is), turn as much of it off as you can. This advice applies to the processor (drop into low-power mode) as much as other subsystems of the hardware.

- Optimisations can live on the server side as well as in the device. A nonpolling or reduced amount of data transferred improves both sides of the solution.

- Avoid premature optimisation. If you hit performance problems, profile to work out where the issues lie.

- Copying memory is expensive, so try to do as little of it as you can.

- Work *with* the compiler, rather than against it. Order your code to help the likely execution path and use constants to help it optimise.

- Choose libraries carefully. One from a standard operating system might not be a good choice for a more embedded environment.

- Tools such as gdb and JTAG are useful when debugging, but you can get a long way with just outputting text to a serial terminal or flashing an LED.

- Careful observation of the environment surrounding the device can help you sniff out problems, particularly when it's connected to the Internet and so interacting with the wider world.

FROM PROTOTYPE TO REALITY

9

BUSINESS MODELS

IF YOU ARE primarily a maker or a programmer, and not an entrepreneur, you may have only a dim idea of what a "business model" is. In casual discussion, this expression seems to refer almost exclusively to how the business makes money. For example, when one is talking about Twitter or Pinterest or the latest social media sensation, a common put-down is "Have they got a business model yet? Sure, they're big now, but do they have any idea how they're going to make money out of it?"

But there is more to a business model than just money. We could define it as a "hypothesis about what customers want, how they want it, and how an enterprise can organize to best meet those needs, get paid for doing so, and make a profit" (www. sciencedirect.com/science/article/pii/S002463010900051X).

This definition brings together a number of factors:

- A group of people (customers)
- The needs of those customers
- A thing that your business can do to meet those needs
- Organisational practices that help to achieve this goal—and to be able to carry on doing so, sustainably
- A success criterion, such as making a profit

All these aspects are relevant as much to hobbyist or not-for-profit projects as they are to commercial enterprises, though for the last point profit might be substituted for "improving the world" or "having fun" as criteria for success.

We start with an overview of business models over time, to get a flavour for the topic, and then look at a commonly used way to evolve a model. We then look at how existing Internet of Things companies have modelled themselves and think about where they may end up. Finally we take a practical look at starting a company, from initial funding, and discuss the advantages of a "lean startup" approach.

A SHORT HISTORY OF BUSINESS MODELS

From the earliest times, and for the great majority of human existence, we have gathered in tribes, with common property and shared resources. This is an almost universal pattern amongst hunter-gatherers, as it means that every member of the tribe can find food and shelter even if they have not been lucky foraging or hunting that day. We could describe this form of collectivism as a basic *gift economy*. Gift economies develop where those with the appropriate skills can provide their products or services—hunting, pottery, livestock, grain, childcare—and expect repayment of this obligation not immediately but with a gift of comparable worth later. This is not a written debt but a social obligation, which the recipient will repay in due course, perhaps when hunting is good, when she happens upon the raw materials for her craft, or even much later in the year at harvest time.

Development of systems such as barter and money developed only at the edges, between different tribes. We could argue that the first of what we could recognise as modern business models developed at these borders and resulted from the technology required to move products and obligations through space and time.

SPACE AND TIME

While neighbouring tribes might have discovered variants in the local area's resources—animal, vegetable or mineral—it is when trade develops with others from far-off lands that it becomes really interesting. A merchant might sell silks made in his village to a region where these cloths are rare and in demand in exchange for aromatic spices which will be highly prized back home. But long-distance trade brings with it a whole set of problems: while nomadic hunter-gatherers were adept at finding food and making a home on the move, merchants have to carry larger quantities of goods for sale and want to maximise the time travelling rather than doing the myriad tasks required for subsistence and shelter. Their goods and food carried will have to last far longer, so they will need to be protected and preserved. Above all, they need to have a reliable means of transport for themselves and their merchandise. Technological advancements such as waterway navigation and portage of boats over land opened up new possibilities, as did the domestication of animals such as the camel, which unlocked trade routes through the Western Arabian deserts.

We touched briefly on the preservation of food, whether through salting or smoking, or simply better storage technology such as grain silos. As well as facilitating transportation through space, preservation is also a way of transporting goods through *time*. A farmer or trader who can afford to not eat or sell all his produce during the glut of harvest can fetch a better price months later at a higher price. So, a merchant trader's business is transporting goods through space and time, and his suppliers, the producers, benefit from that by being able to sell a bulk of their produce in one go, after which they can continue with their daily life and work.

Money, then, abstracted trade further, setting an easy-to-calculate exchange rate between a fixed currency (a certain size disc of gold or weight of grain) and the product being exchanged. In the original gift economies, producers could pay their obligations only periodically or intermittently, according to the rhythms of hunting, farming, or craft. With money, this obligation was abstracted and could be paid back at arbitrary times. In this sense, money is another technology which allows travel through time. The versatility and ease of calculation which this development brought with it made it easier to develop new business models, such as investing in other merchants' trade expeditions in return for a given share or the development of interest on loans.

FROM CRAFT TO MASS PRODUCTION

When Gutenberg demonstrated his printing press circa 1450, books changed from being priceless treasures, hand-crafted by monks and artisans, to a commodity that could be produced. Soon every bourgeois family could afford their own books, at least a copy of the Gutenberg Bible, the first mass-produced book. It is no exaggeration to suggest that the invention laid the foundations for an information culture which is currently exemplified by the Internet and the World Wide Web. Now, painstakingly copying ancient texts onto vellum and stamping them onto paper with the latest innovation appear to end with the same result, a book. That the latter was some thousand times faster was not simply a quantitative change (more books produced) but a *qualitative* one: information is no longer so rare, valuable, and fragile that it must be preserved by gatekeepers (the ruling classes and the church) but can be so widely spread that everyone can have access to it (and will do, whether those former gatekeepers like it or not.)

Trade routes would play their part here too, as the printing press spread to the New World and India via the sea routes that would be discovered by the end of the century. The cost of printing would become ever smaller as the technology spread, leading to new business models with the rise of newspapers and pamphlets. By the time Dickens was writing his novels in the mid-nineteenth century, he could publish them a chapter at a time, by monthly or weekly subscription.

In 1884, the British company Lever Brothers launched Sunlight Soap, the first household soap to be sold not by weight, to be cut in the shop by the grocer, but packaged in bars and branded with a logo. This was an innovation in mass consumerism, whereby the brand established a link of trust direct with the consumer, relegating the middleman, the grocer, to becoming just a way to deliver the product to the consumer.

Mass production, perfected by Ford Motor Company, was another major change in business model, driven not by how Henry Ford sold his cars but by how he made them. Ford moved away from the "craft production" of cars sold by commission to highly custom requirements and made by skilled craftsmen. Rather, his workers specialised on a single task, and he insisted on standard gauges for parts so that the cars could be assembled and fitted together, ending up identical. This approach made it simple to maintain and repair a Ford car, so the average person could afford to buy one without employing a mechanic to keep it working. The fact that mass production also drove down the costs to produce these cars also helped keep them affordable.

The transition to mass production had its own cost, not least that semi-skilled factory labour may not be as fulfilling as the more varied craftsman role that it displaced. As well as social cost, the typical operation can reach bottlenecks in efficiency. The method of lean production pioneered by Toyota in the 1950s retains many aspects of mass production (efficiency, automation, and high volume of production) but instead of producing masses of a single part, assembly, or finished product, can be run to produce them to order, at a specified date. Thus, Toyota is, for example, able to produce a single car of a given colour, configuration of wheels, and so on, and arrange for the right wheels, tyres, and style of door to arrive on the factory line where and when they are needed. This approach allows the company a much greater degree of customisation than does mass production, and the emphasis on continuous improvement of efficiency is believed to lead to a more fulfilling and varied environment for the factory worker.

In other areas, the ethic of mass production resulted in new business models such as supermarkets, which pioneered both "self-service shopping" and the sale of a whole range of products under one roof. The first recognizable supermarkets appeared in the 1930s, evolved into the hypermarkets of the 1960s, and now the concept of self-service shopping has evolved to the automated tills where every shopper can be his own checkout assistant.

Fast-food franchising began in the 1930s and exploded with McDonald's and Burger King in the 1950s. Standardized menus, pre-prepared ingredients, and standard practices for each franchisee to follow meant that you could now eat exactly the same meal in any of a chain restaurant's stores in your country (local tastes, laws, and religious observances mean that menus are tweaked globally). In an interesting turn, many new fast-food chains are fighting against this movement by flavouring sauces made by hand from freshly sourced ingredients instead of mass-produced ones. The U.S.-based Chipotle chain was one of Fast Company's 50 most innovative companies of 2012. Here, injecting the ethical sourcing of food and more responsibility in the hands-on cooking for the employees into the successful fast-food business model has revitalized it. Similarly, Lush created a soap empire in the 1990s by selling natural soap in long strips, to be cut into blocks by weight, just as it had been before Lever Brothers' intervention a century before.

THE LONG TAIL OF THE INTERNET

As we have seen, huge changes in business practice are usually facilitated by, or brought about as a consequence of, technological change. One of the greatest technological paradigm shifts in the twentieth century was the Internet. From Tim Berners-Lee's first demonstration of the World Wide Web in 1990, it took only five years for eBay and Amazon to open up shop and emerge another five years later as not only survivors but victors of the dot-com bubble. Both companies changed the way we buy and sell things. Chris Anderson of *Wired* magazine coined and popularized the phrase "long tail" to explain the mechanism behind the shift.

A physical bricks & mortar shop has to pay rent and maintain inventory, all of which takes valuable space in the shop; therefore, it concentrates on providing what will sell to the customers who frequent it: the most popular goods, the "hits", or the Short Head. In comparison, an Internet storefront exposes only bits, which are effectively free. Of course, Amazon has to maintain warehouses and stock, but these can be much more efficiently managed than a public-facing shop. Therefore, it can ship vastly greater numbers of products, some of which may be less popular but still sell in huge quantities when all the sales are totalled across all the products.

Whereas a specialist shop in Liverpool; Springfield, Oregon; or Florence, Italy, may or may not find enough customers to make its niche sustainable, depending on the town's size and cultural diversity, on the Internet all niches can find a market. Long tail Internet giants help this process by *aggregating* products from smaller providers, as with Amazon Marketplace or eBay's sellers. This approach helps thousands of small third-party traders exist, but also makes money for the aggregator, who don't have to handle the inventory or delivery at all, having outsourced it to the long tail.

E-books and print-on-demand are also changing the face of publishing with a far wider variety of available material and a knock-on change in the business models of writers and publishers that is still playing out today. Newer business models have been created and already disrupted, as when Google overturned the world of search engines, which hadn't even existed a decade previously. Yet although Google's stated goal is "to organize the world's information and make it universally accessible and useful" (www. google.com/about/company/), it makes money primarily through exploiting the long tail of advertising, making it easy for small producers to advertise effectively alongside giant corporations.

LEARNING FROM HISTORY

We've seen some highlights of business models over the sweep of human history, but what have we learnt that we could apply to an Internet of Things project that we want to turn into a viable and profitable business?

First, we've seen that some models are ancient, such as Make Thing Then Sell It. The way you make it or the way you sell it may change, but the basic principle has held for millennia.

Second, we've seen how new technologies have inspired new business models. We haven't yet exhausted all the new types of business facilitated by the Internet and the World Wide Web.... If our belief that the Internet of Things will represent a similar sea change in technology is true, it will be accompanied by new business models we can barely conceive of today.

Third, although there are recurring patterns and common models, there are countless variations. Subtle changes to a single factor, such as the manufacturing process or the way you pay for a product or resource, can have a knock-on effect on your whole business.

Finally, new business models have the power to change the world, like the way branded soap ushered in mass consumerism and mass production changed the notion of work itself. If the Internet of Things does change the world, as we go on to discuss in Chapter 11, "Ethics", it may well be through the business models it permits.

THE BUSINESS MODEL CANVAS

One of the most popular templates for working on a business model is the Business Model Canvas by Alexander Osterwalder and his startup, the Business Model Foundry. The canvas is a Creative Commons–licensed single-page planner.

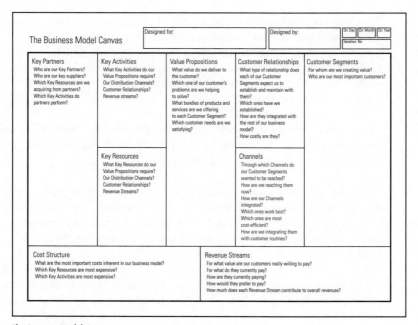

The Business Model Canvas.

At first sight, it looks as though each box is simply an element in a form and the whole thing could be replaced by a nine-point checklist. However, the boxes are designed to be a good size for sticky notes, emphasizing that you can play with the ideas you have and move them around. Also the layout gives a meaning and context to each item.

Let's look at the model, starting with the most obvious elements and then drilling down into the grittier details that we might neglect without this kind of template.

At the bottom right, we have *Revenue Streams*, which is more or less the question of "how are you going to make money?" we used to start this chapter. Although its position suggests that it is indeed one of the important desired *outputs* of the business, it is by no means the only consideration!

The central box, *Value Propositions*, is, in plainer terms, what you will be producing—that is, your Internet of Things product, service, or platform.

The *Customer Segments* are the people you plan to deliver the product to. That might be other makers and geeks (if you are producing a kit form device), the general public, families, businesses, or 43-year-old accountants (famously, the average customer of Harley-Davidson).

The *Customer Relationships* might involve a lasting communication between the company and its most passionate customers via social media. This position could convey an advantage but may be costly to maintain. Maintaining a "community" of your customers may be beneficial, but which relationships will you prioritise to keep communicating with your most valuable customer segments?

Channels are ways of reaching the customer segments. From advertising and distributing your product, to delivery and after-sales, the channels you choose have to be relevant to your customers.

On the left side, we have the things without which we have no product to sell. The *Key Activities* are the things that need to be done. The Thing needs to be manufactured; the code needs to be written. Perhaps you need a platform for it to run on and a design for the website and the physical product.

Key Resources include the raw materials that you need to create the product but also the people who will help build it. The intellectual resources you have (data and, if you choose to go down that route, patents and copyright) are also valuable, as are the finances required to pay for all this!

Of course, few companies can afford the investment in time and money to do all the Key Activities themselves or even marshal all the Key Resources. (Henry Ford tried hard, but even he didn't manage.) You will need *Key Partners*, businesses that are better placed to supply specific skills or resources, because that is their business model, and they are geared up to do it more cheaply or better than you could do yourself. Perhaps you will get an agency to do your web design and use a global logistics firm to do your deliveries. Will you manufacture everything yourself or get a supplier to create components or even assemble the whole product?

The *Cost Structure* requires you to put a price on the resources and activities you just defined. Which of them are most expensive? Given the costs you will have, this analysis also helps you determine whether you will be more cost driven (sell cheaply, and in great volume via automation and efficiency) or more value driven (sell a premium product at higher margins, but in smaller quantities).

WHO IS THE BUSINESS MODEL FOR?

Primarily, the reason to model your business is to have some kind of educated hypothesis about whether it might deliver what you want from it. Even if you don't use a semi-formal method like the canvas we just discussed, anyone who starts up any business will have thought, at least briefly, about whether she can afford to do it, what the business is, and whether she'll get paid.

As a programmer or a maker, you might believe it counterintuitive to think of a piece of paper with nine boxes in it as a "tool", but when you have a well-tested separation of factors to consider, the small amount of structure the canvas provides should help you think about the business and give you ways to brainstorm different ideas:

- What if we target the product at students instead of businesses?
- What if we outsource our design to an agency?
- What if we sell at low volume/high value instead?

Many great product ideas turn out to be impractical, ahead of their time, or unprofitable. Being able to analyze how the related concepts mesh will help you challenge your product idea and either make it stronger or know when to abandon it.

The model is also useful if you want to get other people involved. This could be an employee or a business partner...or an investor. In each of these cases, the other parties will want to know that the business has potential, has been thought out, and is likely to survive and perhaps even go places. With a new business startup, you have no track record of success to point to. Although what will sell the business is primarily the product itself, and of course your passion for it, being able to defend a well-thought-out model of the business is an important secondary consideration for someone who is planning to sink time and perhaps money into your business.

Perhaps to a lesser extent, your *customers* will also be considering whether to invest their time and money in your product. They will ask themselves certain questions about it. Let us look at some of these likely questions, from the wider field of Internet products in general.

- **Why should I waste time trying out Yet Another Social Network? I think I'll wait and see whether all my friends join it first.** This first question is about your "Value Proposition" (that is, the product) and a reasonable concern if you are trying to get into a market that already has good or popular solutions.

- **Will my Internet-connected rabbit become an expensive paper-weight if you go bust?** This happened with Nabaztag, one of the earliest consumer products in the field of Internet of Things. These rabbit-shaped devices delighted their owners by muttering and moving their ears in response to stimuli received via the Internet until the French company Violet went bankrupt. The new owners, Mindscape, factored in this concern by open sourcing the code for Nabaztag (and its successor Karotz) to ensure that customers can continue to use the product no matter what happens to the company. This question is asked with a degree of consumer savvy about business risk. Potential customers have seen other companies fall under and don't want the inconvenience or waste it entails for them.

- **Your online document collaboration looks great, but is it worth my moving my whole business to it? If you stop trading or change the platform, we may have to redo all the work again.** Such customers may well be interested in the details of your business model to calculate whether the risk they've identified is worth their commitment. This isn't just a concern about viability of the company: It's unlikely that Google will stop trading, yet many businesses are still unwilling to rely on Google Drive for editing documents. The reason is, in part, that they don't understand where the product fits in Google's strategy and can't guarantee that the service won't be discontinued or crippled, or predict a cost structure for it in the event that it stops being free.

- **This free service is fantastic, but why don't you let me pay for it, so I can get consistency, receive support, and avoid adverts?** Lastly, many customers are aware of alternative charging models that they would prefer and might prefer a different one. Not all customers vote for the free option. When the social bookmarking site delicious.com started to lose many of the features that had made it popular, Maciej Cegłowski set up pinboard.in, a paying service. Its charging model is designed to keep the user base small enough that he can keep up the development and support by increasing the small sign-up fee by a fraction every time a new user pays for it.

As Cegłowski says, "You don't really know that the cool project you signed up for is in a skyscraper in Silicon Valley, or like me: one dude in his underpants somewhere who has five windows open to terminal servers" (`www.economist.com/blogs/babbage/2011/04/price_fame`). But partners, investors, and informed customers will *want* to know. Though, as we've seen, a commercial enterprise may drop a product as readily as a one-man team; the business model provides, among other things, a useful tool for understanding what plans there are to keep the service running in both cases.

It has been stated about "free" products: "If you're not paying for something, you're not the customer; you're the product being sold". This formulation was popularised by Andrew Lewis in 2010 (`http://www.metafilter.com/95152/Userdriven-discontent`) but builds on a long line of commentary about consumerism, such as Adbusters' classic video of 1999 "The Product Is You" (`http://www.adbusters.org/abtv/product_you.html`). But as elegant as such a phrase may be, is it true? Derek Powazek, CEO of social startup Cute-Fight, challenges several assumptions often made:

- Not paying means not complaining.
- You're either the product or the customer.
- Companies you pay treat you better.
- So startups should all charge their users.

—http://powazek.com/posts/3229

Powazek suggests that the actual lesson to be learned is that:

> *Your business plan cannot be secret anymore. People are too smart for that, too tired of getting burned, too wary of losing their contributions when a startup dies, and too annoyed by sudden changes to the terms. Communicate your business plan from the start and you'll avoid a thousand problems down the road.*
>
> *—http://powazek.com/posts/3250*

MODELS

We have looked at the Business Model Canvas as a tool for generating and analysing models. As we saw from our history, the models have many common variants. It is a good idea to have a look at some of the models that Internet of Things companies have used or might use and consider some of the parameters these models relate to on the canvas.

MAKE THING, SELL THING

The simplest category of models, "make a Thing and sell it," is, of course, valid for the Internet of Things. Adrian sells custom-built Bubblini, and the startup Good Night Lamp is preparing to ramp up production of its eponymous lamps as an off-the-shelf product. As you will see in Chapter 10, electrical products sold in shops (physical or online) may be subject to legislation and certification (RoHS, Kitemarks, and so on), which is an additional factor and cost to consider. Many small-scale projects take the option of selling the product in "kit" form, with some assembly required. Because kits are assumed to be for specialists and hobbyists rather than the general public, the administrative burden may be lower. However, making a decision to limit your target market may well limit the potential revenue also.

SUBSCRIPTIONS

A Thing would be a dumb object if it weren't for the important Internet component which allows the device to remain up to date with useful and current content. But, of course, this ongoing service implies costs to the provider—development, maintenance of servers, hosting costs, and in some cases even connection costs. A subscription model might be appropriate, allowing you to recoup these costs and possibly make ongoing profit by charging fees for your service. Many products could legitimately use this method, but perhaps the more complex, content-driven services would find it more convincing. Paying Bubblino a monthly fee to blow bubbles might seem steep, but the BERG Cloud, which delivers nicely formatted news and entertainment to its Little Printer, might have seemed an ideal product for this model. As it stands, content consumers do *not* pay for either BERG Cloud or for any content subscriptions. In the future, content publishers may pay for certain premium services. Perhaps this example shows that there is not yet a market for paid subscriptions to Internet of Things products. This may mean that there is a market to be built. People happily pay subscriptions to music services, corporate groupware, and of course, mobile phones, so perhaps Internet of Things products in these spaces will find subscription more appealing to their consumers.

The so-called freemium model (a portmanteau of "free" and "premium") has always been a way to encourage paying customers while not alienating free ones. In this model, a smaller or larger part of your product is free, while the users are also encouraged to pay a premium to get additional features or remove limits. This model could be combined with our first two models: Buying the physical device gives free lifetime access to the associated Internet service, but additional paid services are also available.

CUSTOMISATION

We touched on the improvements to mass production whereby the process of buying a car can be tweaked to the buyer's requirements. For an Internet of Things device, at the intersection between solid thing and software, there are options for customisation that we believe may lead to new business models.

For a mass-produced item, any customisation must be strictly bounded to a defined menu: a selection of different colours for the paintwork, options for fittings such as tyres, the trimmings and upholstery inside, and for features like the onboard computer control and display. Fordian logic dictates that all these components must be optimised for manufacture and fit well together.

The world of software is, by contrast, pathologically malleable, if we let it be. Early websites explored the new medium of HTML to its garish extremes, with <blink> tags and animated .gif images. Yet today's equivalent of home pages, offered by incumbents such as Facebook, Twitter, and Pinterest, offer small degrees of customisation within strictly defined boundaries: a selection of (tasteful) colour schemes and a choice of image to use as your avatar.

Many Internet of Things products have some possibility of customisation: Every Bubblino has a name (given to it by Adrian), but the user can also change which phrases he listens to on Twitter. BERG's Little Printer offers a selection of content to be printed but also an option of which smiley face it will print for display while waiting for a new delivery. (Of course, only a limited number of choices are available currently.) Although printer output is as flexible as the software that feeds it, BERG has limited the options to fit into its product aesthetic.

The new manufacturing techniques, such as laser cutting and 3D printing, should allow great possibilities for customising even the physical devices. MakieLab (http://makie.me) make dolls that can be designed online. Built to your specification, they are therefore unique and entirely *yours* in a way that a mass-produced doll couldn't be. Whereas many of the components are indeed chosen from a limited list (wigs, tops, scarves), others are modified using a slider: the "attitude" and "ferocity" of the eyebrows, for example. One could argue that this is effectively the same superficial customisation we mentioned previously, except with a larger number of variables. Yet in some way, the combinatorial explosion of these numerous options *does* make the process of creating "your" Makie seem like a genuine personalization. The Makies are made using a combination of 3D printing, automation, and manual assembly. While a Makie may not be an Internet of Things device in its current iteration, it does already bridge the real and virtual worlds, making an online "avatar" real. In the future, such dolls will certainly cross the line and become Internet-connected devices. In the meantime, they are an interesting case study for new techniques that might be useful for your Internet of Things product, too.

BE A KEY RESOURCE

Not every Internet of Things business will be selling a product to the mass market. Some will sell components or expertise to other companies—that is, component manufacturing or consultancy services. Effectively, in this kind of business, you are positioning yourself as a "key resource" or a "partner" in somebody else's business model. These business models are perfectly valid. Small companies such as Adafruit and Oomlout sell electronic components to hobbyist makers. Manufacturers produce printed circuit boards (PCBs) and other custom electronics for the producers of gadgets such as Things. On the consultancy side, work will be available either simply providing your skills for hire or indeed in providing vision and expertise for strategic planning to a company that wants to engage with the Internet of Things.

These fairly straightforward supplier/consultant relationships make the point that enterprises will need to solve problems, just as consumers will. In this book, we have mostly looked at consumer products because they fit best with our notions of technology for humans and the Geocities of Things. However, the market for enterprise customers may be just as important. Sequoia Capital's Jim Goetz commented that he sees many more consumer startups come to him for funding, yet enterprise startups are significantly more likely to succeed: "It's shocking we don't see more engineers and entrepreneurs interested in enterprise" (www.businessinsider.com/ sequoia-capital-jim-goetz-on-enterprise-startups- 2012-9).

Environmental data consultancy amee (www.amee.com) provides means for not only consumers but also businesses and government bodies to improve their environmental impact by getting hard data about their carbon footprint—not just their direct energy usage but also the energy used to dispose of their waste. Although in many ways amee is a software Internet company, collating data about the carbon cost of various activities or products, its interest in environmental data makes it naturally interested in the Internet of Things also. The company has modelled a factory process for producing bags of coffee beans such that sensor data monitors the carbon cost of grinding and packing each bag in real time, and the final packaged product can be stamped with that data, to help consumers make an informed decision about their purchase.

PROVIDE INFRASTRUCTURE: SENSOR NETWORKS

Sensor data is a fascinating topic in the Internet of Things: Although there are official data sources, often very accurately calibrated and expensive to create, they may be hard to access and of course can exist only where a government body or company has chosen to apply its large but finite resources. The long tail of third-party data sensor enthusiasts can supplement or sometimes outclass the official streams of information. What is needed is a platform to aggregate that data, and one of the companies competing to fulfil that role is Xively (`https://xively.com`—formerly Pachube and Cosm). They allow any consumer to upload a real-time feed of sensor data—for example, radiation levels in Japan after the Fukushima Daiichi nuclear disaster—and for the data from many feeds to be mapped, graphed, and compared. Many of the Japanese engineers and enthusiasts who submitted this data used homemade, and calibrated, Geiger counters. Any one device might be of dubious accuracy, but once they were aggregated, real patterns emerged which a single official body would have struggled to discover.

Xively have, since the beginning, intended to provide a free, public infrastructure for open source data while also providing enhanced commercial offerings with enhanced capacity and privacy options and formal service level agreements (SLAs). While their provision of an Internet of Things "middleware" may be hard to monetize at time of this writing, becoming a major player in the infrastructure for the growing Internet of Things market is a huge potential prize. Xively sold in 2011 to LogMeIn for $15 million, with the new owners bankrolling the startup's estimated $1 million per quarter operating costs and negotiating collaborations with partners such as ARM (`http://readwrite.com/2011/07/20/pachube_acquired`).

Air Quality Egg, sponsored by Xively and funded via Kickstarter, is a project to create the same kind of sensor commons project via a standardised product (`http://airqualityegg.wikispaces.com/AirQuality Egg`). Although the Egg is an open source project, developed by a community beyond the project initiators, it also points a way for similar products which might combine a social intent with a commercial model. For this kind of project to succeed, Australian technologist Andrew Fisher proposes that it must

- Gain trust
- Become dispersible
- Be highly visible
- Be entirely open
- Be upgradeable

—http://ajfisher.me/2011/12/20/
towards-a-sensor-commons

There is no reason why a commercial product couldn't fulfil all these requirements, although we will certainly see companies embrace and extend the good intentions purely for profit. Sensor data is information, which can be shared freely or might simply be sold. Many energy suppliers are rolling out "smart meters", which promise greater efficiency and therefore cheaper bills but also aggregate huge quantities of information (especially when triangulated with other data sources). We look at the ethical questions raised by sensor data in Chapter 11. As regards the business model, you need to consider the legality of such collection (now and in the foreseeable future) and whether it fits with your company values.

TAKE A PERCENTAGE

In the example of sensor networks, if the value of the data gathered exceeds the cost of the physical sensor device, you might be able to provide that physical product for free. In fact, energy companies quite often do this with their smart meters. You could also link devices to advertising to reduce the price. Although this practice is controversial, many US consumers have chosen an ad-supported version of the Kindle e-Book reader to save the initial outlay.

As we suggested earlier, even without charging the *end user* of your Internet of Things device, there will be many options to make a profit from some-where (ad revenues, payment for data services from companies or state organisations, commission for data bandwidth incurred, etc.) Within the burgeoning field of the Internet of Things, exactly what the "product being sold" consists of is a field that remains to be explored. Perhaps future versions of Bubblino could also be triggered for occasional promoted tweets. Perhaps your Internet-enabled fridge will make tutting noises when you fill it and suggest other (promoted) options for your next shop.

FUNDING AN INTERNET OF THINGS STARTUP

As important as future costs and revenues are to a well-planned business model, there will most likely be a period when you have only costs and no income. The problem of how to get initial funding is a critical one, and looking at several options to deal with it is worthwhile.

If you have enough personal money to concentrate on your new Internet of Things startup full time without taking on extra work, you can, of course, fund your business yourself. Apart from the risk of throwing money into a personal project that has no realistic chance of success (which this chapter's aim is to avoid!), this would be a very fortunate situation to be in. And luckier still if you have the surplus money to bankroll costs for materials and staff.

If, like most of the rest of us, you aren't Bruce Wayne, never fear; there are still ways to kick off a project. If the initial stages don't require a huge investment of money, your time will be the main limiting factor. If you can't afford to work full time on your new project, perhaps you can spare a day in the weekend or several evenings after work. You might be able to arrange to work part time on your day job; even an extra afternoon or day might be enough to get things moving. Many people try to combine a startup with a consultancy business, planning to take short but lucrative contracts which support the following period of frantic startup work. Paul Graham advises some caution on this approach, as the easy money from consulting may be too much of a crutch and remove one of the primary motors for a startup, the fear of failure. In an acerbic footnote, he expands on this theme:

> *Consulting is where product companies go to die. IBM is the most famous example. So starting as a consulting company is like starting out in the grave and trying to work your way up into the world of the living.*
>
> —*Paul Graham (*`www.paulgraham.com/`
> `startupfunding.html`*)*

Making sure that you *don't* need to spend huge amounts on the startup is key. You probably don't need an office in the early stages, and perhaps you don't need expensive Aeron chairs. You can work from your kitchen table, a café, or out of a co-working space.

Everything we've discussed in the chapters on prototyping is designed to get a Minimum Viable Product out to show to people and start gathering interest. You can get surprisingly far with a cheap hosting account or a service for deploying apps in the cloud, such as Heroku, an Arduino Ethernet, some basic electronic components, some cardboard, and a knife. Until you get funding, you may be able to scale up your spending on any of these as and when you really need to.

HOBBY PROJECTS AND OPEN SOURCE

If your project is also your hobby, you may have no extra costs than what you would spend anyway on your free-time activity. This is perfectly valid, although if you are reading this chapter with an intent to turn your product into a successful business or community, you may wish to proceed at a less leisurely pace than a pure hobby might entail.

One way to make a project grow faster might be to release all the details as open source and try to foster a community around it. This approach can be hard work and can benefit from a natural talent, experience, or luck in attracting and maintaining good collaborators. After you have open-sourced a project, you can't close-source it again. Yes, you can probably fork the project and continue to work on it in secret, but the existing project may carry on if your collaborators are enthusiastic enough about it. Indeed, your idea, code, and schematics could be used by others in their own commercial offering. Careful consideration of the license used may be critical here: A more restrictive license such as the GPL requires those who build on your work to share their source code also under the same terms. Hence, using the GPL may help restrict commercial exploitation to only those groups that are happy for *you* to, in turn, reap the benefits of their work. Also, when thinking about open source, remember that as the project initiator and owner, you would be the best placed in forming a company around the project and are more likely to reap benefits from the relationship with the community:

- Many pairs of eyes and hands testing, reporting problems, fixing them, and building new features
- Many passionate users with real use cases and opinions about the product—better than any focus group
- The goodwill of that community, with its ready-made network of personal recommendations and social-media marketing

Running an open source project takes work, and the risk of losing control of your project may not be for everyone, but it is certainly an option to consider.

VENTURE CAPITAL

Of course, getting funding for a project from an external investor presents its own work and risks. The process of applying for funding takes time, and although much of this time can be justified as thrashing out the business model, it's not directly related to the work you actually want to be doing on the product itself. Startups often concentrate their fundraising activities into *rounds*, periods in which they dedicate much of their effort into raising a target amount of money, often for a defined step in their business plan.

Before any official funding round comes the informal idea of the *friends, family, and fools* (FFF) round. This stage may be the one in which you've contributed your life savings, and persuaded your aunt, your best friend, and a local small business to pitch in the rest, on the basis of your reputation. Although it's important to consider the possible impact on your personal relationships, this round of funding may be the most straightforward to get hold of.

A common next step would be an *angel* round. The so-called angels are usually individual investors, often entrepreneurs themselves, who are willing to fund some early-stage startups which a more formal investor (such as venture capitalists that we look at shortly) might not yet touch. The reason might be that these angels have a technical or business background in your product or simply that, as individual investors, they may have more scope to go with their own intuition about your worth. Angels typically disburse sums that are significant for early-stage startups—in the region of tens or possibly hundreds of thousands of pounds. However, the personal interest and experience that angels can bring to your company means that their advice, contacts, and other help may well be as useful as any money they provide. Though angels take on a lot of risk in investing so early, before companies have proved themselves, they tend to invest in a number of companies to spread the risk. They usually want equity in your company, a percentage of the value of the company, that will pay back their investment if and when you do well. These angels might also demand a place on your board of directors, to oversee their investment, but also out of interest in helping the company to succeed.

A good place to find an angel in the US could be AngelList, a long tail aggregator where investors can meet startups (`https://angel.co`).

The *venture capital* (VC) round is similar, but instead of your courting individual investors, the investor is a larger group with significant funds, whose sole purpose is to discover and fund new companies with a view to making significant profit. VCs may be interested if angels have already funded you and will certainly be interested if other VC companies are already looking at funding you. VCs will certainly want equity, probably a significant amount of it, and a position on your board of directors. Again, this last role may be as much to help fill gaps that your management team don't cover as much as it is to keep an eye on you and their money. Typically, VC funding will be larger chunks of money, from half a million pounds up.

> *If your idea is a good one, and one of your team has the time and temperament for it, there are opportunities to play the VCs against each other to get the best deal for you, as described in detail in* Venture Deals: Be Smarter Than Your Lawyer and Venture Capitalist, *by Brad Feld and Jason Mendelson (Wiley, 2012).*

A related option, especially in the early stages, would be an *accelerator*, which might be run by a venture capital firm. In this case, part or all of the money that could be awarded to your company is paid in kind, in the form of free office space, consultancy, and specific training and mentoring in areas that the investor believes will make you a success. Accelerators may accept applicants only at set points in time (like rounds of entry) or may accept good startups at any moment (given sufficient capacity). The fact of being collocated in an incubator with other smart new companies may be of great benefit, and the training and contacts you gain could well be valuable.

Current accelerators that may be specialized in the Internet of Things, or cover the field as part of their area of interest, include

- HAXLR8R (`http://haxlr8r.com/program/hack-what`)
- PCH Accelerator (`www.pchintl.com/accelerator/accelerator.aspx`)
- Berlin Hardware Accelerator (`http://www.berlinhardwareaccelerator.com/`)
- Bolt (`http://www.bolt.io`)
- Lemnos Labs (`http://lemnoslabs.com`)

At the time of this writing, more accelerators operate in the US, but the concept is spreading in the UK, Europe, and elsewhere. Every scheme is different, and some are more valuable than others in the quality of their accommodation, mentoring, neighbouring startups, and so on. You would benefit from checking out each scheme and getting recent testimonials about it to make sure it's something that will work for you.

Y Combinator (`http://ycombinator.com`) is also an accelerator, and its founder, Paul Graham, welcomes hardware startups and talks of a "Hardware Renaissance":

There is no one single force driving this trend. Hardware does well on crowdfunding sites. The spread of tablets makes it possible to build new things controlled by and even incorporating them. Electric motors have improved. Wireless connectivity of various types can now be taken for granted. It's getting more straightforward to get things manufactured.

Arduinos, 3D printing, laser cutters, and more accessible CNC milling are making hardware easier to prototype. Retailers are less of a bottleneck as customers increasingly buy online.

—http://paulgraham.com/hw.html

Even though funding may sound like "free money", we've already seen that getting investment comes with conditions: equity and some measure of control via your board of directors. The trade-off is obvious: You couldn't get the money to grow your business otherwise. Even if losing some control in the company is heart-wrenching, a smaller percentage of a valuable company will be worth more than a large percentage of nothing.

We've seen some of the considerations in funding. In addition, you need to be aware that by accepting investment through venture capital, you are committing yourself to an *exit*. An exit strategy is a "method by which a venture capitalist or business owner intends to get out of an investment that he or she has made" (www.investopedia.com/terms/e/exit strategy.asp). Because your investors will want a return, your long-term goal can't just be to make your company successful but to do it in such a way as to pay back the investment. Typically, you have only two exits:

- **You get bought by a bigger company:** In this case, the buyer buys out the investors; that is, the buyer pays the investors the value of their percentage equity of their perceived valuation of the worth of the company.

  Founding members of the company often transfer to the purchasing company, as they constitute one of the company's principal resources. To keep them motivated in working for the new business now that they're no longer in control, they typically are paid a part of their payout in shares; it is "vested" over a certain period (for example, that can be redeemed only after a year's service).

- **You do an IPO (initial public offering)—that is, float on the stock market:** This involves new shares being issued and sold to the stock market. Although this option "dilutes" the value of the shares already issued, the existing holders are able to then sell their shares on the market too, to get back their investment, or to retain the shares if they believe that the shares will grow in value.

Although an IPO is also a good way for the company to raise further money, being on the stock market does mean that you have new commitments: quarterly reports, voting rights for new shareholders, and a duty to be seen to be doing something when the market periodically reassesses your share value.

Obviously, neither of these common exits provides any place for alternative business models, such as cooperatives, or worker-owned capitalist corporations such as John Lewis in the UK. These are perhaps so far outside the standard discourse of contemporary trade that they can exist only if everyone with a share of financial interest agrees in the alternative ideal.

GOVERNMENT FUNDING

Governments typically want to promote industry and technological development in their country, and they may provide funds to help achieve particular aims. Attempting to cover the variety of funding schemes across the whole world would be a project in itself, so we make some mostly general notes based in many cases on the current situation in the UK.

Although governments can and do set up their own venture capital funds or collaborate with existing funds in various ways, they generally manage the majority of their funds differently. For one thing, they also want to fund *existing* companies to do new research and innovation, which might sit uncomfortably with the concept of equity.

The money provided still has "strings attached", but they are likely to be handled differently:

- **Outputs:** Deliverables (aka outputs) are the metrics that an awarding body may use to tell if you are doing the kind of thing that the body wants to fund. This metric may simply be a test that you are managing the money well or may be related to the goals that the body itself wishes to promote. You might be required to write regular reports or pass certain defined milestones on schedule. If your funding is given in stages, the later payments may be conditional on successful delivery of previous outputs. You should be very clear on what needs to be done and how onerous the task is. Even a large sum of money is worth less if you are going to spend significant amounts of time on secondary activities.

  You may be required to *match funds*; that is, if you were awarded £10,000, you would also have to raise £10,000 yourself. Certain UK bodies such as the Technology Strategy Board (TSB) currently operate in this way. It is important to understand the way this matching works.

For example, you may be required to make payments with your matched funds first and then reclaim the amount spent in arrears. If the awarding agency pays these funds irregularly—for example, quarterly—you may be left without money at key moments. You therefore need to understand the process, as it may require additional fundraising, cashflow management, or resources spent begging for money from your awarding body. (This requirement makes perfect sense for large companies that are willing to invest some of their cash reserves in research if the government will match the funds. It is less well suited to funding startups on a shoestring budget.)

- **Spending constraints:** Some funding may require you to spend a proportion of the money on, for example, business consultancy or web development, perhaps with the fund facilitator's company or associates. This requirement may be highly valuable, of course, but the practice appears slightly misleading; it would be better to clarify this as a funding "in kind" rather than cash. If you are running a shoestring startup, you would probably source the service at a much lower cost. You also must consider the time and management overhead in making use of the (possibly unwanted) service. Make sure you understand what expectations the funding comes with upfront!

After having looked at the "rounds" of funding for venture capital, you might be interested to see where government funding fits into the scheme of things. Funding may well cover feasibility studies, research and development, and possibly production rounds designed to help bring a prototype idea into production. From the point of view of a maker or hacker, "feasibility" and "research" may seem superfluous. That's something you do as a matter of course; it's often the next step, of taking the prototype into production, that you could use help with. Governments will, however, try to split their pot of money to fund the outcomes that they are interested in as policy. Quite reasonably, this may tend to favour grants for research over grants to help get to market. After all, after the product is proven, the company should be able to afford to fund it by itself or get VC funding.

It is perfectly normal for companies to work through multiple sources of funding. Having successfully worked through a government innovation award may stand you in good stead for approaching VCs for more money later, for example.

CROWDFUNDING

We've already looked at the long tail as a business model; we can think of crowdfunding as the long tail of funding projects. Getting many people to contribute to a project isn't exactly a new phenomenon. Walter Gervaise built the first stone bridge over the River Exe in 1238 through public subscription by approaching friends and other wealthy citizens (`www.exeter.gov.uk/index.aspx?articleid=2879`). Earlier, after 27 BC, Augustus Caesar sponsored a public subscription for a statue of his physician Antonius Musa (`www.gutenberg.org/files/21325/21325-h/21325-h.htm`). Over millennia many civic and religious monuments and constructions have been funded at least partly by the public. However, such projects have been mostly sponsored and given focus by some influential person or body. With the efficiencies of the Internet's long tail, people can seek funding to print limited editions of their latest comic book, CDs of vocal-only covers of every song by the Smiths (`http://thesmithsproject.blogspot.co.uk`), or perhaps your exciting new Internet of Things product.

As of 2013, the main options for crowdfunding are Kickstarter (`www.kickstarter.com`) and Indiegogo (`www.indiegogo.com`). Historically, Kickstarter was available to use only for funding projects based in the US, whereas Indiegogo set itself up to be "the world's funding platform". Now Kickstarter is available also for UK projects. If you are based in a country not covered by this organization, you might consider Indiegogo. The alternative would be to find a core collaborator in the US or UK, but this, of course, brings on more communication and organizational overhead.

Kickstarter currently has somewhat better traction than Indiegogo. More people have heard of it, and this may make it more likely that people will fund you. Indiegogo is open to all types of projects, including community and charitable ones, whereas Kickstarter is only for those creative projects that end up with a product, be it artistic or technological. With the greater restrictions set by Kickstarter, it is not surprising that there is an application process required to create a project. Not all projects are approved. Indiegogo plays much less of a gatekeeper role, allowing you to start promoting your project immediately without an approval process.

Although a government fund might look favourably at you if you make your application in terms of the outputs it is meant to be supporting, and a VC may wish to know that your business model is sound and the team are competent, the elements that make a crowdfunded project a hit may be harder to determine. A great concept is still important. Appealing text, slick videos, and great design may make the difference between yours and a competing project. Because even some successfully funded projects may fail, older and wiser crowdfunders may be more likely to fund projects in which they see some attention to the business model or a track record for successful completion by the project team.

In short, your funders are real people and will have all the variety of concerns and foibles that any group of real people have. This interaction with a large and diverse group is a key part of the interest of this method of funding: It is far more than just the money. We've already looked at how the long tail allows consumers with all manner of niche interests to find the producers who are interested in satisfying those niches. Crowdsourcing allows you to do this before even investing your time and money in the product! Assuming that the aggregators (Kickstarter, Indiegogo, and the rest) are doing their job well, they will reach a good segment of the potential customers for your Internet of Things product. If there is no interest, perhaps the product is not a winner as currently specified and advertised. If the project goes viral, as happens occasionally, and gains far more than the targeted amount, you know you have a potential hit on your hands. Just as receiving funding from VCs might be valuable as much for the mentoring and networking opportunities, so crowdfunding may be as valuable for the market research and viral marketing as for the money raised.

LEAN STARTUPS

We've looked at the advantages of running a startup on a low budget. The mentality needed to do this includes spending time and money only when it's really necessary—staying hungry and *lean*. The concept of a "lean startup," pioneered by Silicon Valley entrepreneur Eric Ries, springs from this idea (*The Lean Startup: How Today's Entrepreneurs Use Continuous Innovation to Create Radically Successful Businesses*, Crown Business, 2011). The option in the preceding section of crowdfunding a project presented an even more appealing step on this route: running the project only *if* there is a demonstrable niche market for it.

Many lean proponents suggest setting up a landing page for a project with a simple form to register interest. This is quick and simple to do, especially as numerous startups do exactly this (unbounce.com, landerapp.com, and others). These simple pages allow you to propose many projects and focus only on the ones that have most feedback. However, if you've already done some prototyping work and have a good feeling about a single idea, taking things a step further and creating a project on a crowdfunding site may be even more appropriate. Doing so represents more work than creating a simple form, but you will learn far more from it!

In many ways, this "laziness"—doing the minimum now and putting off the hard work till later—is also the reason that we have split the *prototype* from the final product. There is a time to market your project, a time to ensure that the idea works, and a time to build a sellable product. If you are thinking "lean", you should be applying this idea at all stages. For example, at the first stages of production and marketing, you should be working towards the "Minimum Viable Product". This is still a sellable product rather than a prototype, but with all extraneous features removed, it may *feel* like a prototype of your final vision for the product. All the initial efforts are towards making this product because it can be sold. If you have time and money afterward to add additional enhancements to the product, service, packaging, and so on, this will add more value. But adding those enhancements to an incomplete prototype would not result in a working business model.

The essence, then, of lean is to be able to iterate, performing the tasks that are required to get things moving at this stage, without investing time upfront to make everything perfect. The fact that your business model is a *hypothesis* and not set in stone can encourage you to tweak it in response to the feedback you get from iterating your product in the real world. Such tweaks are known as *pivots* and usually work by changing one part of your model—think one of the boxes on the Business Model Canvas. For instance:

- **Zoom-in pivot:** Focus on what was only a part of the value proposition, and turn that into the whole Minimum Viable Product.
- **Customer segment pivot:** Realise that the people who will actually buy your product aren't the ones you were originally targeting. While you can continue to make exactly the same product, you have been marketing it to the wrong people.
- **Technology pivot:** Accomplish the same goals as before, but change the implementation details. While prototyping will almost certainly involve many changes in technology while you establish the best way to make the product from an engineering perspective, this pivot would be a business decision, made to improve manufacturing costs, speed, or quality.

Ries's book goes into much greater detail on the different types of pivot and how best to apply them.

SUMMARY

A business model is a hypothesis about how to run a project well, for commercial profit or some other success criteria, to develop a product that solves problems for a specific group of users. Throughout history, people have invented new ways of doing business; new technology is the factor that is most likely to bring about entirely new models. Faced with the certainty that the Internet of Things, as a technological paradigm shift, will facilitate entirely unexpected new business models, it is increasingly important that you analyse, discuss, and iterate your own model. It is, after all, only a hypothesis and can be changed in the face of the existing evidence. This is one of the important factors of the "lean" approach.

In the fast-moving, competitive, and increasingly business- as well as tech-savvy world of the Internet, it is vital to be able to show your business model to potential investors, partners, and customers. The Business Model Canvas is one useful set of shared categories and terminology that may facilitate your communication and discussion with these groups. This is important because if you are planning to scale up your project into a product, making your vision a reality will rely on their involvement. We looked in particular at investment, from friends and family to angels, government funds, venture capital, and accelerators.

Of course, you need more than funds to create a product. In the next chapter we look at the challenges involved in moving from the project prototype to manufacturing it for a wider market.

10 MOVING TO MANUFACTURE

SO, YOU'VE BUILT an initial prototype and shown it to a few friends (or the rest of the Internet), to wild acclaim. One of the most frequent questions they ask is "Can I get one?", and you start to wonder whether you have the beginnings of a new product on your hands.

Having read Chapter 9, "Business Models", you have some ideas on how to avoid going broke and, we hope, even make a profit on the venture. However, before you launch that Kickstarter campaign, you should consider a number of other issues.

How many devices are you looking to sell? Even if you're just going to make a few in your spare time, what would happen if your idea turns out to be a huge hit and you have half the Internet beating a path to your order page? It's a nice problem to have, but if your costings expect your labour to be free because you enjoy soldering up a few boards, you might need to rework those costs more realistically. Either that or you will soon find out just how much you enjoy soldering boards when you're doing it all day every day to meet demand.

If you don't want to make each item by hand, you will need to find someone who can do the job for you. Hiring out work is an extra cost, naturally, but at the same time you'll usually be buying the components in greater bulk, which will be cheaper, so things often balance out. If you are making enough, the economies of scale of automation kick in, which means you can either lower your prices or increase your profits—or, ideally, both.

Then there are the less obvious things. Will you need to design some packaging so that the products aren't damaged during shipping or to make them appealing when sat on a shelf alongside a host of other gadgets? And what about certification? If you're selling the product in the United States, the Federal Communications Commission (FCC) will want to make sure it is safe and won't be throwing out a lot of unwanted electromagnetic interference. In Europe, you'll need to meet similar requirements to use the CE mark, and there are additional regulations such as the Restriction of Hazardous Substances (RoHS), a directive which bans the sale of products containing certain substances (such as lead and cadmium) above given levels.

In this chapter we dig into both the obvious and the less obvious steps in turning your prototype into a finished product.

WHAT ARE YOU PRODUCING?

Before we get into the specifics of *how* to scale up production of your device, it's useful to pause for a moment and consider *what* exactly you'll be producing.

Depending on your motives and desires for the product, not to mention the amount of time and money that you have available to devote to it, a full spectrum of possibilities is open to you.

If your ambition is just to enable others to build a version of it for themselves, you only need to document the build process and share it, along with any source code and design files you used, on the Internet—either on your own blog or website, or on a site like Instructables (`www.instructables.com`). Aside from maybe a bit of promotion on sites such as Make (`http://makezine.com`) or Hack-a-Day (`http://hackaday.com`) to help people find it, you are basically done.

A huge maker community on- and offline share their projects and experience this way. Joining in is a great way to meet fellow makers and to give something back to the community if they helped you get started. You might find that you become the go-to person for that sort of project, and people might commission you to build related projects for them or want to hire you to work in their company. A well-put-together project can serve as the best CV around.

When you decide that you want to get your invention into the hands of many more people (and hopefully make some money along the way), you can generally split your choices into three categories:

- A kit that your customers can assemble themselves
- A ready-made electronics board which users can use as a sub-assembly in their own projects
- A fully fledged product, complete with its housing, instructions, and even packaging, just waiting to be put on the shelf at your local department store

Each of these options builds on a lot of the work you would already have done for the previous one. A complete device will contain an assembled electronics board, and the electronics board would need a printed circuit board (PCB), much like the one users would need to solder components to in a kit.

We make use of this progression to introduce the different aspects of manufacturing in this chapter. While the section on PCBs focuses on kits, it is equally relevant if you want to take things further; and you will need the section on PCB assembly for both assembled boards and finished products.

DESIGNING KITS

The first step towards selling your idea as a product is to provide it as a kit. Although you might think it is simple to order the relevant parts and then lay them out to follow your schematic, you are likely to be underestimating how much you have learned in working out how to make it. For every person like yourself who gets to the end of building something, there are many more who would have given up halfway through or found it too daunting to even start. Many of those people would jump at the chance to buy a kit in which someone else has done the hard (to them) part of selecting and sourcing the right components and putting them together with a step-by-step guide.

Most kits tend to provide only the electronics and software for a particular application rather than any physical housing. The reason partly comes down to the difficulty, for a cottage kit-building industry, of sourcing custom plastic components. Also, because the main market for such kits is others in the maker community, these makers will perhaps prefer to combine the kit into a project of their own. However, with the growing accessibility of 3D printers and laser-cutters, it is becoming vastly more feasible to provide housing and other physical components even for kits.

Kits tend to piggyback on existing microcontrollers and often take the form of a standard format plug-on board—for example, a *shield* in the Arduino ecosystem or a *cape* on the BeagleBone. This makes sense because it reduces the support overhead for the kit provider; either users will already be familiar with the platform, or, if not, plenty of assistance will be available elsewhere to cover the basics of getting up and running. The kit's documentation can then focus on just what is specific to building the project.

Given that you've built your prototype, you've already done most of the work needed to create a kit. You've worked out which components you need, where to source them, and how to wire them up to create a functioning circuit. And you've written the necessary software to interface to and control the electronics. The parts you might not have done include designing a PCB, documenting the build process, and working out the costs.

If you haven't been building electronics for long, designing a PCB is likely to involve a number of new terms and concepts. Similarly, you can make the PCBs a few different ways after they are designed. As a result, we look at both designing PCBs and making them in more detail later in the chapter.

Documenting the build process isn't too tricky. When you have everything together for one of your kits, run through assembling one of them yourself. As you go, take photos or video of each step and write down the order of each step. The Instructables website (`www.instructables.com`) has a number of guides to help out, and another good approach is to copy the procedures used by other kit makers that you've found useful. For example, we like the tutorials that Adafruit put together for each of its products; the Adafruit Motor Shield for Arduino is typical (`http://learn.ada fruit.com/adafruit-motor-shield`).

Working out what price to charge is harder and more of an art form than a science. Some rules of thumb can help, though. The most obvious is to understand what your costs are. You should create a spreadsheet (or at least a list) of all the items that make up your product, along with their cost to you to buy. You should list every single electronic component, connector, cable, PCB, case, and so on, in addition to the packing box you'll ship it in and the time taken to put things together. This list is called the *bill of materials* (BOM), and it forms the starting point for all your costings and prices.

The BOM gives you the marginal cost for your product—that is, how much extra it would cost to make an additional item when you're up and running with production. It doesn't include any of the fixed costs in setting up for production or developing the software, as they'll be spread out across all the items you sell. You still need to set your prices so that they also cover the fixed costs, but they're harder to specify on a per-item basis, as that will depend on how many you sell.

A good starting point for working out your price (how much you will charge consumers) is to take the total cost of the BOM and multiply it by 4 or 5. That calculation gives you a margin to cover that item's portion of the fixed costs and also some profit. It also provides enough margin for resellers to cover *their* fixed costs and make some profit. This means that if you end up with a hit on your hands, you can enlist some intermediaries to help scale up distribution without losing money on each kit you sell.

Assuming that you want to sell many of your kits, the most important cost to drive down is that of the BOM. That will give you the most flexibility in setting your price so that you can maximise the profits that you make.

Now that you know how much it will cost to make your kit and how much margin to build in, you can think about the price. How much you can charge will depend on how much demand there is for your product. However, by looking at the prices of similar products, you can get a flavour of the market and use that to guide your pricing. You don't need to necessarily find products which solve the same problem; you can also look at ones that are delivered in a similar form. For example, if your kit is a shield for Arduino, you can compare prices of other shield kits to get a feel for the range of prices that people expect to pay.

Because the customer is responsible for assembling and soldering the kit together, usually the only thing you'll need to get custom made just for your application is the bare PCB. That tends to keep your costs down, as you're offloading the labour required to build the circuit to the kit's user. For the target demographic for a kit, the need for assembly can be seen as a benefit because it adds to the sense of achievement and ownership in getting the kit working. However, it can also add to the support overhead, because you will need to deal with remotely debugging your customers' issues, which may be down to their poor soldering rather than defects in your work.

These problems can all be resolved by moving on a step towards a consumer product and selling fully assembled PCBs, populated with all the components. If you aren't selling too many and your design doesn't include any especially fine-pitched or complicated surface-mount components, you might decide to assemble them yourself; otherwise, you'll need to find an assembly house to do the work on your behalf. Either option will also benefit from your working out a way for you to test the finished board, checking that the components are soldered in properly and, ideally, that they function correctly.

Obviously, the final step from kit to consumer product is to manufacture and assemble the housings, linkages, and whatever else is part of the finished device. As this incorporates the assembled PCBs and adds more components or processes, we use that progression to guide the rest of this chapter.

DESIGNING PRINTED CIRCUIT BOARDS

Now you've got your nice prototype made, or maybe your fifth or fiftieth or five-hundredth prototype made, and you're working out what the next step is. Maybe your final prototype is still a bundle of components and wires plugged into a number of breadboards, or you might have gone one step further and soldered it up onto protoboard or stripboard, as we saw in Chapter 5.

Soldering things up is a good step towards making your prototype more robust, because the connections should, if your soldering skills are up to par, mean that you have a solid electrical connection that won't shake loose. After you've done this, you should have something that will survive being given to an end user, unlike a breadboarded prototype which you have to handle with kid gloves. So that means you can just repeat that process for each item you're building, right?

Well, you could, but you will soon get fed up with soldering each item by hand. Now might be a good time to start recruiting a whole army of people ready to solder things up.

There's a relatively natural progression to making more professional PCBs.

Moving beyond stripboard, designing and etching your own custom PCBs gives you more options on how to lay out the circuit and makes it easier to solder up as the only holes in the board will be those for components. It also lets you use components that don't easily fit into the stripboard grid pattern of holes, including some of the simpler surface-mount components.

While a big step forwards, homemade boards will still lack that fully professional finish. That's because they won't have the green solder mask or silkscreen layers that a PCB manufacturer will give you. Moving to professionally manufactured boards further simplifies the assembly process because the solder mask will make the soldering a bit easier, and, more importantly, the silkscreen provides outlines of where each component should be placed.

If you are doing the PCB assembly or selling the PCBs as part of a kit, you will stick almost exclusively to through-hole components, as they are the easiest for the beginner to solder. You might get away with the occasional surface-mount item, but only if the leads aren't too fine or closely spaced.

Other concerns effectively force you to move to a custom PCB: if the routing of connections between components is particularly complex, only a multi-layer PCB will let you cross connections; if any of your components are available only in surface-mount packages, a custom PCB will let you place them without resorting to additional breakout boards; and if you've been using an off-the-shelf microcontroller board (such as an Arduino or a BeagleBone) to provide the processor, and so on, a custom PCB will give you the option of merging that onto your circuit board, removing the need for connectors between the boards and letting you discard any unused components from the off-the-shelf board, thus saving both space on the PCB and the cost of the parts.

The range of options for building a custom PCB runs from etching (or milling) boards yourself, through using one of the many mail-order batch PCB services, to having them made and populated for you. Whichever of those options you choose, the first step in creating your PCB is going to involve designing it. Before we investigate the available software for PCB design, we should look at what makes up a PCB and some of the terms you are likely to encounter.

The PCB is made up of a number of layers of fibreglass and copper, sandwiched together into the board. The fibreglass provides the main basis for the board but also acts as an insulator between the different layers of copper, and the copper forms the "wires" to connect the components in the circuit together.

Given that you won't want to connect all the components to each other at the same time, which would happen if you had a solid plate of copper across the whole board, sections of the copper are etched away—usually chemically, but it is possible to use a CNC mill for simple boards. These remaining copper routes are called *tracks* or *traces* and make the required connections between the components.

The points on the tracks where they join the leg of a component are known as *pads*. For surface-mount components, they are just an area of copper on the top or bottom of the board, which provides the place for the component to be soldered. For through-hole connections, they also have a hole drilled through the board for the leg to poke through.

Single-sided boards have only one layer of copper, usually on the bottom of the board; because they're often for home-made circuits with through-hole components, the components go on the top with their legs poking through the board and soldered on the underside. Double-sided boards, predictably, have two layers of copper: one on the top and one on the bottom. More complicated circuits, particularly as you start to use more advanced processors which come in smaller packages, may need even more layers to allow room to route all the traces round to where they are needed. Three- or five-layer boards aren't uncommon, and even some seven-layer boards are used for really complicated circuits.

When you get beyond two layers, you run out of surfaces on the board to place the copper layer. Additional layers require a more complex manufacturing procedure in which alternating layers of copper and fibreglass are built up, a bit like you would make a sandwich.

This means that the middle layers are embedded inside the circuit board and so don't have an accessible area of copper for the pad. Making a connection to one of these layers for through-hole components is easy because the hole that the leg goes through pierces each layer. When the holes drilled through the board are *plated*—a process in which the walls of the holes are coated in a thin layer of copper—any layers with copper at that point are connected together.

When you need to connect traces on two layers together at a point where there isn't a hole for the leg of a component, you use a *via*. This is a similar, though generally smaller, hole through the board purely to connect different layers of copper once plated. You also can use blind vias, which don't pierce all the way through the board, when you don't want to connect every layer together; however, because of this, they complicate the PCB manufacturing process and are best avoided unless absolutely necessary.

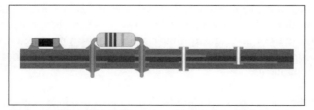

PCB features (left to right): surface-mount component; through-hole component; via; blind via.

In places where you have many connections to a common point, rather than run lots of tracks across the circuit, you can more easily devote most of a layer of the board to that connection and just leave it as a filled area of copper. This is known as a *plane* rather than a trace and is frequently used to provide a route to ground. An added advantage of this approach is that the ground plane provides a way to "catch" some of the stray electromagnetic signals that can result, particularly from high-frequency signal lines. This reduces the amount of electromagnetic interference (EMI) given out by the circuit, which helps prevent problems with other parts of the circuit or with other nearby electronic devices.

The surfaces of professionally manufactured PCBs undergo processes to apply two other finishes which make them easier to use.

First, all the parts of the board and bare copper which aren't the places where component legs need to be soldered are covered in solder mask. Solder mask is most commonly green, giving the traditional colour of most circuit boards, though other colours are also available. The mask provides a solder-resistant area, encouraging the solder to flow away from those areas and to adhere instead to the places where it is needed to connect the components to the tracks. This reduces the likelihood of a solder joint accidentally bridging across two points in the circuit where it shouldn't.

Then, on top of the solder mask is the silkscreen. This is a surface finish of paint applied, as the name suggests, via silkscreen printing. It is used to mark out where the components go and label the positions for easy identification of parts. It generally also includes details such as the company or person who designed the board, a name or label to describe what it is for, and the date of manufacture or revision number of the design. This last piece of information is vital; it is more likely than not that you'll end up with a few iterations of the circuit design as you flush out bugs. Being able to tell one version from the other among the boards on your workbench, or, more importantly, knowing exactly which design is in a product with a user-reported fault, is essential.

SOFTWARE CHOICES

As you might expect, you have many different choices when looking for some software to help you design your PCB. If you are working with a contract electronics design house, the staff may well use something like Altium Designer (`www.altium.com/en/products/altium-designer`), but you're more likely to use one of the following lower-end (and cheaper) options.

Fritzing (`http://fritzing.org`) is a free, open source design package aimed particularly at beginners in PCB design. It deliberately starts with a design screen resembling a breadboard and lets you map out your circuit by copying whatever you have prototyped in real life. It then converts that design to a schematic circuit diagram and lets you arrange components and route the traces on the PCB view.

When you are happy with your design, you can export it for manufacture as a PCB. Fritzing even offers a fabrication service to make it simple to make your design a reality.

You also can export the breadboard design view as an image or a PDF, which has led to Fritzing becoming very popular for people documenting their projects. Even if you don't go as far as designing a PCB, one of the easiest ways to show people how everything is wired up on a breadboard to copy themselves is to re-create your circuit in Fritzing and save the result as an image or PDF.

KiCad (`www.kicad-pcb.org`) is another open source offering but with a more traditional workflow. It has a more comprehensive library of predefined parts and can be used to design boards with up to 16 layers of copper, compared to the double-sided boards that Fritzing produces.

Adrian used KiCad to design the Bubblino PCB shown in the "Journey to a Circuit Board" sidebar in Chapter 5. And in common with the two commercial offerings mentioned next, one of the more recent feature additions has been to see a three-dimensional view of the design. In addition to letting you see what the finished board will look like, it also enables you to export the 3D model. Doing so enables you to import it into your CAD software when designing the enclosure to ensure that the relevant clearances are allowed for all the components.

Probably the most popular PCB layout software for the hobbyist and semi-professional market is EAGLE from CadSoft (`www.cadsoftusa.com/eagle-pcb-design-software/`). The reason for its popularity most likely comes down to its long having a free version for noncommercial use, allowing beginners to get started. That led to a wealth of how-to guides and other helpful resources for EAGLE being developed and shared by the user community. So EAGLE is a good choice to learn PCB design, although in addition to its noncommercial licence, the free version is also restricted to two layers and a maximum board size of 100mm × 80mm.

A more recent rival to EAGLE in the commercial pro-sumer market is DesignSpark PCB (`http://designspark.com/page/designspark-pcb-home-page`). It is provided by electronics distributor RS Components as part of the company's DesignSpark community and, as a result, is free of charge. Unlike EAGLE, DesignSpark PCB does not restrict the size of boards you can design (up to 1m2) or the number of layers (it supports up to 14 layers). However, it is the only program described here which isn't available for Linux or Mac. Compatibility is an issue which RS Components acknowledges and does endeavour to ensure that it works under the Windows compatibility layers Wine on Linux and CrossOver for Mac; however, in practice it's a little clunky.

THE DESIGN PROCESS

Regardless of the exact program you decide to use to lay out your PCB, your task in creating the design is split between two main views: the schematic and the board.

The Schematic

You usually start the design in the schematic view. It lets you lay out the components logically and make the necessary connections without having to worry about exactly where they'll sit in physical space or whether any of the tracks cross.

In the same way that the London Underground map provides an easier-to-grasp understanding of how the stations and lines relate to each other by abandoning the strict layout of their physical geography, the schematic provides a conceptual view of how the circuit is laid out. Components are represented by their standardised symbols, and you usually group them into areas of common functionality instead, which won't necessarily match the groupings they'll have in the physical layout.

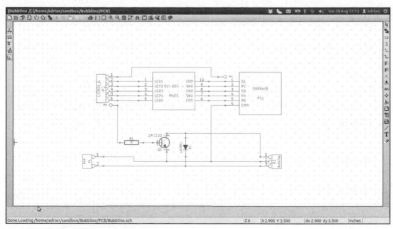

The schematic view of the Bubblino PCB, as designed in KiCad.

Your software package includes most of the common items you need in its library: common resistors, diodes, capacitors, transistors, integrated circuits (ICs), and more. Adding one of those is merely a case of finding the relevant part and sometimes adding the exact part number. For example, with a resistor, you specify its resistance and possibly its tolerance value.

You should also make sure you choose the correct *package* for the component; this is the physical format for it. Many parts are available in a range of different formats, depending on the target application. The manufacturer's datasheet lists the available packages for that part and how they differ. You usually have a choice of packages depending on the soldering style (through-hole or surface-mount) and several other criteria. Over time you will come to recognise some of the package types that you commonly use, so you'll know without checking that a TO-92 is a semi-circular three-pin through-hole package typically used for transistors, or that DIP-16 is a 16-pin through-hole package for ICs arranged in two rows of 8, while SOIC-16 is a similarly arranged surface-mount IC package.

The choice of package doesn't actually affect the schematic because at this point you are interested only in the functionality of the component rather than its physical attributes. However, making the right choices when initially choosing the component will save you having to rework that down the line when you come to the board view.

It's not uncommon to find that you want to use a part which isn't included in your PCB software's component library. If you're lucky, you might find that someone else has provided it in a third-party library. This is particularly common in the case of EAGLE PCB, its popularity within the open hardware movement having led to people sharing parts that they've used. Otherwise, you'll have to design your own. Creating the design is not difficult because all the information you need is in the datasheet, but attention to detail here will pay dividends with how well the part sits on the finished PCB.

When you are happy with the schematic design of your board, you can proceed to laying out the physical board. Although it makes sense to approach the PCB design in this manner, it is not a rigid procedure. You can flip back and forth between the two views of the design, but finishing the schematic as best you can before moving to the physical aspect will minimise the amount of rework you'll have to perform if the design changes.

The Board

There are no hard-and-fast rules on how to arrange the board. It makes sense to keep together groups of components that constitute an area of functionality, such as the power supply, for a more logical layout. And you might find the design has certain fixed aspects—things such as connectors which all need to be along one side for access once in a case, for example, or arrangements of headers to mate with an Arduino board. After that, it's just a case of arranging components in a way that makes the routing of wires easiest. Start by placing the components which have the most connections first and then fitting the remainder around those constraints.

As you move the components around, you may notice a criss-crossing of fine lines joining some of them together, which seem as messy as cheese strings trailing from a slice of pizza. These connections join the various pads on the components to each other. As you position the components, you should try to reduce how tangled they are (rotating or moving them around for the best combination), but don't worry about this issue excessively; you're just aiming for a good starting point for the work of routing the connections properly.

The thin, straight-line connections from point-to-point are known as *air wires*. They show where the connections need to be made but won't appear in the finished PCB design until you turn them into real tracks on the PCB.

Each one needs to be turned into a track on the PCB and routed round the board so that it makes the connection without crossing any of the other tracks or running too close to the pads of other components. If two tracks or a track and a component pad are too close, there's a chance that imperfections in the manufacturing process will result in a connection being made where it shouldn't. By finding enough room for the tracks and stopping them from crossing, you can make the different layers of the PCB come into play. Placing tracks on different layers of the board means that they won't make electrical contact when they cross, and for more complex designs you might run one track on one layer for part of its path and switch it to another layer with a via to continue the rest of its route.

Your PCB software has an auto-route function, which you can use to route all the tracks for you. However, such functions are far from perfect, and in practice, you will find it best to at least lay out the more important tracks first by hand, if not to do all the routing manually.

After all the tracks have been routed, your PCB design is almost finished. You should add any labels to the silkscreen layer to explain things such as nonobvious connectors and to identify the board itself. Also include a version number so that you can differentiate any future revisions, and also add maybe your name or the company name and a website for people to find out more.

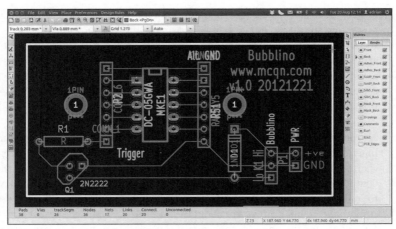

The finished view of the Bubblino PCB board, ready for export.

Then give your PCB a final once-over. Run the design rules check to catch any missed connections or problems where tracks are too close to each other or too thin for your PCB manufacturer to reliably manufacture. The design rules effectively contain the manufacturing tolerances for your PCB manufacturer. They define things like the minimum track width or the minimum distance between pads. Then print out a copy on paper; this way, you can compare the components to their location on the PCB in real life and spot any errors in their footprints.

After you fix any issues thrown up by those last checks, you're ready to make the PCBs.

MANUFACTURING PRINTED CIRCUIT BOARDS

Now that you've designed your PCB, the next step is to make one or lots of them. If you want only a couple of boards, or you would like to test a couple of boards (a very wise move) before ordering a few hundred or a few thousand, you may decide to make them in-house.

ETCHING BOARDS

The most common PCB-making technique for home use is to etch the board. Some readily available kits provide all you need.

The first step is to get the PCB design onto the board to be etched. This process generally involves printing out the design from your PCB design software onto a stencil. If you're using photo-resist board, it will be onto a stencil which masks off the relevant areas when you expose it to UV light; or if you're using the toner-transfer method, it will be for your laser printer to print onto glossy paper ready to transfer.

Your stencil then needs to be transferred to the board. For photo-resist board, you will expose it under a bright lamp for a few minutes; and for the toner-transfer method, you'll use a super-hot iron.

With the board suitably prepared, you can immerse it into the etching solution, where its acidic make-up eats away the exposed copper, leaving the tracks behind.

After all the unnecessary copper has been etched away, and you've removed the board from the etching bath and cleaned off any remaining etchant, your board is almost ready for use.

The last step is to drill the holes for any mounting points or through-hole components. You can do this by hand, or, if you have access to a CNC mill, you can export the drill file from your PCB design package to provide the drill locations for your mill.

MILLING BOARDS

In addition to using a CNC mill to drill the holes in your PCB, you can also use it to route out the copper from around the tracks themselves. To do this, you need to export the copper layers from your PCB software as Gerber files. These were first defined by Gerber Systems Corp., hence the name, and are now the industry standard format used to describe PCBs in manufacture.

To translate your Gerber file into the G-code that your mill needs requires another piece of software. (See Chapter 6 for more on CNC mills and G-code.) Some CNC mills come with that software already provided, or you can use a third-party program such as Line Grinder (`www.ofitselfso.com/LineGrinder/LineGrinder.php`).

The mill effectively cuts a path round the perimeter of each track to isolate it from the rest of the copper. As a result, PCBs which have been milled look a bit different from those which are etched because any large areas of copper that aren't connected to anything are left on the board (to save time milling it away).

THIRD-PARTY MANUFACTURING

If your design has more than two layers, if you want a more professional finish, or if you just don't want to go to the trouble of making the PCBs yourself, many companies can manufacture the boards for you.

The price for getting the boards made varies based on the complexity and the size of the design but also varies quite a bit from company to company, so it's worth getting a few quotes before deciding which one to use.

If you need the boards quickly, a local firm is your best bet and generally has a lead time measured in days. If you have the luxury of more time, you can cast your net further, including to China, which might reduce your costs but could mean a few weeks' wait before you receive your order.

Either way, the Gerber files are what you need to provide to the manufacturer. Make sure you export all the relevant layers from your design, meaning each of the copper layers you're using, plus the solder mask (which gives the PCBs their colour and stops any solder adhering to areas where it shouldn't), silkscreen (for the labels, versioning info, and so on) and drill files.

ASSEMBLY

After your PCBs have been manufactured, you still need to get the components soldered onto them.

If you're selling them as kits, the customers will solder things up, so you just need to pack everything into bags and let them get on with it. Otherwise, you have to take responsibility for making that happen.

For small runs, you can solder them by hand. For through-hole boards, break out your soldering iron. Surface-mount assembly is a little more involved but quite achievable if you don't have any components with particularly complicated package types.

For assembling surface-mount boards, you need one more item from your PCB design Gerber collection: the solder paste layer. You use it to generate a stencil that allows you to apply the solder. You can laser-cut one from a thin sheet of Mylar plastic or have one made for you out of thin steel. Obviously, the steel one will last much longer and let you solder up lots more boards before you need to replace it.

The solder for surface-mount work comes as a paste, supplied in tubs or tubes. Using a squeegee and the solder paste stencil, you need to put down an even layer of solder over all the component locations and then carefully lift the stencil off the board.

Now comes the tricky bit. Using tweezers and ideally a loupe or magnifying glass, place each component onto the relevant spot on the PCB. The paste holds the parts in place to a degree, but take care not to knock the board at this point in case some of the parts get displaced.

When you have all the components on the board, you need to melt the solder to fix everything in place. You can do this with a soldering iron, but doing it by hand is easier if you use a hot-air rework station. This station is something akin to a cross between a soldering iron and a blowtorch, and it uses hot air to provide the necessary heat.

You can solder all the connections at once if you use a reflow oven. As the name suggests, this oven heats up the PCB and components evenly until the solder melts. Professional reflow ovens allow you to set different temperature profiles, allowing you to match the specification in the manufacturers' datasheets for more exacting components.

For most uses, however, the temperature profiling isn't crucial. For hobbyist and semi-professional use, there is a lot of repurposing of toaster ovens or domestic hot plates to provide a suitable heat source. The maker-community retailer Sparkfun Electronics has a good tutorial covering some of the techniques that it has used for surface-mount soldering at `https://www.sparkfun.com/tutorials/59`.

After you outgrow hand assembly, you will need some help from robots. In this case, you will need robots that can pick up components using a tiny vacuum nozzle, rotate and place them in the right location on the PCB, and then repeat that process at a rate of tens of thousands of components per hour. These robots are known as *pick-and-place assembly machines*.

The price of such equipment is starting to drop, such that these days desktop models are available for a price similar to a laser cutter's. However, the cost of the machines isn't the only one you need to take into account. Because they are geared up for mass manufacturing, the components to feed into the machine are supplied in a form known as *tape and reel*. This is literally a long tape with the components on at regular intervals and a row of holes along one (or both) sides to allow a sprocket on the machine to feed the tape through. The tape is then spooled onto a reel, with each reel typically holding a few thousand components.

Obviously, you need a reel for each of the component types in your circuit design. There is also a limit to the number of different reels that can be loaded into the pick-and-place machine at any one time. Swapping reels over takes time and adds to the cost.

Considering all this, if you are running your own pick-and-place machine, having another look at your design may be worthwhile. If you can rationalise the number of different types of parts it uses (maybe some of the resistor values aren't critical, for example, and you can swap out some for ones that have the same value as are used elsewhere), you can reduce the number of parts you end up holding in stock, not-yet-used, on reels.

This complexity might also make it worth your while to offload some of the work to an *assembly house*, also known as a *contract manufacturer*. Contract manufacturers are firms geared up to helping people produce finished, populated PCBs. Often they offer a range of services from PCB design, through dealing with PCB manufacturers, to soldering up the components and even testing the completed boards (which we come to shortly).

Using an assembly house saves you from buying the expensive machinery yourself. But offloading the work to someone who specialises in it has other benefits, too. The extra throughput that they deal with means they will naturally employ dedicated staff to run the production lines. Paradoxically, those staff will most likely be both more skilled than you are at running the pick-and-place machines and doing any hand soldering *and* cost less per hour than you do. This then frees you up for the many other tasks involved in bringing a product to market or to working on your next idea.

If you do decide to use a contract manufacturer, having a conversation about components is worthwhile. For common parts, if you don't have specific requirements for tolerances, and the like, you might be able to specify that the assembler should use the parts it already holds in stock. That might mean you don't have to buy an entire reel just to get a few components.

Even for the parts the contract manufacturer doesn't already carry and that you need to buy in, it may make sense to work with the manufacturer to place the order. If the manufacturer has dealt with the supplier before, its reputation might let you negotiate a better deal.

TESTING

Now your boards are all ready and assembled, but how do you know that they all work as they're meant to? This is where testing comes in.

Actually, through the automated assembly process, you might have had some testing steps included already. Assembly lines can include automatic optical inspection (AOI). In this process, a high-resolution camera inspects some aspect of the board and its components; for example, it could check that the solder paste is laid properly before the board goes into the pick-and-place machine and compare it to a known good version. Any boards which vary from the "golden" reference version by too high a margin are flagged for further checks from a skilled human operator.

After the boards pass the AOI, the next step is to run them through a functional test. This step is something that you can, and should, be doing even with boards that you've soldered by hand.

At its most basic, the functional test just involves powering up the board as it will be used in the finished product and ensuring that it does what it is supposed to. However, that might take a nontrivial amount of time. The focus here is not on ensuring it will run through all normal operations, but just that the PCB and its components are soldered correctly, that none of the components are faulty, and that there aren't any manufacturing defects in the PCB itself.

A better approach is to build a specific test rig to exercise the different parts of the circuit and measure the voltages at set points on the board. These measurements can then be compared against known-good values and a decision made automatically as to whether or not the device under test (DUT) has passed. You might find that adding a few testing points to the PCB—exposed pads on the PCB connected to useful parts of the circuit— will make the testing process easier, so it's worth considering how the test procedure will run before finishing your PCB design.

Building such a rig isn't too complicated, particularly if you're happy building systems with boards like Arduino and Raspberry Pi. If you're not, we recommend (re)visiting Chapter 5, "Prototyping Embedded Devices".

Because you don't want to spend time making individual connections for each test, the normal practice for the test rig is to use the mounting holes for the PCB for alignment and then have it held by some clips against a number of carefully prepositioned, spring-loaded pins. These pins are known as *pogo pins*, and the spring means they can make a good connection to the board without any extra work, such as soldering, when the board is placed into the test rig.

The test program can then run through its tests and measure voltages at different pogo pins at the relevant time in the test to see how the board being tested performs.

If the DUT includes a microcontroller chip, the test rig could flash it with a test program to help with the testing, and even at the end of the test, assuming it has passed, flash it with the final firmware image ready for deployment.

MASS-PRODUCING THE CASE AND OTHER FIXTURES

We've covered how to scale up manufacture of the electronics side of things, but what about any custom casing or other subassemblies used to build up the final product?

A good rule of thumb for keeping down the costs of production is to minimise the amount of time a person has to work on each item. Machines tend to be cheaper than people, and the smaller the proportion of labour is in your costs, the more you'll be able to afford to pay a decent wage to the people who *are* involved in assembling your devices.

If, as discussed in Chapter 6, "Prototyping the Physical Design", your design uses some of the newer, digital manufacturing techniques such as laser-cutting or 3D printing, you might already have little labour in your assembly process.

However, whilst minimising labour costs is a good target, it's not the only factor you need to consider in your production recipe; production rates are also important. Though they're fairly labour free, 3D printers and laser-cutters aren't the fastest of production techniques. Waiting a couple of hours for a print is fine if you just want one, but a production run of a thousand is either going to take a very long time or require a *lot* of 3D printers!

> *Covering all the possible manufacturing techniques is more than enough to fill a book on its own, and in fact many books do just that. One that we particularly recommend as a primer on the breadth of available processes is* Manufacturing Processes for Design Professionals, *by Rob Thompson. (Thames & Hudson, 2007)*

To give you a flavour of the sorts of issues involved, we look at what must be the most common method of mass production: injection moulding of plastic.

As the name suggests, the process involves injecting molten plastic into a mould to form the desired shape. After the plastic has cooled sufficiently, the mould is separated and the part is popped out by a number of ejection pins and falls into a collection bin. The whole cycle is automated and takes much less time than a 3D print, which means that thousands of parts can be easily churned out at a low cost per part.

The expensive part of injection moulding is producing the mould in the first place; this is known as *tooling up*. The moulds are machined out of steel or aluminium and must be carefully designed and polished so that the moulding process works well and the parts come out with the desired surface finish. Any blemishes in the surface of the mould will be transferred to every part produced using them, so you want to get this right. Including a texture to the surface of the part can help mask any imperfections while potentially giving the finished item a better feel. Often for a super-smooth surface, the moulds are finished with a process called *electrical discharge machining* (EDM), which uses high-voltage sparks to vaporise the surface of the metal and gives a highly polished result.

One of the moulds for BERG's Little Printer being finished on an EDM machine.

The mould also needs to include space for the ejection pins to remove the part after it's made and a route for the plastic to flow into the mould. If you've ever put together a model plane or car, you are familiar with those pathways; they're the excess sprue, the plastic scaffolding that holds each piece together in the kit and that you have to snap away. In assembled products, the parts are naturally removed from the sprue during production.

Like any production technique, injection moulding has its own design considerations. Because the parts need to be extracted from the mould after they're formed, very sharp corners and completely vertical faces are best avoided. A slight angle, called the *draft*, from vertical allows for clean parting of the part and its mould, and consistent wall thicknesses avoid warping of the part as it cools.

If you need the thicker walls for strength, an alternative is to use ribs to add rigidity without lots of additional plastic. A look inside some plastic moulded products you already own will show some of the common techniques for achieving maximum strength with a minimum amount of material and also ways to mould mounting points for PCBs or screw holes for holding the assemblies together.

The simplest moulds are called *straight-pull* and consist of the mould split into two halves. If your design needs to include vertical faces or complex overhangs, more complicated moulds which bring in additional pieces from the side are possible but add to the tooling-up cost.

One way to reduce the tooling-up costs and also increase the production rate is to mould more than one part at a time. If your parts are small enough, you can replicate many of them on one mould or, as we saw in the model aircraft kit, collect lots of different parts together.

In a process known as *multishot moulding*, you can even share parts of different colours on the same mould. With carefully measured volumes for each part, one of the colours of plastic is injected first to fill the parts which need to be that colour. Then the other colour is injected to fill the remainder of the mould. Obviously, there is a section of the mould cavity where the different colours mix, but with careful design, that is just part of the sprue and so discarded.

Case Study: BERG's Little Printer

The Little Printer, made by London design firm BERG, is a delightful, tiny Internet-connected printer. It is a great example of a project which has made the full journey that we're covering in this book, from initial concept through to finished product.

The Little Printer.

To follow the story completely, we have to look back to 2006, when Matt Webb, one of the founders of BERG, shared some thinking-out-loud about how the printer connected to his computer could be shared with close friends and family regardless of where they are in the world (http://berglondon. com/blog/2006/10/06/my-printer-my-social-letterbox/). He called this a social letterbox, with the idea being that people he was close to socially would be able to share printed things with him even when they weren't close to him physically. He also mused that maybe he'd be able to subscribe to blogs or similar, less personal but still personally chosen publications and have them delivered at a time that suited him.

As an aside, in the comments to that initial blog post, there's a remark from a certain Adrian McEwen, suggesting that a better approach than repurposing the printer connected to your computer would be to give the printer its own network connection and intelligence.

This initial contemplation led to a number of people, including Matt, some of his friends, and the wider maker community, experimenting with repurposed receipt printers hooked up to Arduino boards and connected to the Internet. They experimented with printing out the weather forecast, their appointments for the day, tweets from friends, and much more.

continued

continued

From those early investigations, they worked through what made sense when printed out and what did not. For example, tweets proved too numerous to bring into being in hard copy. That let them explore the problem space of receipt printing and better understand the qualities of paper and how and why people still use it in preference to purely digital means.

These experiments continued over a few years, operating almost as a background project for BERG as they engaged in a combination of client work and self-directed products. Although those products—Availabot, a physical instant-messenger status display, and SVK, a graphic novel with hidden text revealed by a UV torch—don't immediately seem like test runs for Little Printer, in many ways they let the company learn more about the process of building products.

Not that there wasn't still plenty to do to bring Little Printer into existence.

The physical form required careful design of the printer mechanism and tooling for both injection moulding and metal pressing to provide the housing. The team ran into issues with the way that the injection-moulded plastic cooled around the holes for the button and status light on the top of the case: it introduced a ripple on the surface, and although this was barely noticeable, it marred the piano finish they were after. Solving this problem resulted in a two-stage process for that part of the case. It is now injection-moulded without the holes, which gives the correct finish, and then drilled to provide the holes. Of course, this process is more expensive, but it results in the higher-quality finish they desired.

On the electronics and software side, they wanted to minimise the amount of setup required and to be able to control the look and feel of the whole user experience, from ordering the printer through to using it in the home. This led them to choose a ZigBee-based wireless option which didn't require any username or password to pair with other endpoints. However, while home routers support WiFi (standard 802.11), they don't have ZigBee support built in. This dictated a two-box solution: in addition to your Little Printer, you receive a BERG Cloud Bridge, a box with both ZigBee wireless and Ethernet which you plug into an Ethernet port on your network to talk to the Internet.

That allows the printer to communicate with the BERG Cloud server software, which provides for both the delivery of "publications" to the printers and the user-facing website. Through the user interface of their website, BERG allows users to register their Little Printer and to choose which publications they want to subscribe to and when they should be delivered.

Details of all this work broke cover in November 2011, some five years after the initial blog post.

Even then, there was still work remaining to be done. By August 2012, things were nearing completion, and they had started taking pre-orders. At that point, the predicted shipping date was mid-October 2012. However, because balancing all these different tasks is hard, a few more hiccoughs were still lying in wait.

A combination of the switching frequency of their switch-mode power supply and the PCB design for the Bridge units conspired to make it fail the electromagnetic compatibility emissions test. Solving that problem caused the schedule to slip by more than a month, and then a smaller issue in assembly with the magnetic catches on the case delayed things by another week or so.

At the end of November 2012, these playful Little Printers started winging their way out to customers, bringing more Internet of Things goodness into numerous homes.

CERTIFICATION

One of the less obvious sides of creating an Internet of Things product is the issue of certification. If you forget to make the PCB or write only half of the software for your device, it will be pretty obvious that things aren't finished when it doesn't work as intended. Fail to meet the relevant certification or regulations, and your product will be similarly incomplete—but you might not realise that until you send it to a distributor, or worse still, after it is already on sale.

For the main part, these regulations are there for good reason. They make the products you use day in, day out, safer for you to use; make sure that they work properly with complementary products from other suppliers; and ensure that one product doesn't emit lots of unwanted electromagnetic radiation and interfere with the correct operation of other devices nearby.

You may not have noticed before, but if you take a closer look at any gadget that's near to hand, you will find a cluster of logos on it somewhere…CE, FCC, UL…. Each of these marks signifies a particular set of regulations and tests that the item has passed: the CE mark for meeting European standards; FCC for US Federal Communications Commission regulations; and UL for independent testing laboratory UL's tests.

The regulations that your device needs to pass vary depending on its exact functionality, target market (consumer, industrial, and so on), and the countries in which you expect to sell it. Negotiating through all this isn't for the faint of heart, and the best approach is to work with a local testing facility. They not only are able to perform the tests for you but also are able to advise on which sets of regulations your device falls under and how they vary from country to country.

Such a testing facility subjects your device to a barrage of tests (hopefully) far beyond anything it will encounter in general use. Testers check over the materials specifications to ensure you're not using paint containing lead; zap it with an 8KV static shock of electricity to see how it copes; subject it to probing with a hot wire—heated to 500 degrees Celsius—to check that it doesn't go up in flames; and much more.

Of particular interest is the electromagnetic compatibility, or EMC, testing. This tests both how susceptible your device is to interference from other electronic devices, power surges on the main's electricity supply, and so on, and how much electromagnetic interference your product itself emits.

Electromagnetic interference is the "electrical noise" generated by the changing electrical currents in circuitry. When generated intentionally, it can be very useful: radio and television broadcasts use the phenomenon to transmit a signal across great distances, as do mobile phone networks and any other radio communication systems such as WiFi and ZigBee. The problem arises when a circuit emits a sufficiently strong signal *unintentionally* which disrupts the desired radio frequencies. This is sometimes noticeable in the "dit, dit-dit-dit" picked up by a poorly insulated stereo just before your mobile phone starts ringing.

All the tests are performed on a DUT, which needs to be the final specification for the entire product. As a result, the testing will most likely be a critical point in your delivery schedule, and any problems discovered will delay shipment while you iterate through a new revision to fix the issues.

For the EMC tests, the device is isolated in an anechoic radio frequency (RF) chamber to minimise the chance of external electromagnetic interference confusing the tests. It is then run through its normal operations while any emissions are monitored by a spectrum analyzer measuring at a distance of 3 metres from the DUT. This test gives the level of RF radiation at the different frequencies specified in the regulations. If any of them are close to the limit, the test is redone with the measurements taken at a distance of 10 metres. The acceptable limits are lower at the greater distance, but that checks how quickly the signal attenuates; with luck, you'll still be within limits and gain certification.

The resultant test report is added to your technical file, which is referenced by your declaration of conformity. Assembling this is a requirement for certification and documents the key information about your device and the testing it has undergone.

In addition to the test report, you need to gather together PCB layouts, assembly certificates, the certificates for any precertified modules that you have used, and datasheets for critical components. This information is all held in a safe place by the manufacturer (that is, you) in case the authorities need to inspect it.

The location of the technical file is mentioned on the declaration of conformity, which is where you publicly declare to which directives in the regulations your device conforms.

For certain regulations you must also notify a specific, named body; for example, circuits that perform radio communication and so intentionally emit electromagnetic interference must be registered with the FCC when sold in the US. Such registration is in addition to issuing the declaration of conformity for self-certification.

Because of the added complexity and overhead—both administrative and financial—of some of the more involved directives (the intentional emitter rules being a prime example), it is often wise to use pre-approved modules.

You therefore can include a WiFi module (chips, antenna, and associated circuitry), for example, or a mains power adaptor, without having to resubmit to all the relevant testing. As long as you don't modify the module in any way, the certification done by its manufacturer is deemed sufficient, and you just need to include that in your technical file.

In Europe, you must also register for the Waste Electrical and Electronic Equipment Directive (WEEE Directive). It doesn't cover any of the technical aspects of products but is aimed instead at reducing the amount of electronic waste that goes to landfill. Each country in the EU has set up a scheme for producers and retailers of electronic and electrical products to encourage more recycling of said items and to contribute towards the cost of doing so.

Retailers can either operate a recycling system in which they accept unwanted electronic devices or join a scheme whose operator takes care of the recycling on their behalf, generally for a membership fee.

In the UK, the Environment Agency maintains a list of schemes that producers can join. Some of the scheme providers have tiers of membership, based on company size or the amount of electrical and electronic equipment being produced. For smaller producers, such as those who generate less than a tonne of electronic equipment, there are fixed-price schemes for a few hundred pounds per year. Larger producers report the total weight of devices they've shipped, at regular intervals (usually quarterly), and pay proportionally.

COSTS

As we've seen in the rest of this chapter, you have many things to consider as you move to higher volume manufacturing. Unfortunately, lots of them involve sizeable up-front costs. In fact, the further you get into the process, the less you will need your hardcore coding or critical design skills, and the more time you'll spend balancing cash flow and fund-raising.

However, the upside is that you'll be able to get your *awesome* connected device into the hands of many more people and that's much more important.

If you've raised enough money upfront, the task of managing the "manufacturing project" will be easier, but as with all projects, there will still be time scales and dependencies to look after. If you haven't been through this before, and particularly if you don't have much experience with managing delivery of inter-related tasks and deadlines, it is worth seeking out a trusted advisor or partner to help.

You don't need to be able to wield a Gantt chart or have a PRINCE2 project management qualification, but *someone* on the team needs to keep an eye on how things are progressing; which things must be done before other tasks can proceed; and, peering further into the project timeline, spot (and deal with) problems before they become a roadblock for the rest of the team.

> *Providing a full primer in project management is beyond the scope of this book, but we can give you an idea of the sorts of things to look out for, plus some rules of thumb to help with estimating costs.*

With the relentless optimisation of global supply chains, as consumers we've become used to having our demands satisfied immediately; even ordering physical items, we are often accustomed to their arriving the day after the order is placed.

Mass manufacturing, however, is still optimised for production throughput rather than speed of startup. As a result, the time between ordering an item and its being ready to use can come as a bit of a shock.

You are likely to encounter this situation first with PCB manufacture, where it can often take a couple of weeks from sending off the Gerber files to having something to solder up. Faster turnaround times are possible, but you tend to pay a premium.

The setup and tooling for processes such as injection moulding can be worse. Getting the tool machined and tested and then fine-tuned is likely to take a month or two. Sometimes during that process you're involved, but there also will be big chunks of time while you sit waiting for the work to be done.

With careful planning, you'll be able to work on other parts of the project while you are waiting—maybe finishing the server coding or preparing the marketing materials—but you will still need to block out the time for it in your project plan.

Working out the likely cost for your project is a bit of a black art and obviously depends greatly on the complexity of what you're trying to achieve.

Many of the online PCB services include a quoting tool, so even before the design is finished, you can get a feel for the likely price. You should be able to make a reasonable guess on the size of PCB you need and the number of layers it's likely to require; those are the main factors that the quoting tools use to work out the cost, plus extras if you want something out of the ordinary such as a different coloured solder mask.

For assembling the PCBs, you should budget something around £150–£800 for setup costs—getting the solder paste stencil made, programming the pick-and-place machine, and so on—and then between 3 and 14 pence for placing each component. This doesn't include the cost of the components themselves.

When buying components in small quantities, you will often notice that the price list also shows the cost if buying in greater bulk. This is a good start, but generally lists don't show prices for quantities of greater than 1,000 items.

Assuming you can find a price for a few hundred of something, you can work out a guide price for higher quantities with what its creator half-jokingly calls *Archard's law*. This term was coined by Lawrence Archard, a hardware engineer with much more experience of going to manufacturing than either of the authors. He suggests that after you know the price for a few hundred of a component, each time you increase quantity by a factor of 10, the item cost will drop to three-quarters of the price.

Pricing the plastics or other physical components depends far too much on the design for us to be able to give meaningful numbers here, but getting a hardened steel tool made, which will be good for churning out 100,000 parts before it needs replacing, could easily run to £10,000.

And to get through certification, you are likely to need a similar amount again. Simpler devices being certified in fewer territories might get through certification for around £2,000; more complicated designs, particularly those involving uncertified RF modules, could see costs 10 times that amount (£20,000) to get all the certifications in place.

Naturally, as the project progresses, you will get more accurate quotes (and eventually completely accurate invoices…) as you talk to suppliers and get ready to place orders with them. This will let you update your BOM and cost spreadsheets and have the new information ripple through your plans.

SCALING UP SOFTWARE

Producing a physical *thing* as a prototype or as a manufactured product turn out to be two entirely different propositions. The initial prototype may well be of different size, shape, colour, materials, finish, and quality to what ends up on the shelf. Yet software is intangible and malleable. There are no parts to order, no Bill of Materials to pay for. The bits of information that make up the programs which run in the device or on the Internet are invisible. The software you wrote during project development and what ends up in production will be indistinguishable to the naked eye.

Yet, as with the physical form and electronics of the device, software has to be polished before it can be exposed to the real world. After looking at what is involved in deploying software—both on the embedded device and for any online service you have built—we look at the various factors that require this polish: correctness, maintainability, security, performance, and community.

We only touch upon the issues here, in order to give an awareness of what is involved. The resources you use to learn the particular language and framework you have chosen will cover the ways to build and deploy secure, reliable web services in much more detail.

DEPLOYMENT

Copying software from a development machine (your laptop or the team's source code repository) to where it will be run from in production is typically known as *deployment*, or sometimes, by analogy to physical products, *shipping*.

In the case of the firmware running on the microcontroller, this will (hopefully) be done once only, during the manufacture of the device. The software will be flashed to the device in a similar way to how you updated your prototype device during development. For a simple device like the Arduino which usually only runs a single program, the process will be identical to that in development. For a device like a BeagleBone or Raspberry Pi which runs an entire operating system, you will want to "package" the various program code, libraries, and other files you have used in a way that you can quickly and reliably make a new build—that is, install all of it onto a new board with a single command.

The software for an online service will tend to run in a single location. However, it will generally be visible to the whole of the Internet, which means that it will potentially be subject to greater load and to a greater range of accidental or malicious inputs that might cause it to stop working. In addition, the code tends to be more complex and build on more library code; this greater complexity implies a greater potential for bugs. Finally, as a malleable and user-facing software product, there is always the possibility of updating the code to add value by introducing new features or improving the design.

As a result of all of this, it is not merely possible, but necessary, to update the online software components more regularly than those on the device. Having a good deployment process will allow you to do this smoothly and safely. Ideally, with one trigger (such as running a script, or pushing code to a release branch in your code repository), a series of actions will take place which update the software on the server. If you are using a hosted service such as Heroku, there will be simple, standard ways to do this. If you are running your own dedicated web server or perhaps a virtual machine such as an Amazon EC2 instance, there are many solutions, from shell scripts using `scp`, `rsync`, or `git` to copy code, to deployment frameworks such as Capistrano. A tempting option for the near future is Docker.io, which allows the same application you run on your laptop to be packaged up as a virtual "container" that can run unchanged on an Internet-facing server.

CORRECTNESS AND MAINTAINABILITY

So, you've sold a thousand Internet-connected coffee machines. Congratulations! Now it's time to cross your fingers and hope that you don't get a thousand complaints that it doesn't actually work. Perhaps it makes cappuccinos when the customer asked it for a latte. Maybe it tweets "Coffee's on!" when it isn't, or vice versa.

Clearly, as a publicly available product, your software has to do what you claimed it would, and do it efficiently and safely.

Testing your code before it is deployed is an important step in helping to avoid such a situation, and your chosen language and development framework will have standard and well-understood testing environments to help ease your task.

As it lives in a central place, the server software is easy to update, either to fix bugs or to introduce new features. This is a real boon for web applications, as it removes an entire class of support issues.

The embedded code in the device, however, is particularly important to test, as that is the hardest to update once the product has been sent out to the users. It may be possible, given that the devices will be connected to the Internet anyway, for the code to be updated *over-the-air,* and that is one of the selling points of the Electric Imp platform, for example. However, it should be approached with some caution: what if a firmware update itself caused a failure of a home heating system? And as Internet of Things products become more integrated into our lives and our homes, they become a tempting target for hackers. If your device can update its own code, the channels for delivering and authenticating any updates must be rock solid, lest they be compromised and, as mobile technologist Brian Proffitt warns, "The Internet of Things might try to kill you" (`http://readwrite.com/2013/09/18/internet-of-things-security-disaster-terrorism-war`).

SECURITY

These concerns lead us back to the important issue of security. Though we emphasized this when talking about software prototyping, it is critical to consider the consequences of a mass-market product being attacked in this way.

We have already discussed encryption via HTTPS, and the requirement or otherwise for this may have driven your choice of prototyping or production platform. As well as securing the communication between client device and web server, you should consider the server itself; as an always-on, always-connected device visible to the whole Internet, it is the most obvious target. These considerations are not specific to the Internet of Things, but they should be well known to your system administration and development team. Following are some of the more important guidelines:

- Make sure that your servers are kept up-to-date with the latest security patches, are hardened with the appropriate firewalls, and detect and mitigate against password hacking attempts and rootkit attacks.

- User passwords should never be stored in plain text. If your database were ever compromised, an attacker could easily log in as any user. As we touched upon in the sidebar on "Hashes" in Chapter 2, passwords should be encrypted with a secure algorithm which is not known to be trivially cracked, and "salted" for additional security.

- Never simply trust user input. Check that anything that is entered into a web application fits the type of data you expect, and refuse or clean anything which doesn't. Although you may think input from your connected devices would be okay (because you wrote the code), it is possible that it has been compromised or an attacker may be "spoofing" it. In particular, be wary of passing user input to your database without checking it (otherwise, you risk an SQL injection attack were it to include SQL commands), or including unfiltered user input in your HTML pages, as this could allow a cross-site scripting (XSS) attack. Strip out all HTML tags (or allow only a limited selection of acceptable ones for formatting) or escape the output.

- Be aware of cross-site request forgery (CSRF) attacks from other malicious or compromised websites. For example, if one of your users browses a bad site which uses JavaScript to open `http://some.example.com/heating?switch=off` on your site, and the user is already logged in, he may come home to a cold house.

PERFORMANCE

The first thing many people think of when considering scaling up software is whether it will be fast enough and handle a large number of users, but in fact the other factors we have looked at are usually far more critical. If your web service is running on a modern framework, it should be easy to scale up by deploying the code onto a more powerful machine, or by running multiple servers, with a front-end server or proxy managing the load. In general, you should concentrate on running your web application with appropriate standard infrastructure which is good enough for most problems. If you're lucky enough to have so much traffic that you need to scale, you should always optimise using this algorithm:

1. Identify that you actually have a problem.
2. Measure and profile the tasks which are slow and identify the problem.
3. Fix that problem. The web community does a good job in sharing best practice in how to address such problems, so you often find that others have trodden the path before and documented their tried-and-tested solutions.

USER COMMUNITY

Whether you are launching a mass-market commercial product or an open-source community effort, your project will be successful only if people actually use it. While few large companies can boast Apple's famous commitment to "insanely great customer service", a small, focused startup can often match them for responsiveness and enthusiasm. At a minimum, you need a support email or a bug-reporting tool (ideally a public one, so that users can easily find related issues), but you will probably have a presence on various social media forums (Twitter, Facebook, and the like). As well as responding to queries, however, you should think about the user experience before launching: does your website have documentation, introductory videos, and tutorials? Blogging regularly about product development and related topics helps build a readership of users, both current and potential. Finally, some form of forum, mailing list, or chat room lets users support each other, which reduces your workload, but more importantly helps to build up a community and expertise around your product.

SUMMARY

We've crammed an awful lot of facts, processes, and advice into this chapter, and we hope your head isn't spinning too much.

Building physical products is hard, and products that connect with the Internet take up the complexity another notch. However, the finished items elicit a reaction that is hard to match with a website or an app.

Moving to manufacturing involves many skills and tasks that are quite different from those you used to bring the idea to life, and it can feel quite daunting when you realise all that needs to be done.

However, this process is something that the world has been perfecting for over a hundred years and even in the electronics industry is a few decades old. So if you find the right partners, it needn't be as difficult as you fear.

11 ETHICS

ONE CAN EASILY see any technology in a black-and-white way. Perhaps you could argue that it

- Destroys jobs
- Is intrusive and will enslave us to technology
- Disconnects humanity from ancient traditions
- Encourages us to become lazy and unhealthy
- Tempts us into thinking we are like gods

or that it

- Is shiny and new
- Is progress (with the implication that it is therefore better)
- Will save lives and feed the starving
- Will (at the least) make us happier, healthier, safer, and better educated
- Will free us from drudgery to have more time for leisure
- Will create more interesting, rewarding jobs to replace the drudgery it will make obsolete

Notice how many of the optimistic statements are more complicated than the pessimistic ones. The reason may be that the rejection of the new and the different is deeply embedded in societies and can be phrased in more visceral terms.

Take a moment to reflect on your own stance to technology in general. It may be that you are generally anti- or generally pro-technology (perhaps the latter is more likely, if you are reading this book!) It is also possible that you are optimistic about some classes of technology (Internet, space travel) but pessimistic about others (genetically modified food, wind energy).

The emotions raised by technology may be strong and suggest two competing grand narratives, moving either from or towards the philosophical ideal of the "good life":

- **The downward spiral of mankind from a better state:** This could be identified with religious concepts such as the Christian "fall of man" or simply with traditional values.
- **An inexorable and definingly human advance towards a full self-realization through technology:** This might lead to a new state for the species (the post-human singularity or the spread of mankind to other planets) or simply suggest that every advance leads us to a stable utopia.

Although these narratives are powerful, technologists may be better served by being able to distinguish finer shades of grey: whether to persuade others or to challenge their own beliefs to reframe them in a wider context.

In many traditional disciplines, there are courses on ethics—for example, in university courses on engineering or computer science. As open data and hackspace expert Laura James has suggested (at the OpenIoT discussions, which we return to in detail later in this chapter), "Is the issue that hackers haven't gone through formal Engineering training and so missed it?" Moreover, as we saw in the overview in Chapter 1, the practitioners of the Internet of Things may come from varied backgrounds, from these technical fields, through design, to the fine arts.

In this chapter, we do not present an entire course on formal ethics, although we refer the interested reader to *Ethics in Engineering*, the classic textbook by Mike W. Martin and Roland Schinzinger. Rather, we look at a number of aspects, many of which are related to such an ethics syllabus, and consider them in relation to the Internet of Things. We look at many extreme and challenging ideas, some of which may seem like science fiction or may be politically uncomfortable. As Martin and Schinzinger write in their introduction:

We [argue for particular positions] because it better serves our goal of encouraging critical judgement than would a mere digest of others views. Accordingly, our aim is not to force conviction, but to provoke either reasoned acceptance or reasoned rejection of what we say.

— Ethics in Engineering *(McGraw-Hill, 2004)*

CHARACTERIZING THE INTERNET OF THINGS

Let us start by summarizing what the Internet of Things is, to get a handle on what particular changes it can bring to humanity's relationship to the "good life."

We've stressed the fact that a certain powerful technology (computer chips) is suddenly cheap and plentiful. This is by no means a new observation, nor the first technology that has undergone this explosive transition. Consider the following excerpt from the influential technologist and policymaker Vannevar Bush's masterful essay of 1945, "As We May Think":

Machines with interchangeable parts can now be constructed with great economy of effort. In spite of much complexity, they perform reliably. Witness the humble typewriter, or the movie camera, or the automobile. Electrical contacts have ceased to stick when thoroughly understood. Note the automatic telephone exchange, which has hundreds of thousands of such contacts, and yet is reliable. A spider web of metal, sealed in a thin glass container, a wire heated to brilliant glow, in short, the thermionic tube of radio sets, is made by the hundred million, tossed about in packages, plugged into sockets—and it works! Its gossamer parts, the precise location and alignment involved in its construction, would have occupied a master craftsman of the guild for months; now it is built for thirty cents. The world has arrived at an age of cheap complex devices of great reliability; and something is bound to come of it.

—www.theatlantic.com/magazine/archive/1945/07/
as-we-may-think/3881

This availability of technology brings certain abilities within the reach of not just the powerful but the ordinary citizen. Bush's earlier examples were concerned with publication, transport, and communication. The advances in the Internet of Things are also primarily related to communication, but now allow the publication and transmission of vast streams of data, from the social (did someone mention me on Twitter?) to the environmental (how much energy is used in a typical house in Liverpool? what are the radiation levels in various parts of Japan after the Fukushima incident?), without needing the permission or expertise of a technological or political elite. "Something is bound to come of it" indeed.

We also noted in Chapter 1 how the adage that "form follows function" applies primarily to the physical usage of the "Thing", its affordances, sensors, and actuators, and only minimally to its digital communications. This leads to objects that can look innocuous but have arbitrary and potentially unexpected capabilities.

Connecting the Internet to the real world allows both your physical actions to be made public and, in the opposite direction, for events on the Internet to affect your environment. Applying this bidirectional communication to Things can lead to features that interact with the concept of privacy. When you switch on your Good Night Lamp, the "little lamp" at your mother's bedside will also turn on, letting her know you are home. When you leave the office, the WhereDial at home turns to let your partner know you're travelling.

We have repeatedly noted that the Internet of Things is made up of

> Physical object + controllers, sensors, and actuators + Internet service

Each of these aspects has a part to play in the ethical issues specific to the Internet of Things, and we refer to them in the sections that follow.

PRIVACY

The Internet, as a massive open publishing platform, has been a disruptive force as regards the concept of privacy. Everything you write might be visible to anyone online: from minutiae about what you ate for breakfast to blog posts about your work, from articles about your hobbies to Facebook posts about your parties with friends. There is a *value* in making such data public: the story told on the Internet becomes your persona and defines you in respect of your friends, family, peers, and potential employers. But do you always want people to be able to see that data? With massively increased storage capabilities, this data can be trivially stored and searched. Do you want not just your family and friends but also companies, the government, and the police to be able to see information about you, forever?

A common argument is "if you've got nothing to hide, then you've got nothing to fear." There is some element of truth in this, but it omits certain important details, some of which may not apply to you, but apply to someone:

- You may not want your data being visible to an abusive ex-spouse.
- You might be at risk of assassination by criminal, terrorist, or state organizations.
- You might belong to a group which is targeted by your state (religion, sexuality, political party, journalists).

More prosaically, you *change* and your persona changes. Yet your past misdemeanours (drunken photos, political statements) may be used against you in the future.

Let's look now at how the Internet of Things interacts with this topic. As the Internet of Things is about *Things*, which are rooted in different contexts than computers, it makes uploading data more ubiquitous. Let's consider the mobile phone, in particular an Internet-connected phone with on-board camera. Although we don't typically consider phones as Internet of Things devices, the taking of a photo with a camera phone is a quintessential task for a Thing: whereas in the past you would have had to take a photo, develop it, take the printed photo to your computer, scan it, and then upload it (or take your digital camera to the computer and transfer the photo across via USB), now you can upload that compromising photo, in a single click, while still drunk. The ability to do something is present in a defined context (the personal) rather than locked in a set of multiple processes, culminating in a general-purpose computer.

Even innocuous photos can leak data. With GPS coordinates (produced by many cameras and most smartphones) embedded into the picture's EXIF metadata, an analysis of your Flickr/Twitpic/Instagram feed can easily let an attacker infer where your house, your work, or even your children's school is. Even if *you* stripped out the data, photo-processing technology enables searching of *similar* photos, which may include these coordinates or other clues.

Similar issues exist with sports-tracking data, whether produced by an actual Thing, such as Nike+ or a GPS watch, or a pseudo-Thing, like the RunKeeper app on your smartphone. This data is incredibly useful to keep track of your progress, and sharing your running maps, speed, heartbeat, and the like with friends may be motivating. But again, it may be trivial for an attacker to infer where your house is (probably near where you start and finish your run) and get information about the times of day that you are likely to be out of the house.

When we tell family and friends about the Good Night Lamp or the WhereDial, they often bristle and start muttering about "Big Brother". The idea of people knowing where you are can evoke strong emotions. Yet the idea of knowing that your loved ones are safe is a similarly deep-seated human emotion. To the extent that you allow your location to be shared with people you've *chosen* to share it with, there is no infringement of privacy. But the decision to give your mother a Good Night Lamp might seem less sensible months later when you arrive home late at night. Or you might regret giving your partner a WhereDial if later she becomes jealous and suspicious of your innocent (or otherwise) movements.

Even if these devices are themselves respectful of your privacy, their security or lack thereof might allow an attacker to get information. For example, if it were possible to read an IP packet going from the goodnightlamp.com servers to a household, could you find out that the associated "big lamp" had been switched off? Even if this packet is encrypted, could an attacker infer something by the fact that a packet was sent at all? (That is, will the servers have to regularly send encrypted "nothing happened" packets?) These risks are to be considered very carefully by responsible makers of Internet of Things devices! We would refer the reader back to Chapters 7 and 10, where we discuss the technical details of how to approach securing the online component of your product.

So far we've looked at devices that you, as an individual, choose to deploy. But as sensor data is so ubiquitous, it inevitably detects more than just the data that you have chosen to make public.

For a start, we saw previously that many "things" have little in their external form that suggests they are connected to the Internet. When you grab an Internet-connected scarf from the coat rack or sit on an Internet-connected chair, should you have some obvious sign that data will be transmitted or an action triggered? Urbanist and technologist Adam Greenfield has catalogued interactive billboards with hidden cameras which record the demographics of the people who look at them and vending machines which choose the products to display on a similar basis. He comments that, as well as being intrusions into public space, these objects are not just what they seem to be. Rather, they have an agenda of "predicting behaviours and encouraging normative behaviours", which is not transparent (`http://storify.com/clarered/adam-greenfield-connected-things-and-civic-respons`).

Conversely, perhaps a Thing that is implemented digitally will not give the subtle cues that its analogue counterpart used to give. An e-book is harder to flip through than a paper book because there is no touch feedback from the pages. Many early camera phones had a *faked* camera shutter noise added, simply because society was concerned about their use for silent, surreptitious photography.

Moreover, let us consider the electricity smart meter. The real-time, accurate measurement of electricity has many admirable goals. Understanding usage patterns can help companies to produce electricity at the right times, avoiding overproduction and optimizing efficiency. With humans consuming ever more energy, in a time when our fossil fuel resources are becoming ever more scarce and the impact of using them ever more serious, this is increasingly important. The aggregate data collected by the companies is useful for the noble environmental goals we've mentioned...but how about individual data?

If you could mine the data to see subtle peaks, associated with kettles being switched on for tea or coffee, perhaps you could infer what television programmes a household watches. If there are four longer peaks in the morning, this might suggest that four family members are getting up for an electric shower before going to school or work. Now what if you triangulate this data with some other data—for example, the water meter readings? Smart electricity meters are currently being rolled out across Europe and will, in fact, soon be compulsory. Giovanni Buttarelli, assistant director of the European Data Protection Supervisor, has warned that "together with data from other sources, the potential for extensive data mining is very significant" (`www.guardian.co.uk/environment/2012/jul/01/ household-energy-trackers-threat-privacy`).

The idea of analysing multiple huge datasets is now a reality. There are smart algorithms, and there is the computing power to do it. By combining both ends of the long tail (the cheap, ubiquitous Internet of Things devices on the one hand and the expensive, sophisticated, powerful data-mining processors on the other), it is possible to process and understand massive quantities of data.

How powerful this ability will be may well depend on what data you have available to compare. If an electricity supplier was also able to buy data from, say, supermarket loyalty card schemes, the supplier could compare the information from inside the household with the family's shopping or fuel bills. Of course, it's currently unlikely that a supermarket would sell that kind of individual data. But as our attitude to privacy changes, it is not outside the realms of possibility.

It is very important to note that even aggregate data can "leak" information. If you can see data collected for a street, for example, then comparing a week when a household is away on holiday with a normal week when they are at home might tell you about their usage. Some very interesting questions can be raised about this: should companies be prevented from trading data with each other? Should there be legal limits to what data can be kept or what analyses performed on it? Or do we have to think the unthinkable and admit that privacy is no longer possible in the face of massive data combined with data mining?

At the Open Internet of Things Assembly 2012 in London (`http://postscapes.com/open-internet-of-things-assembly`), there was a great deal of discussion about who owns sensor data. The electricity companies? The householder who has signed the electricity contract? Or all the stakeholders in the house? If you visit a friend's house, data about *you* is collected and "owned" by someone else. This might mean that in future you would be a stakeholder in this valuable data too.

As sensors such as CCTV cameras, temperature meters, footfall counters, and Bluetooth trackers are installed in public and private spaces, from parks to shops, data about you is collected all the time. The term "data subject" has been coined for this purpose. Although you may not own the data collected, you are the subject of it and should have some kind of rights regarding it: transparency over what is collected and what will be done with it, the access to retrieve the data at the same granularity that it was stored, and so on.

While futurology is fun, it's also hard. As the visionary computer scientist Alan Kay famously said in 1971, "The best way to predict the future is to invent it" (`www.smalltalk.org/alankay.html`). Right now, we, as Internet of Things practitioners, are contributing to a discussion about the way privacy will change in the future. It is clear that we are leaking ever more data onto the online world, and some of this data will be vital to dealing with human crises of the near future. Rob van Kranenburg, founder of the think tank Council, predicts that the requirement to smoke out inefficiency, for the survival of our species, will lead to a state of post-privacy. Do we have the "courage to live in the light"? (`www.theinternetofthings.eu/rob-van-kranenburg-what-kind-values-do-we-want-fully-connected-and-connectable-world-0`).

CONTROL

Some of the privacy concerns we looked at in the preceding sections really manifest only if the "data subject" is not the one in control of the data. The example of the drunken photo is more sinister if it was posted by *someone else*, without your permission. This is a form of cyberbullying, which is increasingly prevalent in schools and elsewhere.

Although you, as a loving son/daughter/spouse/parent/friend, may quite reasonably want to share your location or your bedside lamp with your family and friends, what if you are asked to do so? If you are gifted a WhereDial or a Good Night Lamp, is there an *expectation* that you use it, even if you don't really want to?

While the technology itself doesn't cause any controlling behaviour, it could easily be applied by a spouse/parent/employer in ways that manifest themselves as abusive, interfering, or restrictive, in more or less sinister ways. In the case of an employer, we are bound to see cases in the future in which a contractual obligation is needed to share data collected by some Internet of Things device. We will certainly see legal and ethical discussion about this!

Already, companies and organisations are looking at mashing up data sources and apps and may start to offer financial incentives to use Internet of Things devices: for example, reductions in health insurance if you use an Internet-connected heart monitor, have regular GPS traces on a run-tracking service, or regularly check in to a gym. High-end cars already have Internet-connected tracking and security systems which may even be a requisite in getting insurance at all. And as we saw, smart energy meters are currently moving from a financial incentive to a legal requirement.

As with questions about privacy, there are almost always good reasons for giving up some control. From a state perspective, there may be reasons for collective action, and information required to defend against threats, such as that of terrorism. The threat of one's country becoming a police state is not merely a technological matter: institutions such as democracy, the right to protest, free press, and international reputation should balance this. But, of course, with the processing power and information available now, there is a much greater temptation and capability to *become* an effective Big Brother regime. In Tibor Fischer's novel *The Thought Gang*, a character muses on her experiment in hotel surveillance:

> *The biggest lesson was how hard it is to keep tabs on people. I'm not surprised police states tend to be poor. It takes so much effort.*
> —The Thought Gang, (*Scribner, 1997*)

Now that surveillance equipment is cheap, and the processing power required to *analyse* the mountain of data produced by this equipment gets ever more accessible, the simple logistical difficulty of an absolute dystopia vanishes. Commentary on the mourning at Kim Jong-Il's death noted that the, no doubt genuine, grief of many may also have been amplified by the social and political compulsion to express the "histrionics of grief" (*Nothing to Envy: Ordinary Lives in North Korea*, Barbara Demick, Spiegel & Grau, 2010). In a world where pervasive body-blogging is becoming feasible, it is conceivable that not only the *display* of grief but also the physiological symptoms of it could be verified (www.bbc.co.uk/news/magazine-16262027).

As the Canadian open government activist David Eaves has eloquently discussed, it is not only authoritarian states such as Iran and China which are intent on controlling their Internet but also democratic ones. The US, UK, Canada, France, and others have already enacted various laws to give the state and its favoured corporations greater control over its citizens' use of the Internet, and every month one hears news of other suggested legislation which, to a technical specialist, may seem not just badly thought out and unworkable but also immensely dangerous. Just as the printing press gave the state a greater degree of control via propaganda, the Internet gives hitherto unknown possibilities for propaganda and monitoring (http://eaves.ca/2012/06/18/the-end-of-the-world-the-state-vs-the-internet/). Even in a democratic state, with the readily accessibly technology in place, it is up to the institutions that safeguard democracy and the will of the people to become the main bulwark against the threat of authoritarian control.

Of course, it may not be "the State" that profits from the control but corporations. Companies have the expertise and the technology to interact with the Internet. This is particularly true of the Internet of Things, which has largely been driven by monitoring and logistics concerns within large businesses. For those who are keen on the possibilities that the Internet of Things offers, the prospect of it ushering in a "McWorld" style corporat-ocracy is disturbing indeed!

DISRUPTING CONTROL

The other major possibility that Eaves suggests is that "The Internet Destroys the State". This is also a hard and uncomfortable scenario to imagine. However, toning down this idea a little, we can see a more likely one of "the Internet" fighting back against an attempt by the state or corporations to co-opt it. When we refer to a technology as "disruptive", we mean that it affects the balance of power. If one of the fears about the Internet of Things is that it will transfer power away from the citizens, the subjects of technology, to the elite, then perhaps it can also be used to redress that balance.

One extreme example of this would be how surveillance and fears of the Big Brother state (CCTV cameras, remote-controlled helicopter-drones) might be mitigated by "sousveillance". Here, activists might have compromised public cameras, or perhaps installed additional spy cameras, routed through self-healing networks in people's homes, hidden in public spaces, flying in the airspace, or even crawling the sewers.

This last concept of the ratbot network, imagined by sci-fi author Charles Stross, is a fascinating idea from one version of the near future (www. antipope.org/charlie/blog-static/2012/03/pirate-air ships-an-alternative.html).

We can see real steps at disrupting control, however, in a slightly more prosaic but equally fascinating area.

CROWDSOURCING

One fascinating feature of modern Internet life is "crowdsourcing", from knowledge (Wikipedia, et al.) to funding projects (Kickstarter, Indiegogo) to work (Mechanical Turk).

In the Internet of Things world, this concept has manifested itself in sensor networks such as Xively. Founder Usman Haque has said that their original intent wasn't simply "making data public" but also letting "the public making data" (http://haque.tumblr.com/post/25500577232/notes-from-my-talk-at-the-open-iot-assembly-june-16-17). Governments and companies simply do not and cannot have a monopoly on all recording of data: there are infinite combinations of data sources. Choosing which data to record is a creative and engaged act, as well as, perhaps, a political one. After the Fukushima Daiichi nuclear disaster, there were fears that insufficient information was available to track the spread of the leaked radioactive materials. Many hackers around the world built Geiger counters, and Xively was a focal point for Japanese engineers to publish their data to. Perhaps the Japanese government or the management of the Fukushima plant would have provided that kind of accurate, widespread data if they could. But power or financial interests might have worked against this.

Andrew Fisher, a technologist with interests in big data and ubiquitous computing, has written persuasively about a quiet revolution of the "sensor commons", his term for this collaborative voluntary effort to provide environmental data.

Why is this a revolution? Because as a population we are deciding that governments and civic planners no longer have the ability to provide meaningful information at a local level.

—http://ajfisher.me/2011/12/20/
towards-a-sensor-commons/

Former Xively evangelist Ed Borden has led a "call to arms" for a citizen-led air-quality sensor network. As he points out, "The air quality data collected by the government is likely sampled from far, far away and then applied to you on a regional level, almost completely useless from the standpoint of trying to understand or change the local dynamics of pollution that affect you" (http://blog.xively.com/2011/12/07/you-can-help-build-an-open-air-quality-sensor-network/). Crowdsourcing this data is an entirely innocent scientific activity yet is profoundly radical, too. Javaun Moradi, product manager for NPR Digital, clarifies, "These networks aren't trying to replace scientific and government detection equipment, they're trying to both fill a data gap and advance conversation" (http://javaunmoradi.com/blog/2011/12/16/what-do-open-sensor-networks-mean-for-journalism).

This is an important point: local activism may be hampered by lack of available data. Coming together to *produce* such data raises activism from an emotional appeal ("think of the children!") which can be ignored or co-opted by the political elite as expedient, into a reasoned thesis supported by real data (http://blog.xively.com/2011/12/07/you-can-help-build-an-open-air-quality-sensor-network/).

The following figure shows the locations of existing air quality monitors in New York, compared with the projected number of locations in a sensor commons project.

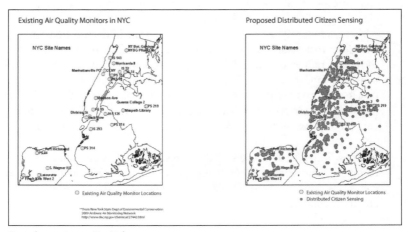

Air-quality monitors in New York.

Fisher's original definition observed five critical requirements for a sensor commons project. It must

- **Gain trust:** Trust is largely about the way that an activist project handles itself beyond the seemingly neutral measurements; understanding local issues, being sensitive about the ways that the sensor network itself affects the environment (for example, local WiFi bandwidth usage), engaging the public with accessible and readable information about the project, and dealing with the local authorities to get access to the systems the project wants to measure.

- **Become dispersible:** Becoming dispersible means spreading the sensors throughout the community. Getting mass adoption will be easier if the proposed sensors are inexpensive (both the physical sensor itself and the ongoing costs of keeping it powered and connected to the network) and if the community already trusts the project. If the sensors are complicated to set up or require massive lengths of cabling, they will get much less take-up! The Xively air-quality project led to the creation of the "air-quality egg", a simple, inexpensive sensor with precisely these features.

- **Be highly visible:** Being visible involves explaining why the project's sensors are occupying a public space. We've already discussed the ethics of hidden sensors. Being honest and visible about the sensor will help to engender trust in the project and also advertise and explain the project further. This may reduce the probability of vandalism too. Advertising not just the sensors but the *data* (both online and in real life) and the ways that data has helped shape behaviour will also generate a positive feedback loop.

- **Be entirely open:** Being open is perhaps what distinguishes the sensor commons from a government project the most. Government data sets are often entirely closed, but the data that *is* released from them will be given a lot of attention because of the rigour and precision that (we expect) their sensor projects will have. A community sensor network may have uncalibrated devices—that is, the readings for a device may be consistently out from the "correct" value and may have additional noise at the extremes of the scale. The openness makes up for this because all the facts about the devices and the possible errors are admitted upfront and can be improved by anyone in the community. In aggregate, the data, and especially the *variations* in the data over time, will still be useful.

The project should also have an API and permissive licensing so that the community can choose to do different, complementary things with the data from the network. A project can't conceive all the possible uses for the data, but other people will always come up with something else.

These factors will allow the data to get "mashed up" with other services; maps, comparisons, and charts also help the project disperse.

- **Be upgradable:** Finally, the project should be designed to be upgradable, to enable the network to remain useful as the needs change or hardware gets to the end of its working life. This requirement interplays with the dispersibility and openness of the project, and the up-front thought to managing the project long term will feed back into the trust in the project.

While Fisher writes specifically on sensor networks, the principles he proposes are, we suggest, relevant to consider for any ethical project in the field of the Internet of Things.

ENVIRONMENT

We have already touched on several environmental issues in the preceding sections, and we'll come back to the themes of data, control, and the sensor commons. First, let's look at the classic environmental concerns about the production and running of the *Thing* itself.

PHYSICAL THING

Creating the object has a carbon cost, which may come from the raw materials used, the processes used to shape them into the shell, the packing materials, and the energy required to ship them from the manufacturing plant to the customer. It's easier than ever to add up the cost of these emissions: for example, using the ameeConnect API (www.amee.com/pages/api), you can find emissions data and carbon costs for the life-cycle use of different plastics you might use for 3D printing or injection moulding. Calculating the energy costs for manufacture is harder.

> *Nobody has really cracked a way of working out the true carbon cost of the products we use.*
>
> — *http://blog.amee.com/developer/labs/*
> *factory-demo/*

amee's prototype of an instrumented coffee production line gives a real-time monitoring of the carbon cost of production for each batch and also stamps a summary on each packet, along with a QR code identifying that batch and a more detailed analysis, in the manner of Bruce Sterling's self-describing "spimes" (*Shaping Things*, Bruce Sterling, MIT Press, 2005).

You may need to consider other environmental factors, such as emissions produced during normal operation or during disposal of the object. For example, thermal printer paper may contain Bisphenol-A, which has health and environmental concerns. BERG's Internet of Things product, the Little Printer, is sold using only BPA-free paper, but initial reactions to it suggested that using paper *at all* is an environmental issue. Of course, a printout the size of a shopping receipt has some carbon cost. On the other hand, the printout will last, perhaps for a long time, whereas a digital device needs to constantly use electricity to display the same information on its LCD. This kind of trade-off may sound like splitting hairs, but these are the sorts of discussions that you may need to have to be able to consider your environmental cost and to be able to market and defend your product in that area.

In the preceding chapter, we discussed RoHS regulation. Whether or not your market requires you to comply with this European directive, doing so may be the environmentally ethical decision. Nowadays, most consumer electronics do indeed conform to it; health benefits are obtained both at the point of manufacture and at waste disposal/recycling (Ogunseitan, Oladele A. July 2007. "Health and Environmental Benefits of Adopting Lead-Free Solders". *Journal of Materials*. New York: Springer).

Human Cost

As well as the environmental cost of production, there is a human cost. You might prefer to manufacture locally, but globalisation is an important factor. We saw earlier that technology has been a driver for the change in jobs. Although "globalisation" is not a technology per se, the communications, transport, and logistics required are certainly rooted in technology. Manufacturing has not been killed by globalisation, but it has largely moved from the Western First World to the developing world and especially to those, such as China and India currently, that have the combination of massive technical expertise and relatively low labour costs. It may be so vastly cheaper to outsource manufacture of some or all components to such a country that it would be a competitive disadvantage not to do so.

Large companies that use offshore manufacturing have been criticised for using "sweatshops". Consider the controversy with Apple and its Foxconn factory in China (www.washingtonpost.com/wp-dyn/content/article/ 2006/06/15/AR2006061501898.html). Although ignoring the working conditions in the factory of a supplier might seem convenient, it is arguably weak from both the ethical and the PR standpoint not to do due diligence on an offshoring supplier.

The advances in operator-less manufacturing tools such as 3D printers and laser cutters are, however, enabling small-scale industry to return to the First World (albeit without generating a huge number of jobs). These devices power many of the prototyping techniques we have looked at and may scale to small-scale manufacture. The ethical discussion and futurology around these technologies are also fascinating and uncertain.

ELECTRONICS

The electronics contained in a Thing have their own environmental cost. Buying PCBs locally or from a foreign manufacturer affects the carbon cost of shipping the completed units. Considering the potential cost savings, even a responsible manufacturer may find it reasonable to offset the extra carbon emissions.

If your product needs to conform to RoHS legislation, then every single component that could be extracted from it must be RoHS compliant. As we have seen, this is not too onerous.

More worryingly, many electronic components rely on "rare earth minerals" (REMs) which have been extracted in China or from other locations worldwide. The mining process must be managed properly; otherwise, slurries formed of mildly radioactive waste minerals will be left behind long after the mines cease production. Refining them involves the use of toxic acids. Shipping the raw material from mine to refinery to manufacturer has its own carbon cost too. Perhaps little can be done to reduce this environmental cost currently, but as companies in other countries start to mine REMs, being aware of the parameters may allow improvements in purchasing choices.

Every electronically enhanced Thing that you produce will incur these costs and will also need to be powered to run. As mentioned in Chapter 8, speaking to the Internet (via WiFi or 3G) is a major part of the power cost of running an Internet of Things device. Anything that can be done to reduce this cost will make the devices more efficient. Choosing suppliers of WiFi chips wisely and following the low-power IPv6 developments (6LoWPAN) closely will be helpful here.

INTERNET SERVICE

As Nicholas Negroponte (founder of MIT's Media Lab) preaches, "Move bits, not atoms" (*Being Digital*, Vintage, 1996). In the digital world, moving data rather than physical objects is faster, is safer, and has a lower environmental cost. Of course, "data" doesn't exist in the abstract. The stone tablets, parchment scrolls, and libraries of paper books or microfiche that have historically been used to store analogue data always had their own environmental cost. Now, running the Internet has a cost: the electricity to run the routers and the DNS lookups, plus establishing the infrastructure—laying cabling across the sea, setting up microwave or satellite links, and so on.

As well as the cost of transferring the data across the Internet, running your own web server uses power. Many server hosting specialists now offer carbon-neutral hosting, where you pay extra to offset your emissions. Running inefficient code or services may cause higher power usage. So, of course, will having more customers, although of course we won't go as far as suggesting that you cut down on those!

SOLUTIONS

Compared to a simple, physical object, an instrumented Internet of Things device does seem to use vastly more resources in its production, daily use, and waste disposal. Considering our starting point—that this kind of instrumentation is now cheap enough to put *everywhere*—it seems as though the mass rollout of the Internet of Things will only contribute to environmental issues! Assuming that you want to go ahead with manufacturing a Thing regardless, we hope that you will be aware of the various possibilities and consider ways to reduce your impact and also consider contributing to offsetting schemes.

From a more optimistic point of view, it's also true that the realisation that the number of Internet-connected devices will be exploding in the coming years is spurring massive research into low-power efficient chips and communications.

THE INTERNET OF THINGS AS PART OF THE SOLUTION

Gavin Starks, former CEO of amee, has spoken convincingly of instrumenting the world precisely to *save* it. The trade policy scholar Brink Lindsey argued that the 1990s was the "age of abundance", but now the *Economist* calls the 2010s the "age of scarcity" in comparison (www.economist.com/node/15404916). Within 13 years, humans will have modified 50 percent of the planet. We are approaching (or have passed) the peak of the planet's oil reserves. *Water* may be the next commodity to be fought over. The world's industrial nations cannot agree on effective ways of turning back anthropogenic climate change....

While Starks's lectures are timely and necessary, as a good hacker, he prefers to *do* something about the problem: try to solve it through technology, information, and awareness. We already discussed distributed sensor networks as a social and political act: the potential for global environmental action is also massive. A UN Environment Programme report warns that the lack of reliable and consistent time-series data on the state of the environment is a major barrier to increasing the effectiveness of policies and programmes (www.unep.org/geo/pdfs/GEO5_SPM_English.pdf).

If community-led sensor networks can help supplement government and international science measurements, then we should be doing everything we can to help.

Instrumenting production lines, home energy usage, transport costs, building energy efficiency, and all other sources of efficiency might seem extreme, but it may be a vital, imperative task.

Other technologies which aren't principally linked with the Internet of Things will also be important. If 67 percent of the world's water usage is in agriculture, then are there ways to reduce that quantity through technology? Meat farming uses a disproportionate amount of resources, so perhaps the latest advances in lab-grown meat will be critical. Even here, instrumenting the supply chains, measuring to be certain that new methods really *are* more efficient, and reducing inefficiencies by automation could well use Internet of Things solutions to help measure and implement the solutions. The Internet of Things could become a core part of the solution to our potentially massive environmental problems.

Projects such as a carbon score for every company in the UK will help change attitudes, perhaps simply by gamifying the process of improving one's emissions, but also by having an objective measure that could, in future, be as important to a company's success as its credit score.

In the face of these suggestions—collective sensor networks and massive business process engineering not for profit but for environmental benefits—you might wonder whether these calls to action amount to critiques of capitalism. Is the status quo, capitalism as-is, still viable as the global operating system? Of course, capitalism's great success has always been how it routes around problems and finds a steady state which is the most *efficient* to the market. There is no reason why capitalism as-could-be should not be part of the process of striving towards efficiency on an environmental as well as monetary level.

There is a real sense that the technology we have discussed in this book could be revolutionary. Adam Greenfield has used the iconography of Occupy in discussing citizens' uses of the Internet of Things. Rob van Kranenburg has similarly called to "Occupy the [Internet of Things] gateways" with open source software and hardware (www.designspark.com/blog/an-open-internet-of-things).

Van Kranenburg also makes alternative, starker proposals: not only may privacy become obsolete, but even those currently personal possessions such as cars might also become communal, through the increasing move from ownership to rental models. Why have the inefficiency of a car for every person, when your apartment block could have enough cars for all, from city run-arounds, to a few four-wheel-drive cars and formal cars too, to be used as needed? As resources become ever scarcer, a greater percentage of income might be spent on covering rental of all goods—cars, food, possibly even housing. This kind of futurology leads to scenarios such as the death of money itself: a fixed proportion of income to rent needed services from a commercial supplier is more or less indistinguishable from taxation to pay for communal services. Whether the death of privacy and of money sounds like utopia or dystopia to you, it is worth considering the impact tomorrow of the technologies we implement to deal with the problems of today.

As a counterpoint to these messages of doom, Russell Davies of London's Really Interesting Group (RIG) often tries to bring the discussion of Things back to *fun*. Although this may not sound as engaged or political an attitude, by looking for the unintended uses for technologies, the end users, rather than the political elites, can turn them into platforms for human expression. Davies makes the examples of Christmas lights for house-fronts being repurposed to animate singalongs (`www.creativelighting displays.com/`), something that the manufacturers could never have imagined! Similarly, the World Wide Web was originally conceived to share academic papers but has taken on the roles of brokering business on the one hand and publishing pictures of kittens on the other without breaking its step. The Internet of Things will also, if we let it, become a platform for whatever people want it to be. Although this may be less *important* than saving our species from environmental disaster, perhaps it is no less ethical in terms of asserting our humanity through, and not simply in spite of, the technology that we might have feared would dehumanise us.

CAUTIOUS OPTIMISM

Between the tempting extremes of technological Luddism and an unques-tioning positive attitude is the approach that we prefer: one of cautious optimism. Yes, the Luddites were right—technology *did* change the world that they knew, for the worse, in many senses. But without the changes that disrupted and spoilt one world, we wouldn't have arrived at a world, our world, where magical objects can speak to us, to each other, and to vastly powerful machine intelligences over the Internet.

It is true that any technological advance could be co-opted by corporations, repressive governments, or criminals. But (we hope) technology can be used socially, responsibly, and (if necessary) subversively, to mitigate against this risk. Although the Internet of Things can be, and we hope will always be, *fun*, being aware of the ethical issues around it, and facing them responsibly, will help make it more sustainable and more human too.

As a massively interdisciplinary field, practitioners of Internet of Things may have an opportunity (or perhaps responsibility) to contribute to providing moral leadership in many of the upcoming ethical challenges we have looked at. Before we let that get to our heads though, we should remember an important lesson on humility from Laura James's keynote at the OpenIoT assembly:

> *Don't assume you know it all. The [I]nternet of [T]hings is interdisciplinary and it stretches most of the individual disciplines too. You will need help from others. Be ready to partner with other organisations, collaborate with people from very different backgrounds to you.*

When designing the Internet of Things, or perhaps when designing *anything*, you have to remember two contrasting points:

- **Everyone is not you.** Though you might not personally care about privacy or flood levels caused by global warming, they may be critical concerns for other people in different situations.
- **You are not special.** If something matters to you, then perhaps it matters to other people too.

This tension underscores the difficulty of trying to figure out overriding concerns about any complex area, such as the Internet of Things!

THE OPEN INTERNET OF THINGS DEFINITION

The Open IoT Assembly 2012 culminated in the drafting of the "Open Internet of Things Definition". An emergent document, created after two days of open discussion, it seeks to define and codify the points of interest around the technology of the Internet of Things and to underscore its potential to "deliver value, meaning, insight, and fun". This document touches on many of the topics that we discussed in this chapter, so let us walk through some of them to see the conclusions that this more formal treatment has come to.

A particularly interesting consensus in the definition was that, even though the Data Licensor (usually the person who has set up the sensor or paid for that data) should quite reasonably own the data from that sensor, some rights should also apply to individuals whose data is recorded (the Data Subjects). They *must* be granted licence to any data that regards them and *should* be allowed to license the anonymised aggregate data for their own purposes. We can summarize the main goals of the definition as follows:

- **Accessibility of data:** As a stated goal, all open data feeds should have an API which is free to use, both monetarily and unrestricted by proprietary technologies with no alternative open source implementation.

- **Preservation of privacy:** The Data Subjects should know what data will be collected about them and be able to decide to consent or not to that data collection. This is a very strong provision (and most likely unworkable for data which is inherently anonymous in the first instance) but one which would provide real individual protection if it were widely followed.

  As with any information gathering, "reasonable efforts" should be made to retain privacy and confidentiality.

- **Transparency of process:** Data Subjects should be made aware of their rights—for example, the fact that the data has a licence—and that they are able to grant or withdraw consent.

  In addition, where the data is collected from a *public* space, the public should get a right to participate in decision making and governance of that data. We could imagine that planning-permission notices might be posted, as they are in the UK for building developments.

The importance placed by these principles on data is unsurprising: the Internet of Things brings the gathering and collation of data into the everyday world and has real consequences on individual privacy and power.

SUMMARY

Technology often creates new possibilities with one hand and new problems with the other. We have looked at the capabilities of connected devices throughout the book and noted in Chapter 10 how new technology fosters new business models. Yet just as these new possibilities were born of the defining characteristics of the Internet of Things, so the ethical concerns raised spring from the same essence.

Inherent in the physical "thing" produced are environmental concerns: the carbon cost of manufacture and of the raw materials required for its complex electronics. Then there is a moral question over whether the workers tasked to construct it are treated fairly. Taking complex electronics off the desk and putting them into the fabric of the world and your personal possessions allows sensors to read sensitive data on an unprecedented scale. Combined with the ability to aggregate this data via the Internet, it becomes possible for companies to monitor their customers through their telephones, electricity meters, or their air fresheners. Similarly, government bodies can monitor their citizens in locations and ways that might not be obvious. This raises questions of transparency and privacy and the issue of our right to have access to data that concerns us.

As technologists, we don't have to see these concerns as prophecies of doom but as a reminder to consider our responsibilities while we are engaged in designing and building our magical objects to delight our customers and bring us profit or amusement. We have also touched on how the technology of the Internet of Things can act as counterbalance to its own potential flaws. The widespread sensors and powerful processing can lead to better information and possible mitigations to our impact on the environment. The accessibility of the technology permits crowdsourced sensor networks which tips the balance of civic power to let citizens make their own informed decisions about issues that concern them.

As the field of the Internet of Things develops, we will see more clearly the next most immediate steps to take. Perhaps some of the futures we've envisaged will come to pass, and perhaps they won't. With a strong understanding of the ethical decisions we need to make as technologists, we should be ready to help guide the Internet of Things in such a way that it need not become an invasive, oppressive instrument but instead a framework in which we can learn better what it is to be human.

Index